PEOPLE OF ANCIENT

EGYPT

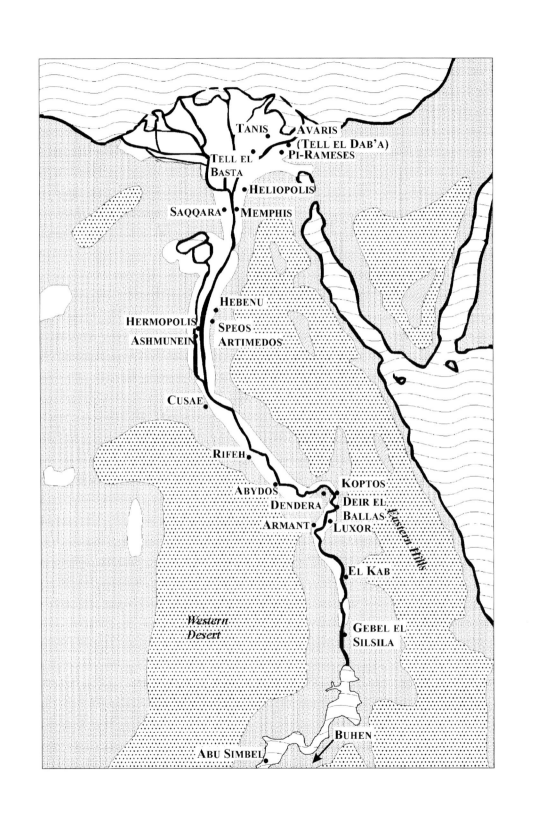

PEOPLE OF ANCIENT

EGYPT

CHARLOTTE BOOTH

TEMPUS

Frontispiece: Map of Egypt. *Produced by Peter Robinson*

First published 2006
This edition 2007

Tempus Publishing Ltd
Cirencester Road, Chalford,
Stroud, Gloucestershire GL6 8PE
www.tempus-publishing.com

British Library Cataloguing in Publication Data.
A catalogue record for this book is available from the British Library.

ISBN 978 0 7524 4343 0

Typesetting and origination by Tempus Publishing Limited

CONTENTS

ACKNOWLEDGEMENTS

I should like to thank everyone who has helped me to publish this book, including the editors at Tempus Publishing for all their hard work. I would also like to thank the Petrie Museum, the British Museum, Robert Partridge, Clare Banks, Geoff Webb and Ulla Kaer Andersen for providing some of the illustrations and Peter Robinson for the map. Additionally, I would like to thank Wayne Frostick and Lesley Kelly for reading draft copies and providing invaluable suggestions.

INTRODUCTION

Every year there are hundreds of Egyptology books published on various aspects of the subject, including architecture, religion and royalty. However, there are very few on the actual individuals that lived in ancient Egypt. It must always be remembered that any historical period is made up of people, who have the same motivations, strengths and weaknesses as we all have today. This is what has inspired me to write this book and to introduce some of the interesting characters from the past. Each chapter will look at all aspects of the lives of the Egyptians, from a period of 2500–30 BC; the entire Pharaonic Period. The individuals all fall into at least one of five categories although Hatshepsut (chapter 5) and Horemheb (chapter 10) change their role and both become king from unexpected positions.

     ♦   Kings   (chapters 2, 4, 5, 8, 11 and 15)

     ♦   Queens   (chapter 19)

     ♦   Priesthood   (chapters 3, 16, 17, 18 and 20)

     ♦   Officials   (chapters 1, 6, 7, 12 and 13)

     ♦   Military   (chapter 10)

     ♦   Workmen   (chapter 14)

Although each of the individuals in the following chapters all hold variants on these positions it would be useful to outline the basics of each of the more common occupations.

TYPICAL ROLES FOR MEN

Scribes

Once an individual had mastered the art of reading and writing they could enter the career of scribal administration either in the palace, military or priesthood. There was no formal schooling system in ancient Egypt but from the New Kingdom onwards there is evidence that there were a number of official scribal schools, situated at the Mut complex and the Amun temple at Karnak, the Ramesseum and perhaps in the region of Deir el Medina. These schools would primarily have been for the children of the upper elite, although the *Instruction of Khety for his son Pepi* tells of his journey from Sile in the Delta to 'the school for scribes, among the children of the Magistrates, with the elite of the Residence', indicating that children of non-elite families could have been accepted into these schools. This particular school appears to have been purely for those who expected a future in the central government, whereas there may have been different institutions for military or priestly applications. For those who were not accepted into these elite educational institutions, there were local alternatives. Children were often educated by their father, or they were 'adopted' by a local scribe who taught them his craft. It is possible that Ramose (chapter 12) and Kenhirkhepshef (chapter 13) may have taught their skills to the children of the village of Deir el Medina. Although these students were given the honorary title 'son' or 'staff of old age' the student was 'adopted' more as an apprentice than as a child. This education was also only normally open to boys although there was no official ban on girls gaining an education.

The young boy started his primary scribal education at approximately five years old. This training was difficult and should he not excel at his studies he would have been beaten. A proverb from ancient Egypt states: 'A boy's ear is on his back; he hears when he is beaten.'

The students were taught reading, writing and arithmetic which enabled them to enter into varying professions. Initially the children were taught hieratic phrases and sentences rather than alphabetical signs, which they copied onto gesso-coated wooden or stone tablets. These could be wiped clean after use and examples have been found where the earlier texts are visible beneath. They learnt by chanting, famous texts from the Old and Middle Kingdoms, written in a version of the language that was alien to these New Kingdom children. Some of these texts may have been written by the revered sage Imhotep (chapter 1), and learnt by rote by these young children. Once they had learnt the texts they would write them down, initially by copying and then as more advanced students, from memory. This primary education lasted for four years.

Then the student entered into an apprenticeship scheme for 10 or 11 years before choosing whether to go into the military, priesthood or palace administration. The army and the scribal profession appeared to have been in competition in the New Kingdom, especially at this stage of the education system. The life of the soldier promised glory, foreign trips and potential acknowledgment by the king, whereas the scribal profession offered knowledge and wealth. A number of texts have been discovered praising the life of the scribe over that of the soldier. The *Miscellanies* addressed the weaker, non-sporty boys, by praising the life of a scribe:

> Be a scribe! Your body will be sleek; your hand will be soft. You will not flicker like a flame, like those whose body is feeble. For there is no bone of a man in you. You are tall and thin. If you lifted a load to carry it, you would stagger. Your feet would drag terribly, you are lacking in strength. You are weak in all of your limbs, poor in body. Set your sights on being a scribe, a fine profession that suits you.

The *Satire of the Trades* describes the life of the scribe as a means to encourage able-bodied young boys to enter the scribal profession rather than any other:

> It's the greatest of all callings, there's none like it in the land. Barely grown, still a child, he is greeted, sent on errands, hardly returned he wears a gown. I never saw a sculptor as envoy, nor is the goldsmith ever sent.

This indicated that even the young scribal apprentice would receive wealth and respect. Once an apprentice had completed his training as a scribe he was able to move through the ranks to positions of great power, such as vizier (chapter 7) or high priest (chapter 20).

The highest rank that a scribe could reach was that of the vizier, and this was often a stepping stone to the throne itself (chapter 10) should there be no royal successor. The vizier would have worked at the palace and all the internal operations were under his control. He received daily reports from all the enclosures within the temple grounds, which he would then summarize and report to the king. He was responsible for controlling everything entering and leaving the palace grounds including all messengers delivering to various cities throughout Egypt. This meant he was privy to all the information entering and leaving the palace. He also was responsible for the opening of all the palace workshops and stores, although he would have worked closely with the 'Overseer of the Treasury' in these areas. The vizier kept records of all materials entering the workshops and all products leaving.

The vizier would also have been heavily involved in the security of the king, whether in the palace, or on tour, as well as the general security of Egypt. He was responsible for the hiring of policemen, therefore putting the police under his jurisdiction. He would have dealt with the 'Overseer of the Police Force' on a daily basis for the receipt of reports from the guard posts throughout Egypt. The vizier would also have been in control of the security within the palace and was responsible for questioning anyone who may have been involved in a crime. He also resided over the court that dealt with the daily petitions of the ordinary people which were normally concerned with crimes or other minor offences. Although many of the petitions were dealt with by his subordinates some of the more serious crimes were referred to him directly. He then would give his judgement on the situation which, although it could be questioned, was tantamount to the judgement of the king.

The most important role of the vizier was as a personal assistant and secretary to the king. He compiled a weekly or monthly report for the king of all the key information on the whole of Egypt, compiled from the daily reports received by the vizier's office. At times, the vizier would act as the king by proxy, when he would be given the authority of the king to carry out certain tasks. They would include the distributing of land and spoils of war to town districts or as rewards for services rendered. As this property belonged to the king it was his responsibility to distribute it. The responsibilities of the vizier were varied and would have made him the most powerful man in Egypt other than the king.

Priesthood

It was possible for an individual to enter into the priesthood even if they were illiterate, as there were many roles within the priesthood for those with varying skills and abilities.

The priests of the House of Life were scribes and scholars and would have worked in the place where all the religious texts were written, restored and archived. The works of the House of Life were greatly respected, and Greek and Latin texts praise Egyptian wisdom. The House of Life is reputed to have knowledge of medicine, medical herbs, geography, geometry, astronomy and the history of kings. Strabo (64 BC–AD 24) records that the true year was unknown to the Greeks until it was translated from the Egyptian priests' writings into Greek, indicating that the House of Life had detailed astronomical charts. Various library inventory lists have been recovered including one at the temple of Edfu and the smaller temple at Tod, near Luxor. The library at Tod included books on:

◇ The entrance of the god Montu into Thebes

◇ The ritual of completing the eye of Horus

⋄   A book of offering in the altar of the temple of Amun

⋄   A book of the Festival of Thoth in the temple of Khonsu

This indicates the smaller libraries may have only housed books relevant to the cult of the local temple or the nearby area. Numerous other texts have been discovered that record the information stored in the House of Life, including religious knowledge, temple plans for building and decorating, and spiritual secrets. In the first story of Setne (Late Period) it mentions that if a particular text is read, it will allow the reader to understand the secrets of the universe, as well as possessing the ability to understand what the birds and fish are saying. If some of the text is recited the reader will see the sun god Re in the sky. This is clearly a very powerful text, and would have been stored in the safety of the House of Life of one of the larger more secure temples.

Most large temples incorporated a House of Life, including Memphis, Abydos, Amarna, Akhmim, Koptos, Esna, Edfu and Karnak. It is possible that in the later periods a school functioned in the House of Life, and there is at least one mention of a 'Teacher of the House of Life'.

Many of the priests of the House of Life were trained physicians and many prescriptions were written by them. The lector priest carried the sacred book during rituals, and recited the prayers as well as being present during the divine oracles. These are known from the second dynasty. These priests were regarded by the Egyptian community as magicians, and are referenced in some Middle Kingdom literary tales.

There was a large number of funerary priests (*sem* priests) who carried out all the rites and rituals on the body before burial, as well as the prayer recitations, water sprinkling, lighting of incense and the 'Opening of the Mouth' ceremony. This ceremony was particularly important as it ensured that the deceased individual was able to breath, eat and speak in the afterlife. The *sem* priest was normally the deceased's heir, and this ensured that the line of succession was clear, but was also the traditional role of the eldest son. However, as early as the first dynasty there were professional *sem* priests who could be paid to carry out these rites. *Ka* priests were also associated with the funerary cult; in particular supplying the offering tables and libation stands with food for the sustenance of the deceased. The mortuary temples of the king were managed by a contingent of *ka* priests.

As well as funerary and lector priests there were a number of cult priests, the most important of which were the hour priests who were responsible for specifying the exact time and day that temple rituals needed be carried out. They were familiar with the daily path of the sun and identified the exact time from their observations. They were also familiar with the stars and could identify the nightly hours by these observations. They were closely connected to the Greek *horoskopoi* who devised the calender of unlucky and lucky days, which defined each day according to divine legends. Those born on certain days would die in a specified manner which could be identified by these priests. The calender also listed whether days were lucky or unlucky and what activities should be carried out or avoided on certain days. In the Graeco-Roman Period the *horoskopoi* priests matched the birth date and time with the star signs for a more accurate horoscope although this was not practiced in the Pharaonic Period. The horoscope priest had an in-depth understanding of astronomy and astrology and the astrological ceilings in the eighteenth-dynasty tomb of Senenmut (chapter 6) and nineteenth-dynasty tomb of Sety I indicates that their knowledge was at a high standard even in the earlier years. Records have survived of the stars and planets that had been identified and the titles given to them by the Egyptians.

◇ 'Unwearying stars' – planets

◇ 'The star of the evening and the morning' – Venus

◇ 'The Red Horus' – Mars

◇ 'The Dazzling Star' – Jupiter

◇ 'Horus the Bull' – Saturn

◇ 'Ox's leg' – Big Dipper

◇ 'Man with arms extended' – Cygnus

◇ 'Man running whilst looking over his shoulder' – Orion

It was only with the intervention of the Greeks that the zodiacal signs were introduced, as can be seen in the zodiac ceiling at the Ptolemaic temple of Dendera. Using stars to predict the future was a foreign concept and also was not introduced until the Graeco-Roman Period.

There were many part-time priests from the Old Kingdom onwards known as phyle priests who worked for three months a year. They worked for one month in four and would return to their villages when they were not required in the temple. The changeover of phyle priests would be an opportunity to conduct an inventory of all the religious paraphernalia, to keep track of any petty pilfering that may have gone on!

The lower clergy were known as the *wab* priests (chapter 3) which meant the 'pure ones' and played a supporting role, including the carrying of the sacred bark, cleaning the temple, supervising the painters and draftsmen and other general tasks around the temple. If they themselves were craftsmen before they came to the temple, they may have been given the task of making sandals for the deities. For a large temple like Karnak even the *wab* priests divided further with the 'Foremost of the Pure Ones', being in charge of the lower *wab* priests.

The title 'Bearer of the Bark', although a low clergy post, was an important one. The lower clergy may have taken it in turns to carry the bark, especially over long distances. Way stations were situated every few hundred feet where the bark was put down and incense, food and prayers were offered. This also may have been a chance to change the bearers. This role was quite prestigious in the community and a Ramesside inscription reads: 'I carried Ptah at the length of my arms, may this god grant that I may be beautified with his fervour!' indicating that he may have been held in high esteem by other Egyptians for this role. In addition to carrying of the sacred bark, there was the title of 'Carriers of Sacred Objects' whose responsibility was to carry objects in sacred processions or to the sacred shrine at the back of the temple. Natsefamun (chapter 16) held the title 'Incense Bearer' and participated in the processions within the temple, and his title would fall into this category. There were also 'Sacrificers' whose role consisted of slitting the throats of the sacrificial animals including cattle and fowl. They were not butchers as the animals used for sacrifice were carefully chosen, and needed to be killed according to ritual in order to make them suitable for the food of the gods.

The 'Interpreter of Dreams' was a scribal position and may have been held by someone in the House of Life. They were responsible for the interpretation of the dreams of the devotees who stayed in the temple. These devotees would be searching for help with an illness or problem and the interpretation of their dream would tell them how to appease the gods. Taimhotep's husband (chapter 20) received a dream from the god Imhotep which would have been interpreted by one of these priests. It is also possible that there were local scribes who were able to interpret dreams, as Kenhirkhepshef's (chapter 13) *Dream Dictionary* would suggest.

Each temple employed a number of auxiliary workers who were not priests, including caretakers, janitors, workmen, bakers, butchers and florists; all essential to the successful running of the temple.

Army

In the New Kingdom, after the expulsion of the Hyksos (chapter 4) the military became a full-time profession. Prior to this period armies were conscripted as and when they were needed. At the start of the New Kingdom the army was a single entity, but by the reign of Horemheb (chapter 10) there were two divisions, one for the North and one for the South of Egypt. By the time of Ramses II and the battle of Kadesh (chapter 11) it had risen to four. This ensured that the power held by the generals was limited to a small division. These divisions were further divided for easier control:

✧   A division had 5000 men

✧   A host had 500 men (consisting of two companies at least)

✧   A company had 250 men (consisting of five platoons)

✧   A platoon had 50 men (consisting of five squads)

✧   A squad had 10 men

There were also specialist units made of charioteers, spearmen, infantry and foreign mercenaries. From the early dynastic period mercenaries from Nubia, known as the Medjay, were often used as scouts and light infantry troops. By the reign of Amenhotep III the army also had Syrians, Libyans, Sherden (grouped as one of the 'Sea People' – chapter 15) and even Hittites. These mercenaries were conquered enemies, who were taken as prisoners and were given the option to fight in the army or be executed. This could be advantageous as their knowledge of their own homeland and tactics could help the Egyptian campaigns. However, mercenary companies were never sent to fight their own race in case issues of loyalty arose.

Scribes would also have been an essential part of the army entourage, in addition to the soldiers, as they were needed to record the events of the campaigns. They accompanied the military on campaigns and were responsible for counting of the body parts which were cut off to calculate the enemy dead as well as the amount of booty and prisoners which were collected.

Another essential non-military member of the campaign entourage was the standard bearer. Military standards were an important part of the battle and the individul who carried the standard held a very important position. The standard was taken into battle and, amongst other things, was vital for seeing where the troops were situated on the battlefield. It was difficult to identify friend from foe once everyone was covered in dirt and blood. They also were a focus of pride for the troops, to fight under a banner in the same way that it is in the army of modern nations.

It is thought that there may have been a type of martial music to encourage the troops to march in time, as trumpets have been found in the tombs of soldiers. Modern musicians who have used them describe a very limited note range indicating that they may have been used as signals during the battles to alert the troops to a change in tactic or manoeuvre.

Evidence shows that drums were used throughout dynastic Egypt and reliefs have survived showing them in use. Actual examples are rare although metal ones have been found. The main use was probably to keep the army in step whilst marching by creating a monotone beat. The drums were made from an open-ended cylinder of wood or metal, with skin or leather stretched over the end and tensioned with leather thongs. It could be played with one or two hands, with or without a drumstick.

Although a dangerous career the military was one that led to wealth and glory as soldiers loyal to the king would have been rewarded well.

TYPICAL ROLES OF WOMEN

Although there are few chapters dedicated solely to women in this volume, there are women present in the lives of all the individuals discussed. Most women, spending the majority of their time in the home, would essentially be housewives. However during harvest time the women would also be involved in the manual harvesting work as all hands would be needed. Winnowing was generally women's work and girls were sent to glean. Women were also responsible for the grinding of the grain and the baking of bread, which was unleavened flat bread cooked by laying it on the outside of the clay oven or on hot stones. This method is still used in modern Egypt.

Although women could not hold bureaucratic positions, in the Middle Kingdom women held titles like treasurer, major doma, or superintendent of the dining room, all held in private houses. In the royal house or independent workshops women held positions of:

♢ 'Overseer of the Singers'

♢ 'Overseer of Amusements'

♢ 'Mistress of the Royal Harem'

✧ 'Overseer of the House of Weavers'

✧ 'Overseer of the Wigshop'

In the Old Kingdom women held administrative titles like stewards in charge of storehouses, food supplies and cloth. They were generally in the service of other women and were not allowed to oversee the work of men. There is, however, one example of a female vizier in the sixth dynasty, which was very unusual. It is possible that the title may have been honorary.

From the Old Kingdom and the First Intermediate Period eight women were given the title 'Sealer'. Their job involved sealing boxes, rooms and letters on behalf of the house holder. The 'Sealer' held the authorised seal of the house and therefore was in a position of great responsibility and trust.

The linen trade in particular was dominated by women as both workers and supervisors. In the New Kingdom, the royal harem in the Faiyum was responsible for the production of a large amount of linen. The royal women were responsible for the training and supervision of textile workers and it is highly probable that some did some delicate work themselves to pass the time.

The most prestigious profession for women was to enter into the priesthood. From the fourth dynasty women were priestesses mainly for the cults of Neith and Hathor but could also work for the cult of any other god. Unlike the male priesthood these positions were not necessarily hereditary, although some were passed down for generations. Priestesses were held in high esteem and they were considered to be respectable and intellectual. As priestesses they primarily acted as impersonators of goddesses or played instruments during the temple rituals. Old Kingdom evidence shows that women could also be *ka* servants working for the funerary cult. However, most women involved in the funerary cult fulfilled the role of professional mourners. It was not a priestly title but they were hired for both royal and noble funerals. They threw dust over their heads, ripped their clothes, scratched their cheeks and wailed in distress. It was considered unseemly for the women of the deceased's family to be shown in such grief so women were hired for the occasion. In these groups of mourning scenes there are often images of young girls, indicating that like most professions it was passed down from mother to daughter.

In the New Kingdom so many women had the title priestess it lessened the importance of the position, at a time when the male priesthood was professional and held in great esteem. Like most of the male priesthood, priestesses also worked one in four months on a rotation system and then returned to their families and villages.

Midwife

Within the villages many women trained as midwives, to aid the birth of the many children born. There was a school of midwifery at the temple of Neith at Sais where elite women were trained by temple staff in the skills of midwifery. Most forms of medicine were dealt with by men and other temples trained male doctors and gynaecologists. Most midwife skills were learnt, however, through experience by assisting the village midwives, and the vast majority of midwives received no formal training. Midwives were in great demand in any village, as most women had at least five children, and most had more.

Wet nurses were hired by the upper classes to nurse the very young children. A number of contracts between wet nurses and employers have survived indicating how common the role was. Royal wet nurses were held in very high esteem, and in the New Kingdom high officials often married royal wet nurses for political advantage. In their tombs it is carefully recorded that their wives nursed princes. Children of a royal wet nurse were considered 'milk siblings' to the king and it is likely that they grew up with him and would be in his circle of friends. It was normal for children to be nursed for three years as it was felt to be a safeguard against pregnancy and also a way of ensuring uncontaminated food. There is, however, no record of what happened to the royal wet nurses after these three years were over; presumably they were kept in employment for the next royal child.

There were a number of professions open to women in the entertainment business. Dancers were hired for banquets and religious festivals. Many of the processions of Hathor involved elaborate dances, and there is one where the dancer holds a mirror in one hand and uses it to reflect the other hand. Another dance shows the dancers with balls attached to their hair which are used to weight the hair as it is dragged along the ground. The dancers would often be accompanied by musicians. Religious musicians would mostly play sistra, or menat necklaces and banquet musicians would mostly play lutes (New Kingdom) and clappers. Women also played stringed harps, either full length or hand-held, which would be played whilst seated. Drums were played as a background rhythm for the rest of the music. There is no evidence that nobles played instruments in public, although musicians were well respected. However, nobles could play instruments and in the tomb of Mereruka (chapter 2) his wife sits on the end of a bed playing a harp indicating music and singing may have been a pastime of the elite.

EVIDENCE

The evidence for all the people in this volume comes from a variety of places. For the kings there is often a great deal of written evidence as well as stone monuments, tombs and in many cases the mummies themselves. For the non-royal individuals finding details of their lives is more difficult. Luckily the individuals from Deir el Medina have left plenty of written evidence in the form of ostraca (limestone sherds). For the Third Intermediate Period priests (chapters 16, 17 and 18) all that remains is the mummies themselves but using modern scientific methods we can identify a number of diseases and ailments that would have affected their later years, as well as in the case of Asru identifying her career. As methods of research improve and new finds are uncovered, whether they are of a textual nature or new tombs, such as the newly discovered KV63, we hope to become increasingly knowledgeable about the people of ancient Egypt. Despite the varying resources and information available it is often possible to create a clear picture of the lives of the people concerned, and I hope by the end of this volume the people of Egypt will be more alive and accessible to the reader.

ONE

IMHOTEP
FROM ROYAL BUILDER TO GOD

INTRODUCTION

One of the most obscure and yet well-known officials from the Old Kingdom is the architect and vizier, Imhotep. He is famous for two things: for building the Step Pyramid of King Djoser and as the patron god of medicine in the Late Period. He is a perfect example of how an ordinary individual was raised to the status of a god.

CHILDHOOD AND FAMILY

There is sadly very little information available about him prior to his deification in the late Rammesside Period. However, an inscription from the Wadi Hamamat lists the male family members of Imhotep starting with his father Kanefer, through 25 generations ending with Khnumibre. Each generation held the title of architect indicating it was a profession passed down from father to son. Imhotep's father's titles included that of 'Architect of South and North Egypt' indicating he may have been a royal architect throughout Egypt, which also appears to have been the role of Imhotep.

Kanefer was married to Keredankhu who gave birth to Imhotep in Ankh-Tawy (a suburb of Memphis), on the sixteenth day of Epiphi (12 June), third month of summer, in approximately 2650 BC.

Imhotep married Renpetnefret and they had one son called Rahotep who followed in his father's profession and became an architect. Whether Imhotep and

Renpetnefret had any other children is not recorded, although in later years it was recorded that Renpetnefret died in childbirth.

CAREER

Imhotep held many titles whilst alive; and many were attributed to him after his death. It is generally undisputed that Imhotep was the vizier and architect of King Djoser of the third dynasty (2668-2649 BC). Imhotep had a close relationship with the king, and was mentioned on a statue base originally belonging to Djoser:

> The Chancellor of the King of Upper and Lower Egypt, the First after the King of Upper Egypt, Administrator of the Great Palace, Hereditary Lord, Greatest of Seers, Imhotep, the Builder, the Sculptor, the Maker of Stone Vases.

This was a great honour, and the list of titles show that he was a prominent individual in the royal household which for someone of common birth was a great achievement. He obviously rose through the ranks due to his genius, natural talents and dedication.

TITLES AND ROLES

'The Chancellor of the King of Upper and Lower Egypt' identifies Imhotep as vizier, and 'the First after the King of Upper Egypt', indicates he was the second most powerful man in Egypt, and may have advised the king on matters of state. His duties as a vizier included 'Chief Judge', 'Overseer of King's Records', 'Royal Seal Bearer', 'Chief of all Works of the King', 'Chief of that Which Heaven Brings, Earth Creates and the Nile Brings'; clearly a very powerful position to have.

A late inscription on the rock at Sehel Island, south of Aswan (323–30 BC), records the legend of the seven-year famine. The Nile failed for seven years due to Djoser's neglect of the god Khnum, god of the first cataract who controlled the Nile. Djoser approached his vizier (Imhotep) for advice. On his advice the king wrote to the Viceroy of Kush and asked what gods or goddesses of the Nile would help him fill his granaries. On their information he visited the temple of Khnum and gave offerings. Khnum appeared to Djoser in a dream and promised the Nile would rise and fall normally. On further advice from Imhotep, Djoser gave a strip of land to the god including all revenue and taxes, a new temple and numerous gifts, thus ending the seven-year famine. This inscription indicates that the vizier was close to the king, and available for advice whenever needed.

'Administrator of the Great Palace' is one of the roles that automatically accompanies that of vizier as he would be responsible for all the record keeping for the king including tax records, building progress, farming and the inundation. This title also indicates that Imhotep was literate and in the Ptolemaic Period he became patron god of scribes. In later years Imhotep became famous for his writings and is mentioned in a New Kingdom harper's song, who claims to be aware of the teachings of Imhotep as well as other scribes and sages of years gone by. An inscription in a Nubian temple of Ptolemy V states that Imhotep was 'Chief Scribe of Grain for Upper and Lower Egypt', responsible for keeping record of the harvest primarily for taxation purposes.

'Hereditary Lord' is an honorary title that holds no responsibilities but ensures that the role will be passed down from father to son.

The title 'Greatest of Seers' indicates that he was high priest of the solar cult at Heliopolis, 25 miles north-east of Memphis; the religious capital during the Old Kingdom. The high priest was a powerful individual and performed the daily statue rituals in the temple, and royal funerary rituals assisted by a *sem* priest. The high priest of any cult was a representative of the king and performed the rituals on his behalf for those occasions when the king could not attend himself.

Imhotep was particularly famous for being a 'Builder, the Sculptor, the Maker of Stone Vases' which indicates he was skilled with specialist items that would only have been owned by the wealthy. In later years of his career, he was primarily responsible for the supervision of the royal building works throughout Egypt. As he was an official, it is unlikely he would physically have done any building or sculpting, but rather supervised those who were, which is reflected by his title 'Chief of Works of the King of Upper and Lower Egypt'.

The most important achievement of Imhotep is the building of the Step Pyramid at Saqqara (1). It was the biggest monument constructed in this period and contained a large number of buildings in the surrounding complex. In this surrounding complex, the use of space and stone shows Imhotep had an eye for detail and was a true architect and a talented manipulator of stone.

The Step Pyramid was the first stone building to be built in the world and the limestone enclosure wall contains an area of approximately 146,000 square metres. The wall itself is built in the 'palace façade' style reminiscent of earlier reed structures. The mortuary temple was used for ritualistic offerings of food and sustenance of the deceased king Djoser. There are a number of dummy buildings within the complex and the reason for this area has been greatly debated, although it is thought to

1 Step Pyramid of Djoser, Saqqara. *Photograph Wayne R. Frostick*

represent a collection of temporary buildings traditionally made of flimsier materials, in order for the king to have a kingdom to rule in the afterlife.

The Step Pyramid complex includes not only the king's tomb but those of his family, a pillared hall, an open courtyard with altars dedicated to the sun god, and a festival courtyard where he performed his rejuvenation ceremony or *heb sed*. The festival would in life have been carried out in Memphis at the palace, and the one in the Saqqara complex served the king in the afterlife for the same purpose.

There were also two *ka* mansions fin which the spirit of the king could reside. The Northern Mansion was identified by papyriform columns symbolic of the papyrus plant that grows in the north and the Southern Mansion was identified by lotus bud columns representing the plant that grew in the south. These two 'mansions' symbolised the king's rule over both Upper and Lower Egypt.

On the north side of the temple was a mortuary temple with an enclosed chamber attached to it, known as a serdab, which contained a statue of Djoser which served as the main focus of the offering cult of the king (*2*). There were holes cut into the front wall of this chamber so the statue was able to look out, and probably may have been a little disconcerting for the priests, who would just have seen a pair of crystal eyes sparkling in the dark.

One of the statue rooms contains graffiti showing the site was visited as a tourist site during the New Kingdom. One of the inscriptions dates to the winter of year 47 of Ramses II when two scribes of the treasury, the vizier, and two brothers, named Hednakht and Panakht recorded their visit. Other graffiti connects the name Netjerikhet with that of Djoser, therefore identifying the owner of the pyramid.

DEIFICATION

The fame of Imhotep was widespread long before he was deified, as he was revered for his intellect and prophecies (3, 4). A harpist's poem from the reign of Ramses II suggests that the writings of Imhotep were still popular during the New Kingdom, and he was quoted as an ancient scholar. Although not deified in the New Kingdom his teachings were taught at school.

2 Serdab of Djoser, Saqqara. *Photograph Wayne R. Frostick*

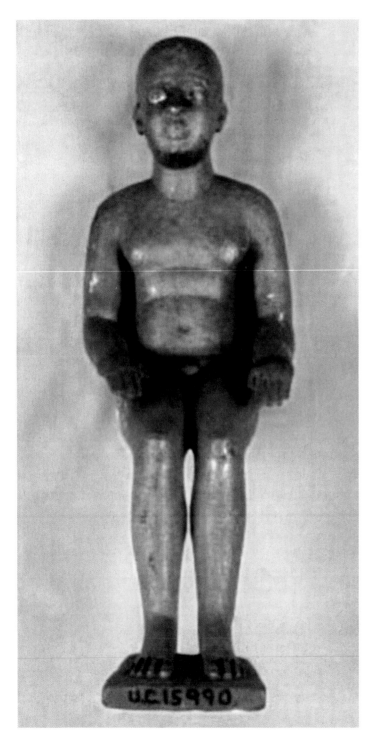

3 Imhotep as a youth
– twenty-sixth dynasty,
Memphis. *Copyright:*
Petrie Museum of Egyptian
Archaeology, University
College London, UC 15990

4 Imhotep as a priest, Late Period. *Copyright: Petrie Museum of Egyptian Archaeology, University College London, UC 8709*

By the Late Period Imhotep was deified and was given the title 'Imhotep the Great, Son of Ptah, the Great God'. Although deified and now the son of the creator god, Imhotep was still connected to both the divine and human world. Ptah was the god of craftsmen and therefore a household god, and Imhotep became primarily a god of medicine, also adopted as a personal god. As the son of Ptah, Imhotep became part of the powerful Memphite triad along with Ptah and Sekhmet, and in the temple of Ptah at Karnak he is shown alongside these deities (*5*).

Although Imhotep's father was now recorded as being the god, Ptah, his mother Keredankhu maintained her human status, and her position as the mother of Imhotep, therefore placing his origins both in the mortal and divine realms. As the son of Ptah, Imhotep received the epithets:

> Beneficent god, begotten by the god of the South Wall (*Memphis*), giver of life, who gives to those he loves, ... who provides remedies for all diseases. Great one, son of Ptah ... who comes to him that calls upon him wherever he may be who gives sons to the childless, ... the image and likeness of Thoth the wise.

5 Imhotep, Ptah and Sekhmet, temple of Ptah, Karnak. *Photograph Wayne R. Frostick*

These outline his medicinal attributes and the association with Thoth the god of scribes and knowledge. As a god of scribes, there are numerous statues of Imhotep seated as a scribe with a papyrus roll on his knee (*colour plate 1*).

By the time of Manetho (300 BC), Imhotep's role was primarily that of a god of medicine:

> Djoser reigned for 29 years, in whose time was Imhotep, who is equated by the Egyptians with Asklepios (Greek god of medicine) because of his medical skills and his invention of building with hewn stone; also for the excellence of his writings.

At the temple known as the Asklepieion, in Memphis, Imhotep was worshipped in this association with Asklepios. This temple housed a statue of the seated scribe in the central shrine and the priests laid offerings at his feet. Julius Caesar and Cleopatra visited the pyramid at Saqqara and it is likely they visited the temple and tomb of the 'Egyptian Asklepios'. Imhotep had a reputation for helping women conceive and during this trip, Cleopatra herself was pregnant with her son Caesarion and may have visited his monuments to ensure a safe pregnancy and birth. It was common for people on these pilgrimages to Imhotep's temple and tomb to sleep in the temple to receive divine intervention through dreams and visions. This temple is still recorded in the ninth/tenth century AD by Arabic writers, although it is now lost.

It has not since been rediscovered, although numerous statues and fragmentary inscriptions have been found from the shrine indicating that at the fall of paganism the temple was sacked and plundered.

On the late *Oxyrhynchus Papyrus* the story of Necrautis describes the cult of Imhotep in the Late Period. Necrautis and his mother were taken ill, so they both went to sleep at the sanatorium in the temple of Imhotep. Whilst in the sanatorium, both of them had a vision – the mother whilst awake and Necrautis whilst asleep. The vision was of someone with superhuman stature in shiny clothes carrying a book. He observed the patients from head to foot thoroughly and then vanished. Both Necrautis and his mother were cured of their illness, but Necrautis had to fulfil a promise to re-edit in Greek an Egyptian book in honour of Imhotep, which he completed and then donated to the temple as an offering. It was common for people to sleep in the sanatorium of Imhotep to be cured of their ailments. Those who were cured, or those just arriving at the temple, dedicated a small bronze statue with an inscription thanking him, promising him or asking for 'great length of days and a long and happy old age'. Sometimes models of the afflicted part of the body in the form of an amulet were left at the temple (e.g. head, leg, ear and eye).

In addition to Memphis, the top terrace of Deir el Bahri was used as a sanatorium of Imhotep during the Ptolemaic Period, and the devotees left graffiti describing their experiences. The cult of Imhotep as god of medicine eventually spread throughout Egypt to Nubia although the only surviving purpose-built sanatoria is at Dendera.

Although primarily a god of medicine, Imhotep was still revered as a builder and is mentioned in this capacity at Edfu temple:

> The master craftsmen was Imhotep, son of Ptah, the Great God of Memphis, and father
> and son united their powers and built the first temple at Edfu.

However, if Imhotep had built a temple on this site it is now lost as the temple on the site now is of Ptolemaic date.

Imhotep, as well as being part of the Memphite divine triad, is also mentioned alongside other principal deities like Osiris, Re, Ptah, Isis and Nephthys, and therefore became an active part of the Egyptian pantheon. He also appears in relief alongside Thoth, and another deified scribe and vizier, Amenhotep son of Hapu (reign of Amenhotep III) and they were worshipped together at Medinet Habu and Deir el Medina (6).

A statue pedestal of the Priest of Ptah, Imhotep Pedibast, lists six festival days covering different events in the life of the deified Imhotep:

◇ Sixteenth day, third month of summer, month of Epiphi – Imhotep is born of Ptah and Keredankhu

◇ Eleventh day, second month of winter, month of Mekhur – Ptah and Sekhmet ordain and glorify his image. Imhotep appears before these two gods

◇ Tenth day, fourth month of summer (5 July) – Sekhmet slays Asiatics by tearing their limbs and burning them and capsizing their boats (maybe the Asiatics injured Imhotep in some way)

◇ Seventeenth day of the fourth month of summer (13 July) – lamentation by Ptah after the death of his son Imhotep

◇ Twenty-third day, fourth month of summer (19 July) – Imhotep reclines before his father after death. Reunion of the spirit with the body

◇ Fourth day, second month of summer (1 May) – Imhotep goes to spirit world

DEATH AND BURIAL

The statue pedestal states Imhotep died on the seventeenth day of Mesore (13 July), fourth month of summer, and was buried on the twenty-third of the same month. The year is not recorded although the numerous titles that he held indicate he lived to an advanced age. Imhotep's name has been found written in ink on the girdle wall of the unfinished pyramid of Djoser's successor Sekhemhet, indicating that he outlived Djoser and gained favour with the new king. He has also been accredited with the architectural design of Sekhemhet's pyramid. It is thought that he may have died in the reign of King Huni (2637-13 BC) the third king after Djoser.

6 Imhotep, and Amenhotep son of Hapu, temple of Ptah, Karnak. *Photograph Wayne. R Frostick*

In the harper's poem the tomb of Imhotep appears to have been lost during the Rammesside Period, although by the twenty-sixth dynasty it had been located and had become a major site of pilgrimage. His tomb, although not yet located, is likely to be in the region of Ankh-Tawy (just outside Memphis).

In 1987 a Polish archaeological team excavated to the west of Djoser's Step Pyramid in Saqqara, searching for Imhotep's tomb. This area has mostly been ignored by archaeologists as the majority of the Old Kingdom tombs in this area are to the east and north of the pyramid complex. They discovered a wall running parallel to the enclosure wall of the pyramid dating to the same period. The archaeologists also discovered that the wall surrounded an open-air courtyard, part of a second- or early third-dynasty structure yet to be fully excavated. All indications show that this tomb belongs to a king or an equally prestigious person.

The open-air courtyard displays clear traces of ritual fires, which may have been used for burnt offerings to the deified Imhotep, if this was indeed his tomb. Archaeologists found small faience tiles and vessels similar to those used to decorate the subterranean chamber of Djoser's complex, indicating the tomb undoubtedly belongs to an important person who could afford equally precious decoration. The tomb itself has two rock-cut shafts, 4m long and 3m wide, which are covered with a complicated ceiling structure of many layers. Unfortunately, the walls are uninscribed so we do not know with certainty who was buried here.

CONCLUSION

Once Imhotep's tomb is discovered it could shed some light on his personal life, and that of his family. If his body is discovered it could indicate his age and cause of death as well as any illnesses he may have suffered from. Unfortunately until that day we will have to speculate on the character of the man that went from architect and vizier to god.

TWO

TETY

THE ASSASSINATION OF AN OLD KINGDOM KING

TETY'S EARLY REIGN

Tety was the first king of the sixth dynasty and ruled Egypt for approximately 12 years between 2345–33 BC. There is very little information about this king other than what has survived in the records of Manetho (300 BC), who records that the sixth dynasty originated in the Memphite region due to their cemetery being situated in this area.

When Tety came to the throne at the end of the fifth dynasty it was amidst a period of political unrest, caused by the increased power of the nomarchs or provincial governors, weakening the power of the throne. Tety's newly appointed Horus name was Seheteptawy 'He who pacifies the Two Lands' further supporting the troubles present at the start of his reign. Royal names starting with 'Sehetep' were normally only used during problematic periods, as a way of starting the healing process, by showing that the king was renewing political unity.

The problems at the end of the reign of the previous king, Unas, appear to have involved the last two viziers of his reign. They lost the favour of Unas and then they lost their tombs, which were recarved and reused. This was a terrible punishment as without a tomb and regular offerings the deceased would not have an afterlife. This would condemn them to an eternal damnation without rebirth.

In order to try and increase the power and support of the throne one of the first things Tety did as king was to erect a stela at Abydos exempting all temples from taxation, ensuring the temple administration supported and remained loyal to him,

7 Façade of mastaba, Saqqara. *Photograph Wayne R. Frostick*

therefore strengthening the throne against the growing power of the nomarchs. However, to gain control within the temple cults to prevent a religious uprising, Tety increased the use of phyles (part-time priests) who included both work-crews and cult priests. As this role was considered desirable the king gave them to his trusted officials. Between the reign of Neferirkara (2477-67 BC) and Tety (2345-33 BC) there were 20 temple cults using the phyle system, whereas between the reign of Pepy I (2332-83 BC) and Pepy II (2278-2184 BC) this had decreased to only six. The use of phyles ensured that one individual did not gain great power within one temple, which could potentially threaten the throne. This system also ensured that the phyles were reliant on more than one temple for their income, as well as reliant on the king for gifts and bonuses. This system doubled the number of people the king would need to reward, but would also have doubled the number of people who were loyal and dependant on him.

FAMILY

In order to reinforce his right to rule Egypt Tety married Princess Iput, the daughter of King Unas, the last king of the fifth dynasty. Princess Iput held the titles 'Daughter of the King of Upper and Lower Egypt, Wife of the King of Upper Egypt, and Mother of the King of Upper and Lower Egypt' in reference to being the daughter of Unas, wife of Tety and mother of Pepy I. This marriage could suggest Tety should be considered a king of the fifth dynasty rather than the founder of a new dynasty. However, the father of Tety is thought to have come from outside the royal family of the fifth dynasty indicating Tety was not of royal blood.

Tety and Iput had at least four children in their marriage. One son Pepy, became king after Tety died. However their eldest son, Tetyankh, died at the start of Tety's reign. Both Tetyankh and a young daughter were both buried in the mastaba tombs (7) at Memphis which originally belonged to the two viziers from the reign of Unas; their names and titles had been erased and replaced with those of the royal children.

These viziers probably were not connected to the death of the royal children although their untimely deaths could indicate a violent takeover, where they were victims. Tety and Iput had a third son, Nebkawor, who also died young, leaving the third son Pepy as heir to the throne.

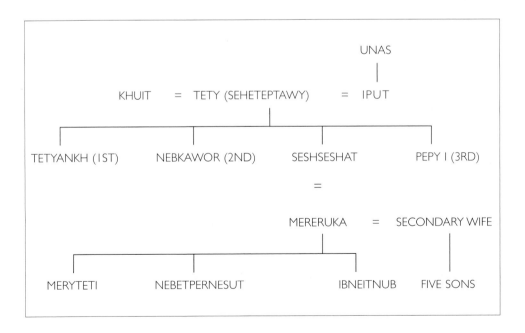

THE OFFICIALS

One of the first things Tety did to ensure a peaceful reign was to fill the official positions with people he could trust. It would appear that he may have felt threatened due to the increased number of personal attendants and bodyguards employed by him.

The most important official in the administration would be the vizier, who controlled the craftsmen, law, general administration as well as being an advisor to the king. The first vizier of Tety's reign was Kagemi, who had risen to this position during the reign of Djedkara (2414-2375 BC). Therefore it is clear that he had shown himself loyal to the king and had given no cause for concern to Tety. Kagemi's mastaba tomb was very close to the pyramid of Tety, showing he was a greatly trusted official. Another mastaba in close vicinity to Kagemi's is that of Khentika, the last vizier under the reign of Tety, who also held the title of 'Priest' under Tety and Pepy I. It would appear that Tety may have had up to five viziers during his short 12-year reign. However, the decline in the power of the viziers through the reign of Tety is represented in the decline in size of the mastabas of these officials. Kagemi's mastaba is four times the size of the later vizier Khentika.

Each of Tety's officials and guards were hand-picked, and the autobiography of an official called Hesi claims he was a relatively junior official until:

> It was Tety, my Lord, who promoted me as a Judge and Administrator, and who promoted me as Royal Chamberlain. His Majesty caused it to be done for me because His majesty knew my name when selecting a scribe because of his ability, and without any backer. He remembered the one who spoke to him wisely.

Tety obviously trusted Hesi's judgment, and was reassured that he would be loyal as he held a low position prior to his promotion, and did not have any elite support at this time – people who may have ambitions to overthrow the royal house.

Every aspect of Tety's life was protected by guards. For example the official Seankhuiptah held the title of 'Overseer of the Guards of Tety's Pyramid' indicating that even the process of building his pyramid included extensive security. Seankhuiptah was also the 'Chief Physician' responsible for the health of the king and the royal family, and was therefore a man of great responsibility and trust.

Another official called Semdent who was close enough to the king to be buried in the Tety cemetery at Saqqara held the title of 'Overseer of the King's Repasts in all his Places' indicating that wherever he went Tety had someone to check his food, in case of poisoning.

This entourage would also have consisted of a number of personal attendants including a man called Inyemsaf who was 'Overseer of the Two Bathrooms of the Palace' and 'Controller of Clothing'. The royal family at this point were clearly wealthy enough to have two bathrooms which was a sign of affluence and Inyemsaf no doubt helped Tety with his daily hygiene routines including application of cosmetics, and body oils as well as arranging his wardrobe and laying out his clothes for the day.

Mereruka (8) was the most famous of the officials from the reign of Tety and in his mastaba he is shown with numerous personal guards of his own, supporting the idea that it was a time of danger and unrest. His mother, Nedjetempet, held the title 'Royal Acquaintance' before he was given the prestigious titles of 'Overseer of the House of Weapons', and 'Overseer of the King's Harem', indicating that he rose from within the royal court. His titles may seem like a strange combination but many conspiracies started in the royal harem amongst disgruntled wives who wanted their sons to be the heir to throne, consequently giving them the power associated with the title 'Mother of the King'. Therefore by putting the control of weapons and the harem into the hands of someone he trusted, Tety felt he had protected another avenue of potential danger. The trust that the king had in Mereruka is further reinforced by his marriage to Tety's daughter, Seshseshat, making him son-in-law to the king. Mereruka and Seshseshat had three children, two daughters and a son. Within the mastaba of Mereruka, six rooms were included as the funerary suite of his wife, which may have been financed by the king to ensure that his daughter had an appropriate burial. Within the mastaba there are some charming scenes of family life with Mereruka and Seshseshat seated on a couch as she entertains him with her harp, and another scene where they are holding hands while their bed is prepared for them.

Further attestation of the king's favour is when Mereruka is given the title 'Foster Child of the King'. He later became the 'Chief Priest' of the funerary cult of Tety, taking the place of the eldest son, perhaps suggesting that the two older sons of Tety had already died and Pepy was too young to participate.

TETY'S PYRAMID

Tety was buried in a pyramid in Saqqara, built on a diagonal line with the earlier pyramids of Djoser, Sekhemkhet, Userkaf and Unas (9). His pyramid stands on high ground and needed a huge embankment for the causeway which is now sadly missing. This pyramid complex was called 'The pyramid which is enduring of Tety's

8 Mereruka, Saqqara. *Photograph Wayne R. Frostick*

places' indicating it was designed to last for eternity. However the pyramid was built at a time when rubble rather than stone blocks were used as building material, hence it is in rather poor condition. The pyramid core is made up of five steps which were then built up by using small quarried stone and debris fill. The outside of the pyramid was originally covered with casing blocks which have mostly been removed for other building works, although some have survived on the eastern side. The removal of these casing blocks caused the core of the pyramid to slump resulting in the mound that is visible today. The pyramid originally stood over 53m high, and the inner chambers were constructed from a 10m-deep trench cut into the rock beneath ground level. The burial chamber is roofed with three layers of stone slabs.

The pyramid entrance is at ground level on the central axis of the pyramid, sealed with large flagstones. The funerary chapel was constructed over the entrance. The chapel had large wooden double doors, which rotated in the sockets that are still visible. The walls of the chapel were decorated with painted reliefs of offering bearers, and the roof was constructed of a limestone slab decorated with painted stars representing the sky. In the back wall there was a false door made of black basalt, which acted as a doorway for the *ka* of the king to enter into the chapel to participate in the food offerings. A further false door at the west end of the attached mortuary temple, against the pyramid, allowed the *ka* access to the pyramid through the temple.

It would appear that the pyramid had been used for the burial of the king although it had been robbed in antiquity, as in the burial chamber there was a basalt sarcophagus with a band of *Pyramid Texts* inscribed around the edge. This was the first time that the *Pyramid Texts* had been used on a sarcophagus. Robbers had broken the lid, ransacking the body, leaving only a few fragments of the mummy intact (*colour plate 2*). The pyramid of Tety is only the second pyramid to include the *Pyramid Texts*, although he makes it clear that the texts are from an older source, and makes reference to a period when burials were much simpler (namely pit burials).

Two queens, Iput and Khuit, were also buried in the complex of the Tety pyramid, south of the inner temple, and are the only two queens of Tety's royal court furnished with their own pyramids. Iput, Tety's principal wife, was originally buried in a mastaba tomb at the site, but her son Pepy decided, as king, to turn it into a pyramid. This pyramid did not have an entrance as most pyramids would, as it was an extension onto a mastaba, but there was a red granite false door in the offering chapel, allowing the *ka* access. In this chapel there was a statue chamber with three statue niches and a granite offering slab. The mortuary priests laid offerings before the statues of the queen in the niches, which reached her *ka* and nourished her in the afterlife. The remains of Iput were found in a cedar coffin within a dressed-

9 Pyramid of Tety, Saqqara. *Photograph Wayne R. Frostick*

limestone sarcophagus, although all that remained was a skeleton due to ancient tomb robbers. These remains were found alongside a necklace and a gold bracelet, indicating that she had a wealthy burial with numerous funerary goods. Five crude canopic jars were also found, indicating that more than one person was buried within this pyramid. The burial chamber was filled with limestone chips up to the height of the sarcophagus lid, which may have been added after burial as a deterrent to robbers. On the sarcophagus lid a number of model items were placed including alabaster vessels, pottery, copper and alabaster slabs each inscribed with the names of sacred oils and model copper tools and fragments of gold leaf. Each of these would serve a purpose for the afterlife and would turn into a useable object.

TETY'S TEMPLES

The mortuary temple of Tety included a pillared court made up of square pillars, and a large rectangular alabaster altar in the centre of the temple which show traces of painted images. The bottom register of the paintings show images of Nile gods bearing offerings, each with a nome standard on their head. In total it would appear that there were 22 images of these nome standards, representing the 22 nomes of

Lower Egypt, supported by the presence of the standard of Memphis. The top of the altar was probably decorated with two *htp* signs (the hieroglyphic sign for offerings) reinforcing the purpose of this altar. Similar altars were found in the mortuary temples of the surrounding pyramids of earlier kings. These temples accommodated the priests of the funerary cult who left offerings to the *ka* of the deceased, officiated at the royal funeral and performed the burial rites. There were numerous magazines on either side of the pillared court, used to store items needed for the maintenance of the 'cult of the *ka*' of the king. From this pillared hall there was a short staircase leading to a statue chapel, which had five statue niches, housing statues of the king and his *ka*; a focus point of prayers and offerings of the priesthood.

During the pyramid age it was common for each pyramid to have a valley temple in addition to the mortuary temple, as well as a village in which the builders of the complex lived. However the location of his valley temple and pyramid town have not yet been found.

A *ka* temple of Tety was built at Tell el Basta in the Delta and was 108 x 50m and was built about 250m north-west of the temple of the cat-headed goddess Bastet. Nearby is the *ka* temple of his son Pepy I of which only two rows of pillars have survived. These temples would also have served the funerary cult of the king, and the priests made offerings and recited prayers to aid him on the journey through the afterlife.

THE BURIAL COMPLEX AT SAQQARA

The pyramid of Tety formed part of a large burial complex where the top officials, and the royal family were buried. However, Tety's choice of cemetery was unusual as there were already a number of fifth dynasty mastaba tombs on the site. At the start of his reign he built an enclosure wall around the complex which prevented expansion of the site. If he had ruled for longer than 12 years, officials from the later years would not have had the space to be buried within the royal cemetery. It was usual to have a wall around a royal enclosure but particularly unusual to have a wall built around an official cemetery. It would appear that the cemetery was designed as a single project with each official in position at the start of the reign being assigned a space to erect their mastaba tombs. Tety either did not expect to rule for long, indicating he may have been elderly, or he felt he had chosen his officials so well they would remain with him until their death, meaning he would not need to choose another set of officials.

Tety's pyramid was to the south of the necropolis and his queens were buried to the east of the site. Important officials of the royal court were buried to the north of the pyramid and less important officials were buried further north or to the west of the queen's burials. The numerous guards of Tety all had small but wealthy mud-brick mastabas in the north-west of the cemetery. As they were considered important by the king they were buried close to him so they could continue to protect him in the afterlife.

The Tety funerary complex was in close proximity to the pyramids of Djoser (2668-49 BC), Userkaf (2498-91 BC), and Unas (2375-45 BC), each of whom was a pioneer of his time in pyramid construction and Tety wanted to associate himself with these kings. All of these kings, like Tety, abandoned the use of Re in their names despite the growing popularity of the solar cult in Egypt. None of Tety's children has Re included in their names, indicating a further distancing from the solar cult. This may have been a conscious action by these kings against the growing power of the priests, although none of these kings abandoned the solar cult altogether. King Userkaf built a sun temple, and Tety also promoted two of his viziers Kagemi and Mereruka to the position of 'High Priest of Re' and between them they cover almost the entire reign of Tety. During this period the introduction of Osiris into the *Pyramid Texts* and inclusion of the texts in the Pyramid of Unas and Tety deflects some of the power from the priesthood of Re as the *Pyramid Texts* alone can aid the dead in the afterlife, without the need of priests. It is possible that at the end of the fifth dynasty and the start of the sixth dynasty there was a power struggle between the priests of Re and the royal family.

ASSASSINATION

Manetho recorded that Tety I was assassinated by his bodyguards, which would be ironic considering the lengths Tety went to in order to protect himself. This statement of Manetho has caused a lot of research into this king's reign. There is no evidence of this however, other than this record, written 2000 years after the event. This does not however mean that there was not a record similar to the *Instruction of Amenemhat*, available to Manetho, which is unavailable now. The *Instruction of Amenemhat I for his son Senusret I* describes how to prevent assassination:

> Beware of the subjects who are nobodies, of whose plotting one is not aware. Trust not a brother, know not a friend, make no intimates, it is worthless. When you lie down, guard your heart yourself …. He who ate my food raised opposition, he whom I gave my trust used it to plot …. It was after supper, night had come. I was taking an hour of rest, lying on my bed, for I was weary. As my heart began to follow sleep, weapons for my protection were turned against me …. I awoke at the fighting, alert, and found it was the combat of the guard. Had I

quickly seized weapons in my hand, I would have made the cowards retreat in haste. But no one is strong at night: no one can fight alone; no success is achieved without a helper.

Thus bloodshed occurred while I was without you; before the courtiers had heard I would hand over to you, before I had sat with you so as to advise you. For I had not prepared for it, had not expected it, had not foreseen the failing of the servants.

It is, however, possible that such an event would not have been recorded as the assassination of a king would undermine the divine kingship ideology, and the texts that have survived recording such events may be anomalies.

If Tety was assassinated by his bodyguards the severity of their punishment would depend on his successor. If the successor was a usurper benefiting from the murder the assassins may have been rewarded. If the successor was a supporter of Tety the punishment would have been harsh.

THE AFTERMATH

After Tety died, whether by foul play or natural causes, his successor was King Userkara. Although the relationship between Tety and Userkara is uncertain it appears that Userkara usurped the throne from the rightful heir Pepy I, although he only ruled for about a year before Pepy took his place (*colour plate 3*). There are many ideas regarding who this usurper may have been, including:

◇ A usurper supported by the growing power of the priests of Re, who may have aided with his ascension to the throne in order to gain more power, wealth and status

◇ The next legitimate king, who may have descended from the fifth dynasty, making Tety the usurper

◇ A 'stopgap' to oversee the regency of Queen Iput, Tety's widow, whilst her son Pepy came of age. This seems unlikely as he only ruled for a year, and if Pepy was only a year shy of coming of age he would have ruled with his mother as his regent

◇ Userkara may have been a son of Tety, by a secondary wife and therefore a legitimate heir

As Userkara only ruled for about a year practically nothing has survived of his reign; a few monuments, no titles, or personal names, making it difficult to identify who he really was. This absence of information could suggest Pepy I wiped out the existence of this reign when he came to the throne a year later. If Userkara was the son of a secondary wife, it would also be likely that his and her tomb would be destroyed by Pepy I. This would fit in with the evidence from the Tety cemetery as many of the tombs show evidence of deliberate damage. Those tombs that were not damaged were those who died during the reign of Tety, and those who were not in the personal service of the king; whereas those present at the end of his reign had intentionally damaged tombs. A number of Tety's guards were punished by having their names removed from tombs, or the infliction of damage to the face and feet of the figures, ensuring the deformity of the deceased in the afterlife. Three men also had their entire figures and names erased; the 'Chief Physician' Seankhiptah, the 'Overseer of Weapons', Merire who shared the title with Mereruka, and the 'Vizier' Hesi, suggesting they had committed a crime of greater magnitude than the others. The punishments were therefore for offences committed at or near the end of Tety's reign.

Some officials, including Tetyseneb and Mehi, at the end of the reign of Tety wanted to disassociate themselves from him, indicating it may have been dangerous for them to still be associated with him during King Userkara's reign. Tetyseneb replaced his name meaning 'Tety is healthy' with another name; Iri. The son of Khentika, the vizier at the end of the reign of Tety changed his name from Tety-Djedi to Pepy-Djedi, therefore showing allegiance to the rightful heir. Evidence would suggest that he changed his name during the building of his father's mastaba which may have started very near the end of the reign or even after Tety's death. Other officials also changed their names on the accession of the new king, further indicating there was a troublesome change of kings; an official called Tetyhotep changed his name to Pepyhotep to honour the new king. Mehi carved out Tety's cartouche from his personal tomb, and replaced it with that of Userkara. However, during the reign of Pepy I, Mehi removed the new block and replaced it with the old block. This strongly suggests that both Tetyseneb and Mehi both outlived King Tety and, for whatever reasons, during the reign of Userkara they disassociated themselves from Tety, and then during the reign of Pepy I pledged allegiance to Tety again; this indicates that Userkara was not a supporter of Tety, and those loyal to him may have been persecuted. Despite this change, Mehi's sarcophagus was unfinished and it would appear that a burial did not take place, at least not in this mastaba, indicating that he did not win Pepy's trust after his earlier disloyalty to his father.

Although evidence is circumstantial it would appear that there may have been a conspiracy that brought about the end of Tety's reign, meaning that Userkara could usurp the throne from the very young Pepy I.

THREE

KHNUMNAKHT AND NAKHTANKH

TWO BROTHERS

INTRODUCTION

Two brothers, who lived in the twelfth dynasty, were buried together in a joint tomb at the cemetery at Rifeh close to where they lived. These two brothers were called Khnumnakht and Nakhtankh and their bodies and funerary equipment are currently in the Manchester Museum.

TOMB

The tomb of Khnumnakht and Nakhtankh was discovered by a workman called Erfai, who was working under the British Egyptologist Ernest Mackay, for Petrie's excavations in 1906. Petrie described it as 'one of the finest collections of its kind that has ever been discovered in Egypt'. Bearing in mind this was before the discovery of Tutankhamun, and the Tanis tombs, an almost undisturbed tomb of two nobles was remarkable. The tomb itself was a large unsculptured rock-cut tomb, cut into the corner of a courtyard of a grander tomb, dated to the reign of Ramses III and as the tomb had not been cleared in antiquity it could be suggested that the entrance of the tomb was not visible at the time of Ramses III. Their tomb was so full of furniture there was very little space for the excavation to take place, and in the early stages a small boy crept in and passed the moveable objects out to the archaeologists until there was space for them to enter. The tomb contained two sets of coffins, one set for each brother, one set of canopic equipment belonging to Nakhtankh (*10*), pottery vessels and three carved wooden statues of the tomb owners.

One small statue was placed in the coffin of Khnumnakht and the other two were in the coffin of Nakhtankh; these two seemed less stylised and more natural than that in the coffin of Khnumnakht. However, the names written on the wooden figures did not match the coffins they had been placed in. One of Nakhtankh's statues was in his own coffin and the other two were the wrong way round; Nakhtankh therefore had a figure of himself and one of his brother and Khnumnakht only had a figure of his brother. When Nakhtankh, as the older brother, buried Khnumnakht he may have placed a small statue of himself in the coffin as a sign of the bond they held in life. Two model boats (*11*) were amongst the funerary goods, which are thought to have belonged to Nakhtankh although they are not inscribed with his name. One of the boats was for the journey upstream equipped with sails and the other for the journey downstream equipped with oars. They were designed for the journey to and from Abydos, where all Egyptians were expected to make a pilgrimage. The model boats within the tomb were painted red with white decks and were equipped with a full crew of sailors. On the boat with oars the steersman and the lookout are wrapped very tightly in their cloaks in protection against the cold north wind. There were also two statue figures of female offering bearers, who provided food for the brothers' afterlife.

The study of their mummies, from the very beginning, has played a significant role in the development of Egyptian palaeopathology (the study of disease in ancient bodies). In 1908 the first Curator of Egyptology at Manchester, Dr Margaret Murray, gathered together a multi-disciplinary team, who undertook an autopsy and scientific study of the mummies of these two brothers. The two brothers were unwrapped in the Chemistry Building of Manchester University. The unwrapping of Khnumnakht was a public ceremony with 500 people present and only took 90 minutes, and contrary to the scientific approach of the unwrapping it is recorded that:

> At the close of the ceremony members … who wished to have a piece of the mummy wrappings were invited by the chairman to leave their names and addresses.

As scientific as this autopsy was, it caused irreversible damage to the brothers' bodies, as well as to the bandages which were freely distributed afterwards. At the time of the unwrapping there were soft tissues on both of the bodies but now only the skeletons remain. The mummies were both in a very different state of preservation, with the mummy of Khnumnakht being extremely dry, and Nakhtankh being moist – most of his bandages were wet.

10 Canopics of Nakhtankh. *Photograph from Petrie 1907*

11 Boat of Nakhtankh. *Photograph from Petrie 1907*

Each of the brothers' bodies was discovered in an anthropoid coffin, within a rectangular wooden coffin. From these coffins we learn that they were both sons of a woman called 'Aa-Khnum'. Their father, however, is not named, although he has the title of 'Mayor' on the coffin of Nakhtankh, and 'Son of the Mayor' on the coffin of Khnumnakht. Through examination of the bodies it is suggested that they were in fact half-brothers due to an apparent race difference between them, indicating that their fathers were different. Khnumnakht displays Negroid features on his skull (*colour plate 4*) whereas his brother Nakhtankh does not. Nakhtankh's skull has numerous feminine qualities, being smaller with a lighter brow ridge, and his long bones were slighter than expected for a male skeleton and there are less pronounced joints for the muscles, all indicating a petitely built man (*colour plate 5*).

It is generally believed that Khnumnakht's father may have been a Nubian, although from studies of his body there is not enough evidence to say this for definite. It is also possible that one of the brothers may have been adopted which was a common practice in ancient Egypt. The Manchester Mummy Project eventually plan to do DNA tests to find out the truth regarding their relationship. The autopsies also show that the brothers had been mummified using two different methods, indicating either an inequality of status or a change in financial wealth.

NAKHTANKH

Nakhtankh was in a poor state of preservation before unwrapping, although his face was almost perfectly preserved showing brown skin, and stubble on the side of his face. He also had remains of grey hair on his head which was visible in 1908 but has since disappeared. His body had been mummified traditionally and his internal organs had been removed and preserved. His chest cavity had been filled with matting to retain a natural shape. Underneath the bandages of the mummy were the remains of beetles, indicating the body might not have been buried straight away after embalming. There is evidence from the Ptolemaic Period that bodies were sometimes stored in back rooms of the home to wait for other family members to die before opening family tombs, and this may have been practiced in this period too. There is also evidence that his brain had been removed in the traditional fashion and his nails had been tied onto his fingers and toes to prevent lifting during the mummification process. He was furnished with a set of pottery canopic jars and a wooden canopic chest which was found near his coffin. The canopic jars are painted yellow and inscribed. The bodies of the jars are made of pottery and the stoppers were made of carved wood covered with stucco. Each compartment of the chest was padded out with natural fibre.

A study has been done on the build and stature of the two brothers and it has been discovered that they were quite short with Nakhtankh standing just 5ft 6in tall and his brother standing at 5ft 5in. Despite this small height difference Nakhtankh has a very petite skeletal structure, and it has been suggested that he may have been a eunuch.

Due to the very poor condition of his mummy there was very little soft tissue remaining and most of that fell off when he was unwrapped. This was luckily stored in a jar and kept until it was re-examined in a study in 1975. Unfortunately the remainder of his genitalia does not confirm or deny the possibility of his eunuch status. However it would appear that Nakhtankh may have undergone some genital modification. It would appear that he had suffered a bisection of the underside of his penis, which is a practice known to have been carried out by Australian aborigines although evidence of this practice in Egypt is rare. In Australia when this operation was carried out it was accompanied by the extraction of the upper right incisor, as a visible sign that this operation had been performed. The Egyptologists originally unwrapping Nakhtankh were delighted to discover his incisor was also missing. However, further examination by the Manchester Mummy Project indicated all his teeth were present in life and some had fallen out post mortem. As the evidence from his soft tissues is inconclusive it has been suggested that rather than being a castrated male he may have been born as a natural eunuch.

In two of Nakhtankh's four canopic jars were preserved internal organs; the liver with the gall bladder attached, and lung tissue with part of the wall of the heart attached to it. It is thought that near to his death Nakhtankh may have had an inflamed heart, possibly due to pneumonia resulting in it being partially extracted with the lung. Tissue from his lung showed various diseases including sand pneumoconiosis (caused by breathing in sand), and silica discovered in his lung has been identified as sand particles. This condition is common with desert populations and many Egyptians suffered from this. The inflammation of the lung surface indicates pleurisy and a condition of the heart known as pericarditis. The combination of these conditions made breathing very difficult and painful, and Nakhtankh probably would frequently wheeze and cough. The only remedy available for this was a honey mixture which probably would not have soothed his coughing fits.

As well as breathing difficulties Nakhtankh also suffered from osteoarthritis seriously affecting his back, making standing, sitting and lying down a painful experience. He may also have had a stoop due to these problems, which may have been quite disabling. Nakhtankh, however, may have been the more active of the two brothers as he had extensive development of the facets of the femora and tibiae due to constant squatting.

Nakhtankh died at about 60 years old, probably of old age, although it is possible that his breathing problems became fatal, aggravated by pneumonia.

The rectangular wooden coffin of Nakhtankh is currently in the British Museum (BM EA 35285) and is a typical Middle Kingdom coffin with minimal decoration, and a common offering inscription. Within the rectangular coffin was an anthropoid coffin which was laid on its left side so the body could look out through the eyes painted on the side of the rectangular coffin to the east. The east was both the place of the newborn sun, as well as where the funerary chapel was normally situated. The anthropoid coffin of Nakhtankh was in better condition than that of his brother. It had a painted black face, which was not an indication of race but is a colour associated with the rich fertile soil of the inundation, therefore associated with fertility and rebirth. The face has inlaid eyes and eyebrows. He is shown wearing a plain nemes headdress and a dark green beard incised with yellow horizontal lines representing hair. He is also shown wearing a coloured bead collar; a permanent example of the floral garlands often laid over mummies in the coffin.

KHNUMNAKHT

Khnumnakht's body was in a much worse state of preservation than Nakhtankh's. It was very dry and as soon as it was touched it crumbled into dust. Where fragments of the body had survived the skin was white, due to the drying process rather than ethnic origin. Unfortunately this poor state of preservation meant a full study in the 1970s was not possible. From rudimentary studies it would appear that Khnumnakht was about 45 years old when he died, but he did not have any canopic equipment with him in the tomb indicating that perhaps his burial was not of the same standard as Nakhtankh. Unlike his brother, when Khnumnakht was unwrapped there were no insect remains in the wrappings indicating that Khnumnakht had been buried straight away.

Studies show that Khnumnakht also suffered from osteoarthritis, in his hip and neck leaving him with a disfiguring and disabling stoop, hindered by abnormal curvature (scoliosis) in the thoracic region. It is thought that this may have been caused by persistent squatting throughout his life which was a common problem as most people in ancient Egypt worked in this position. Through study of the skull it was discovered the configuration of his front teeth show a rare condition called double germination resulting in the fusion of the upper left incisors; the left one was larger than the right one, and was formed with two roots which has caused a tusk-like appearance of his incisors.

It was originally believed that Khnumnakht also had a clubfoot, which affected walking, although further study has indicated that rather than a congenital deformity this damage to his foot may have been caused by excessively tight bandaging during mummification.

His fingers had been separately bandaged but there was no evidence of trying to protect the fingernails during the mummification process. There is also no evidence that Khnumnakht's brain had been removed, although there were no remains of it within his skull. It is therefore clear that the mummification of Khnumnakht was inferior to that of his brother.

Some of the bandages of Khnumnakht were inscribed with 'Year three – good (*in reference to the linen*), 'The Great *Wab*', and on Nakhtankh his bandages read 'Year four – good' indicating that Khnumnakht died first and was followed the next year by his older brother. Nakhtankh's bandages also stated he was 'Foremost of the two Living' perhaps in recognition of his senior status to Khnumnakht. All of Khnumnakht's bandages are dyed yellow whereas only a few of Nakhtankh's bandages are dyed. They were both dyed using the safflower which was a cheap method of producing colour.

Khnumnakht stood at 5ft 5in, and was of a bigger build than his brother. He also had a larger skull with a large jaw pushing his teeth forward, giving him a rather prominent mouth. As the larger of the two brothers he may have been more robust, and there is evidence that he suffered a broken rib in life which had healed.

The rectangular wooden coffin of Khnumnakht was very similar in design to that of his brother, with minimal decoration, mostly consisting of traditional offering formulas. His coffin had three false doors on each of the long sides and one on either end to enable Khnumnakht to participate in the offerings in the tomb. Both of the brothers' rectangular coffins were made of *ficus sycamors* (sycamore wood), native to Egypt, and the coffin pegs holding the planks together were made of acacia, also native to Egypt. Laurel leaves and stalks were also found in some of the pottery vessels located in the tomb.

Within Khnumnakht's rectangular coffin was an anthropoid coffin, also discovered lying on the left side in the coffin so he could look through the eyes painted on the exterior. Both of the brothers' coffins are different, but both have a decorative pattern between the horizontal strips, which are thought to represent net or bead shrouds that were sometimes placed over the body before the introduction of the anthropoid coffin. The face of Khnumnakht's coffin is painted yellow, which is normally the colour used to denote women. His striped nemes headdress hangs further down the chest of the lid than Nakhtankh's and he also has inlaid eyes of limestone and obsidian, inserted into bronze rims, inlaid eyebrows and a false beard with the appearance of plaited leather. This coffin is very badly damaged with the decoration flaking in various places.

IDENTIFICATION

Khnumnakht is thought to be half Nubian and he shows slightly more Negroid features on his skeletal remains than Nakhtankh although it is not enough to attribute him firmly to any racial type. However, it is generally agreed that the skull and mouth type are too different on the mummies for them to be full brothers, or indeed of the same race.

The inscriptions on the coffins can perhaps shed some light on the situation. Khnumnakht held the title 'Great *Wab*-priest' of the cult of Khnum at Rifeh and his grandfather held the title of local mayor. Nakhtankh on the other hand is identified as the son of a local mayor, and neither names are given. Both men had the same mother and it could indicate that she in fact married twice, and perhaps her second marriage was to the son of her first husband (by a first wife). However whether Khnumnakht's father was Nubian is unknown. It has also been suggested that Nakhtankh, as the older brother by 20 years, may have adopted Khnumnakht to take over his position when he died, as he was unable to have children himself due to his eunuch status. However his profession is not made clear.

CONCLUSION

The extensive study of the mummies of Khnumnakht and Nakhtankh has told us many things about the later lives of these brothers. The study also indicates that people did not die as young as generally believed as Nakhtankh was 60 and Khnumnakht was 45 at death. We also can gather some information about families, as we know that they were of the same mother, but apparently different fathers, indicating that Nakhtankh suffered either the death or divorce of his father, and then the birth or adoption of his new brother. The coffin of Khnumnakht was placed into the tomb first indicating that he died before his older brother Nakhtankh and this is supported by the wrappings of the bodies. Nakhtankh's is dated to year four and Khnumnakht is dated to year three indicating that he died first.

If one of the brothers was adopted then that suggests that their father may have needed an heir for his occupation to be passed down to. Often if there was not a son, or if the son did not want to or could not continue with the father's profession

12 Khnum, Late Period.
Copyright: Petrie Museum of
Egyptian Archaeology, University
College London, UC 52785

they would adopt another boy to be trained as an apprentice. Due to Nakhtankh's very slight build he may not have had the constitution for the occupation of mayor. However, as potentially a eunuch, Nakhtankh may have wanted to pass his own profession onto someone but was unable to father a son, hence he may have adopted the younger Khnumnakht. Whatever their relationship they obviously were very close in life hence they were buried together for eternity.

FOUR

AHMOSE
THE END OF AN ERA

INTRODUCTION

King Ahmose was the first king of the eighteenth dynasty, and of the New Kingdom. He is famous for ending the conflict between the Theban seventeenth dynasty and the Hyksos kings of the Delta region.

FAMILY

Ahmose was the son of Seqenenre Tao II and Ahhotep, and had one brother, Kamose. His parents were brother and sister, a standard practice for the Egyptian royal family. His grandparents were Seqenenre Tao I and Queen Tetisheri. He was born in approximately 1580 BC and came onto the throne in 1570 BC when he was still a child, at only 10 years old.

Ahmose grew up in Thebes, during a time of political instability in the Second Intermediate Period, when Egypt was divided, with the Hyksos ruling the north and Ahmose's family ruling the south. The *Sallier I Papyrus* talks of the conflict between Apophis, the Hyksos king, and Seqenenre Tao II, and describes the elaborate palace that Ahmose and his brother would have grown up in. The papyrus is in the form of a letter from Apophis to the Theban king who complains of the hippopotami in the pool of Seqenenre's palace keeping him awake in the Delta, a distance of over 500 miles. Although it was designed to antagonise the Theban king the papyrus could indicate that Seqenenre Tao II really had a hippopotamus pool in his palace in Thebes. This would suggest a very elaborate palace which could accommodate these large animals.

Ahmose had a childhood of upheaval, as his father died in battle when he was still very young, about five or six years old, leaving him to be raised by his mother, and grandmother. Ahmose learnt to read, write and was taught at an early age the art of warfare in the military town of El Kab, 40 miles south of Luxor. It is probable that as a child and teenager he would also have visited the new military town built by his father at Deir el Ballas which was the staging post for all of the battles with the Hyksos. Kamose ascended to the throne in 1573 BC when he was a teenager and Ahmose was still a child, and Ahhotep, Kamose's mother, acted as co-regent whilst he was engaged in battle.

Ahmose's mother was a strong woman who not only acted as regent, when his brother Kamose was king, but also when he was king. A stela at Karnak describes her role as regent:

> She is one who has accomplished the rites and cared for Egypt. She has looked after Egypt's troops and she has guarded them. She has also brought back fugitives and collected together the deserters. She has pacified Upper Egypt and expelled her rebels.

This stela suggests she held a military role which was unusual for a queen. This may have been necessary as both her husband and her eldest son had been killed in battle, which could have caused the army to lose heart.

Whilst the men were at war it was important to provide a stable figurehead, so the army were motivated in what would prove to be harrowing campaigns and this may have been Ahhotep's role. Her funerary equipment included a necklace of the 'Order of the Fly' which was a military honour (13), weapons, including a jewelled dagger, and a lapis axe with Ahmose's cartouche amidst images of smiting scenes. During the time of military campaigns, when the king and princes were fighting, the domestic administration of Egypt was probably left to Ahhotep, throughout both her husband's and her son Kamose's reign.

In addition to the death of his father and his older brother, Ahmose also had to cope with the death of his grandmother Tetisheri in 1541 BC. He lived with her influence until he was 39 years old and therefore her death would have been a great loss. Her mummified body was found in the Deir el Bahri 1881 cache known as the 'Unknown woman B' but the location of her original tomb remains a mystery. The mummy is elderly, partially bald with artificial hair braided to the remains of her white hair. She was quite short and had a substantial overbite which was characteristic of the royal family in the eighteenth dynasty (14).

Only 11 years after the death of his grandmother, Ahmose also lost his mother Ahhotep, in 1530 BC, therefore losing another of his best advisors and his last relative.

Above: 13 Golden Fly of Ahhotep,
Luxor Museum. *Photograph
Charlotte Booth*

Right: 14 Mummy of Tetisheri.
Photograph from Elliot Smith 1912

She was buried at the royal cemetery Dra Abu el Naga in Thebes, and she had many funerary goods, including elaborate rishi coffins decorated with wings, jewellery and a number of weapons. As mentioned earlier this reflects the military nature of the period and also her active role in the military. Many of the weapons have the cartouches of Kamose and Ahmose and may have belonged to them and been kept by Ahhotep. There are also items that look like they are from Minoan Crete indicating there was an alliance between Egypt and Crete at some point during her life.

Despite losing the two most important women in his life – and his father and his elder brother – Ahmose had the companionship of a number of wives. It has been suggested that Ahmose may, in his later years, have married a Minoan princess, which may have sealed the alliance between Egypt and Crete. His palace at Avaris, built after the Hyksos expulsion, was decorated with Minoan frescoes, normally found only in Cretan palaces, indicating a princess from the Cretan royal family may have resided at Avaris. If Ahmose had married a Minoan princess she would have been happier living in an environment decorated in a recognisable fashion, and the palace may have been decorated this way just for her and her entourage. In addition to this political marriage, his Egyptian chief wife was Ahmose-Nefertari (*colour plate 6*), who was also his sister, as was traditional for the Egyptian royal family. They had at least two children, a son Amenhotep who later became Amenhotep I, and a daughter Meritamun who married her brother.

Ahmose-Nefertari was still alive in 1523 BC, in the first year of the reign of Thutmosis I, her grandson, although the exact date of her death is unknown (*colour plate 7*). Her mummified remains were found in the 1881 Deir el Bahri cache. She was probably in her 70s also with a severe overbite, and was suffering from hair loss, which had been disguised with 20 strings of twisted human hair plaited into her own. She was obviously a fashionable woman and did not want to be 'seen dead' with thinning hair (*15*). It would seem that Ahmose-Nefertari did not get buried straight away as her body had started to decompose before it was mummified, which was a practice to prevent embalmers from defiling important female bodies.

CAMPAIGN AGAINST THE HYKSOS

There were three campaigns against the Hyksos rulers of Egypt (*16*). After a century on the throne of Lower Egypt the Hyksos gradually started moving south until they were the legitimate rulers of both Upper and Lower Egypt; the Theban seventeenth dynasty retaliated and started the first campaign against the Hyksos rulers. This was during the reign of Seqenenre Tao II, the father of Ahmose.

15 Mummy of Ahmose-Nefertari. *Photograph from Elliot Smith 1912*

SEQENENRE TAO II'S CAMPAIGN

Although we know Seqenenre Tao started a campaign against the Hyksos, no records have survived of the battle itself. Injuries on his mummy indicate he was killed in battle, with numerous wounds to his head (*17*). He was relatively young and dying in his 30s. He probably died on the battlefield and his body may have lain for some time before being removed for mummification, as his body had started to

16 Hyksos women, Beni Hasan. *Photograph Ulla Kaer Andersen*

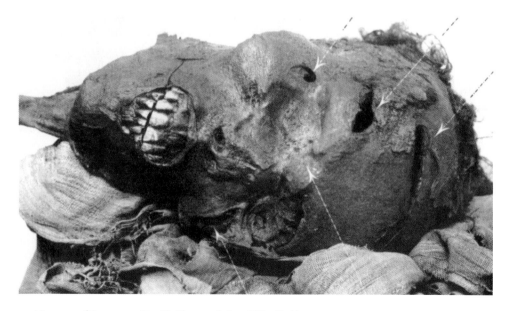

17 Mummy of Seqenenre Tao II. *Photograph from Elliot Smith 1912*

decompose and the grimace, the head angle and also the angle of the arm is due to the way he had lain and the embalmers were unable to do anything to rearrange the body. He would no doubt have had a typical royal burial but his tomb has not been found, although his body was later placed in the Deir el Bahri cache.

KAMOSE'S CAMPAIGN

At the death of Seqenenre Tao, his teenage son Kamose took over the throne and the campaign against the Hyksos. Kamose may have been more motivated than his father due to wanting to avenge his father's death. However as he was quite young he initially signed a treaty between himself and the Hyksos king Apophis. The treaty stated that Apophis could control land and sea trade routes between Egypt, the East Mediterranean and the Near East. The Nubian rulers at that time controlled trade from Nubia and the Hyksos had an alliance with them and used a route through the oasis to trade with them, therefore cutting out the Thebans altogether. It is likely that Kamose was pushed into signing this treaty and he soon devised a plan abandoning the treaty, starting a new campaign against the Hyksos which he recorded on the *Kamose Stela* from Karnak temple currently in the Luxor Museum (*18*).

In year three of his reign, Kamose planned a surprise attack on the Hyksos. He was heartless and made examples of any Hyksos prisoners or Egyptians who supported them that he could capture. The *Kamose Stela* records how Tety, son of Pepy, a supporter of the Hyksos, captured at the site of Nefrusy, was subdued by the king and his wife taken as prisoner. The Egyptians were brutal in their subjugation of prisoners and would have executed and displayed them in public places as examples to others.

When the Egyptian army reached the fortified town of Avaris they took possession of the trading ships of the Hyksos, which were full of various goods, including wood and oil being imported into Egypt. However they then hit a stalemate. The Egyptian army were outside the walls of the fortified town, without the strength to proceed and the Hyksos looking out were completely unwilling to engage in battle.

The Egyptian army eventually left Avaris shouting insults at the Hyksos, and arrived in Thebes celebrating a victory. As there would not have been any media other than the king and his spin-doctors no-one would know that it was not a victory until some time later.

The Egyptians, once back in Thebes, blocked communication between the Hyksos rulers and those of Kush by securing the oasis routes, west of Thebes. This prevented the Hyksos from getting support from Kush, as well as blocking trade

18 Kamose Stela, Luxor Museum. *Photograph Wayne R. Frostick*

routes, and therefore goods reaching Avaris. The Egyptian army had also managed to retake the towns north of Hermopolis, placing them under the jurisdiction of the Theban seventeenth dynasty.

Kamose died in 1570 BC when he was approximately 25 years old, possibly in battle. The coffin in which he was buried has been found but the body itself had disintegrated, preserving the secrets of his death. Ahmose would probably have been named the successor at or prior to the death of Kamose, in order for the army to have a figurehead, and to prevent any problems regarding succession. However, no official coronation took place until a more stable time. Ahmose took over the throne when he was 10 years old, and it probably would not have looked like such a promising career, considering he had seen the last two kings killed on the battlefield. His earliest memories of both his brother and his father were in the form of battle reports and plans, no doubt with much detail of the brutality administered to the enemy, as well as the dismembered, decapitated bodies of the enemies captured in battle. This no doubt dictated how he viewed his future as the king of Egypt.

AHMOSE'S CAMPAIGN

Ahmose, being a child when he became king, waited a few years before continuing with the campaign of his father and brother. He would probably have been about 15 when he took his first army into battle against the Hyksos. The battles of Ahmose are recorded at El Kab just south of Luxor, in the tombs of two army officers, Ahmose son of Ebana and Ahmose Pennekhab.

Ahmose son of Ebana, a naval officer from a military family, and probably a childhood friend of King Ahmose. He boasts: 'I used to attend the king … when he went forth in his chariot' indicating he was close to the king.

The *Rhind Papyrus*, mentions that in year 11 (1559 BC) King Ahmose entered Heliopolis in early July and the city of Sile in mid-October indicating that they were moving quickly north towards the fortified town of Avaris. Along the way they cut off the route for any potential troops from Canaan isolating the Hyksos at Avaris. Ahmose reached Avaris amidst a number of small battles between enemy troops and the Egyptians. Ahmose son of Ebana records his capturing of a prisoner for which he was rewarded by the king with the 'Gold of Valour' which may have been in the form of a 'golden fly', or gold jewellery, either armbands or necklaces.

After many small battles Avaris was sacked, and the important buildings and temples were ransacked and burned to the ground. There are a number of group burials at the site indicating that the Hyksos soldiers were buried quickly and without ceremony. Some Hyksos were captured by the Egyptians and trained as servants in exchange for their lives. Ahmose son of Ebana was personally given four Hyksos prisoners as servants in payment for his role in the battle.

King Ahmose then built two buildings at Avaris, which became the campaign residences of his army whilst he continued to chase the Hyksos completely out of Egypt. Manetho records that the Hyksos initially tried to make a treaty with the Egyptian king stating they would be allowed to leave Egypt unharmed but Ahmose did not want to risk them regrouping and returning to Egypt. He had now probably decided to avenge both his father's and brother's deaths. For three years he pursued the Hyksos out of Egypt to Sharuhen and sacked all cities on the way, to make it difficult for them to return and also acting as a warning to those thinking of supporting them.

On his return to Egypt Ahmose started to reinforce the borders, make foreign alliances (to prevent invasion) and to generally strengthen the country. At that time Crete was the strongest naval power in the area, and an alliance with them was very advantageous for the Egyptians against naval attacks, as they themselves were not a sea-faring nation. This alliance may have been further sealed through the political marriage of the Egyptian king with a Cretan princess. Ahmose also launched a number of rapid campaigns to Syria to ensure that this border was also secure.

Once the northern borders were secure Ahmose campaigned southwards and focused his attention to Nubia which was still governed by the Kushite rulers. Ahmose was uncertain of their loyalty even after explaining the advantages to them, in the only way he knew how, as recorded by Ahmose son of Ebana: 'His Majesty made great slaughter among them and I brought booty from there. Two living men and three hands'.

There were numerous small rebellions in Nubia, all recorded as a victory for the king of Egypt. Just north of the second cataract a Nubian rebel called Aata attacked the Egyptian army with a small band of rebels: 'his fate brought on his doom. The Gods of Upper Egypt grasped him'. He was captured by King Ahmose and taken as a servant.

Another uprising was by an Egyptian soldier called Tetian, and a small army of rebels. King Ahmose crushed the rebellion and killed them all, so as to eliminate any threats to his reign. He introduced the title and position of the 'Viceroy of Nubia' ensuring that there was someone in Nubia loyal to the Egyptian state, in a position to report on potential problems and uprisings. The settlement and fort of Buhen in Nubia was also restored and a loyal Egyptian man, Turi, was posted to this fort as 'Governor of Buhen'. He collected taxes and organised administration of the gold mines under Egyptian control, and would report everything to the king.

Ahmose also established a centralised government with viziers of Upper and Lower Egypt reporting directly to him on any problems, uprisings, income or taxes. This ensured complete control over the whole of Egypt.

With this completed, Ahmose had successfully evicted the foreign rulers, reunited Egypt and secured both the northern and southern borders, therefore maintaining the sacred rule of *maat*, and appeasing the gods which could only be beneficial for Egypt in the long term.

Ahmose then started to strengthen the role of the king and the royal family and to re-establish a positive relationship with the god Amun.

As women had been a large influence in his life, Ahmose introduced a religious title of 'God's Wife of Amun', for the wife or daughter of the king to be passed down to female heirs. They played the role of Amun's wife in religious ceremonies and reinforced the ideology that the royal family were closely linked to the gods, and were themselves divine. His mother Ahhotep was the first 'God's Wife of Amun' followed by his wife Ahmose-Nefertari. She made a number of gifts to various temples at Thebes, Abydos and Serabit el Khadim in the Sinai, where turquoise was mined. 'God's Wives' were given land which would provide income through rent, tax and produce, which then went back into the temples through offerings to the god. This title in later periods was sometimes used as a replacement for the title 'Great Royal Wife' indicating it was a high-status position. This title rewarded Ahmose's female relatives and increased their personal wealth whilst making a show to the populace that the worship of the gods was re-established.

In addition to re-establishing trade routes between Egypt and the Sinai, Ahmose also reopened limestone quarries at Tura near Memphis for building works, primarily for the temple of Ptah in Memphis, and the temple of Amun at Karnak. Ahmose also started his own building works with a small temple and cenotaph with a pyramid at Abydos. This was the last royal pyramid to be built in Egypt. He chose to build a pyramid to show a connection with times before the Hyksos, as a way to archaise and legitimising his reign. The temple attached to the pyramid at Abydos had a causeway decorated with images of his campaign against the Hyksos, with images of horses and chariots, all with archers shooting arrows into the air, as Asiatics with small pointed beards fell beneath the wheels.

Ahmose also built a small terraced temple near his cenotaph, which housed caches of votive vessels, model stone vases and boats with oars. At the back of the temple is a pedestal where a statue of the king was placed for offerings to be made to his *ka*.

Near this pyramid Ahmose set up a chapel to Tetisheri, his grandmother. He erected a stela describing this act:

> Now it came to pass that his majesty sat in the audience hall, ... 'great king's wife' Ahmose Nefertari was with his majesty. She asked him 'Why has this been remembered why are you talking about this what has come into your heart?' he replied 'It is I who have

remembered the mother of my mother, and the mother of my father, "great king's wife" and "king's mother" Tetisheri, triumphant. She has a tomb and a memorial chapel on the soil of Thebes and Abydos. I have said this to you, in that I have desired to have for her a pyramid and a house at Abydos as a monumental donation of my majesty.'

This stela is unusual as it shows that during his reign it was normal for his wife to be involved in discussions where she aids with important decisions. This reflects the influence women had on Ahmose's life, and that it was normal for him to consult the royal women on a number of matters. The chapel dedicated to Tetisheri was an elaborate affair with a lake, a garden, livestock and a priesthood in order to carry out the funerary rituals for her *ka*.

After the expulsion of the Hyksos, Ahmose set up a stela at Karnak, which refers to the mass destruction of temples and monuments by the Asiatic rulers of Egypt. It was found from within the third pylon in fragments and is known as the *Unwetterstela*.

The text on the stela refers to the damage being caused by a storm, as a metaphor for the Hyksos. However the phrases used suggest that these monuments may have fallen into disrepair naturally: 'His majesty then ordered the repair of the chapels which had fallen in ruins in all the country'. Another line refers to the sacred chambers of the temple being invaded by the water and the subsequent need to restore them. However, if the Hyksos were a ruling faction in Egypt then their king was entitled to enter these sacred chambers, especially after they had conquered Thebes and were the undisputed rulers of Upper and Lower Egypt. The *Unwetterstela* could be referring to the metaphorical sense of invasion, the feeling of violation that foreigners were allowed in the places reserved for Egyptian rulers. Rebuilding and restoring was a way of eradicating the existence of this invasion.

DEATH AND AFTERMATH

Ahmose died in year 26 of his reign (1546 BC) when he was in his 30s. His tomb has not been found but he was probably buried at the royal cemetery of Dra Abu Naga in western Thebes. His body was found alongside his wife, mother and grandmother in the Deir el Bahri cache (*19*). His brain had been removed during the mummification process unusually via a cut in the back of his neck; his skull was then filled with a ball of resin soaked linen. The only funerary equipment found belonging to Ahmose is a single shabti figure which is currently in the British Museum.

His wife Ahmose-Nefertari outlived him by a number of years. Their son Amenhotep succeeded him as king and ruled initially as a co-regent with his father

19 Mummy of Ahmose. *Photograph from Elliot Smith 1912*

from 1551-46 BC, and then as sole ruler until 1524 BC. As he was still a child when he succeeded the throne his mother Ahmose-Nefertari acted as regent with him for the first few years. He was probably buried in Dra Abu el Naga, and fragments of his *heb sed* images have been found near the area indicating that his funerary temple would also have been in this area. Ahmose-Nefertari outlived her son and was still alive during the reign of the next king, a military man, Thutmosis I. Although her exact date of death is uncertain a cult dedicated to her and her son Amenhotep I was popular in the later New Kingdom at Deir el Medina. The temple of 'Amenhotep of the Garden' is situated around the back of the Ptolemaic temple currently on the site.

After the death of King Ahmose, Ahmose son of Ebana and Ahmose Pennekhab both remained in the army. It is also recorded that Ahmose Pennekhab took part in campaigns during the reigns of Amenhotep I, Thutmosis I, II, III and even the co-regency between Thutmosis III and Hatshepsut, indicating that he lived to an advanced age.

Ahmose son of Ebana went on campaigns to Nubia during the reigns of Amenhotep I and Thutmosis I and the Syrian campaign of Thutmosis I. His son Itruri and grandson Paheri were tutors to the pharaoh's children indicating that through his military career he achieved a great level of trust within the royal family, and this is reflected through the privilege of his children.

CONCLUSION

From the life of Ahmose, we can see he liberated Egypt, from what was seen as the barbaric, destructive reign of the Hyksos. Despite his disrupted childhood he seemed to be very methodical in his campaign against the Hyksos and then in his 'clean up' of Egypt after they had left. He sensibly restored and secured the borders and then concentrated on obtaining allies in the surrounding area through trade, or placing Egyptian loyalists in position in the country. He was able to concentrate on rebuilding the religion and with it the favour of the gods through extensive temple building.

It is hardly surprising that Ahmose grew into a great military king, considering his aggressive and unstable upbringing. He was born during a time of foreign rule and witnessed his father's and brother's campaign to reunite Egypt under an Egyptian king. This ambition meant Ahmose witnessed the death of family members and numerous friends. He spent much of his formative years amidst soldiers, and the military minded women of his family. Despite this unstable background Ahmose honoured his ancestors and seemed to be deeply attached to his mother and grandmother, so although a military king he clearly had a softer side.

FIVE

HATSHEPSUT
THE FEMALE PHARAOH

INTRODUCTION

Hatshepsut is one of the most famous women of ancient Egypt. She lived in the eighteenth dynasty at a particularly wealthy time in Egyptian history and was one of the few women who ruled Egypt in her own right rather than settling for the secondary role of queen or co-ruler, where she had power, but the final decisions were decided by the king regardless of his age or experience.

FAMILY

Hatshepsut's father was Thutmosis I, although his parents are unknown. His predecessor, Amenhotep I died without children leaving the accession to the throne unclear. It is thought that Thutmose I may have been either a minor royal (the son of a minor wife) or the son of a prominent noble family. Hatshepsut's mother, Ahmose, is thought to have been the sister of Thutmosis I and therefore her parents are also unknown. As only royalty married their sisters it suggests that Thutmosis I must have been of royal birth as he married her a few years before he came to the throne in 1524 BC. Hatshepsut was probably born at the end or year one or two of her father's reign in 1522 BC.

Hatshepsut had one full brother and two half-brothers that are known; Prince Amenmose was older than Hatshepsut and was probably approximately 10 years old in year four when he obtained the honorary title of 'General'. He is likely to be the son of Ahmose, as Thutmose I could not have taken another wife until he was crowned. He was named as heir to the throne but died prematurely and never became king.

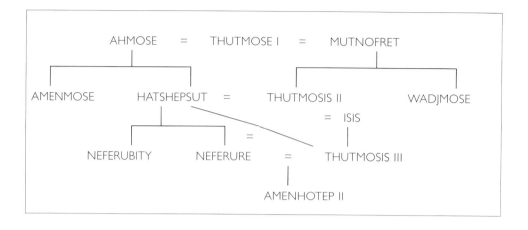

The mother of Wadjmose and Thutmose II was a secondary wife, Mutnofret. Wadjmose was shown with Prince Amenmose and their tutor so they were probably all raised together.

Thutmose I died in year 12 month 9 (1512 BC) when Hatshepsut was approximately 12 years old. She was very close to her father and his death would have had a devastating effect on her. His sarcophagus was found in her tomb rather than his own, indicating that she had ordered it to be moved there at a later date so she could spend eternity with him.

Upon her father's death Hatshepsut married her half-brother Thutmose II who would also have been about 12 or 13 years old. This was a marriage in every sense of the word, and Hatshepsut had two daughters, Neferure and Neferubity, at approximately 14 years old, not long before the death of her husband. Neferubity appeared to have died young as there are few records of this little princess. Thutmosis II also had a son by a minor wife, Isis, who later became Thutmosis III. As a child Thutmosis III was given priestly training at the temple of Amun at Karnak, and it was here that he was proclaimed heir to the throne by the oracle of Amun.

As the queen of Thutmosis II, Hatshepsut had a tomb which was never used in a valley west of the Valley of the Kings. It still holds the sarcophagus intended for her, made of quartzite which at the time was normally only part of a king's funerary equipment and therefore unusual for a queen.

Thutmosis II died in 1504 BC leaving Hatshepsut widowed. His son Thutmosis III took over the throne, even though he was still a young child. Hatshepsut and Thutmosis III married and co-ruled together (*colour plate 8*). As he was young Thutmosis III needed a mentor and regent and Hatshepsut was the most obvious candidate. The biography of a Theban official, Ineni, describes her co-regency:

Thutmosis II went up to heaven and was united with the gods. His son arose on his throne as King of the Two Lands and ruled on the seat of the one who begot him. His sister, the 'God's wife', Hatshepsut controlled the affairs of the Land according to her own plans. Egypt was made to labour with bowed head for her, the excellent seed of the god, who came forth from him

From this description it would appear that whilst Thutmosis III was young Hatshepsut had full control of Egypt, and she made herself quite prominent in the minds of the officials and the people of Egypt. Despite the important role that she played and the extent in which her prominence grew after the death of her first husband, at the start of the co-regency Hatshepsut used traditional queenly titles like 'Principle Wife' or 'God's Wife'. It is suggested that she was testing the political waters by playing the role of the dutiful queen even though she really held the power in this co-regency. After year two she started using titles modelled on those of kings for example 'Mistress of the Two Lands'. She also adopted a throne name, Maatkara, 'Truthful is the spirit of Re', in the manner of kings, which was written in a cartouche. Queens' names were rarely written in cartouches, although after Hatshepsut it became more common for powerful queens.

After year seven, Hatshepsut completely abandoned her queenly titles and adopted the five-fold titulary of a king, and is shown on monuments wearing the masculine attire of a king including the false beard (20). Some people have made the suggestion that she was a transvestite and that these images are proof of this. However if she is to be taken seriously as a king she needs to be represented as a king, due to the symbolic meaning of the kingship iconography.

She even partook in activities normally reserved for kings; very rarely performed by queens. For example she commissioned and dedicated four obelisks at Karnak temple; two on the eastern side of the temple behind the hall of Thutmosis III and the other two between the fourth and fifth pylons. Obelisks represent the first ray of sunshine that appeared at the dawn of creation, and they are long and thin representative of sun-rays. The pyramidion on the top was normally tipped with gold or electrum (21), although Hatshepsut went one step further, as the obelisks on the east side of Karnak were completely covered in gold and the other two were covered to approximately half way down the shaft.

On two obelisks she states she was present at the dawn of creation and knew the thoughts of the creator. She describes herself as 'the luminous seed of the almighty one' and continues:

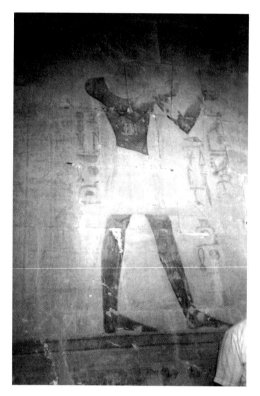

Left: 20 Hatshepsut as a king, Deir el Bahri.
Photograph Wayne R. Frostick

Below: 21 Fallen obelisk of Hatshepsut, Karnak.
Photograph Wayne R. Frostick

> Those who shall see my monument in future years and shall speak of what I have done, beware lest you say 'I know not, I know not how this has been done, fashioning a mountain of gold like something self created' Nor shall he who hears this say it was a boast, but rather 'How like her this is, how worthy of her father.'

These obelisks were set up in front of the hall of her father Thutmosis I who she credits for starting the trend of erecting obelisks, which is only true of Karnak, as other obelisks had been erected by previous kings throughout Egypt from the Old Kingdom. In monumental inscriptions she is also shown making offerings directly to the gods which was also an act reserved for the king, in his role as high priest.

In statues although she is shown in the kingly attire, she is generally represented with a feminine face and body (*colour plate 9*). She basically adapted the traditional Thutmosid style of narrow faces and angular noses and made it her own. It is possible they are true portraits of what this incredible woman looked like. As was traditional, Thutmosis III also adopted this feminine style and sometimes it is difficult to tell the two apart.

Even though she had proclaimed herself king Hatshepsut did not ignore the authority of Thutmosis III and dated her regnal years in line with his, and she often depicted him alongside herself in temple inscriptions. In fact they seemed to share responsibilities; with Thutmosis III concentrating on foreign policy and Hatshepsut concentrating on home affairs. It is also thought Thutmosis may have led two military campaigns to Palestine and a couple into Nubia to quash small uprisings.

In a small rock-cut temple in Middle Egypt, known as the Speos Artemidos (*22*) Hatshepsut describes her campaign to rebuild Egypt after the Hyksos rule of Egypt, 80 years prior to her rule. She claims that the 'barbarians … overthrowing that which was made, ruled in ignorance of Re' and it was not until her reign that the ruins were restored, and she 'raised up that which was unfinished since the Asiatics were in the midst of Avaris'. This is pure propaganda as the restoring of monuments was undertaken by the Theban seventeenth dynasty, which was contemporary with the Hyksos dynasty. It is possible that, during the troubled period before the Hyksos takeover, the temples fell into disuse and consequently into disrepair. Any building works started prior to this period could not be continued if the country was suffering from plague and famine. Once the Hyksos were in power, their priorities were primarily concerned with the building of their new capital, so the old projects were soon forgotten. Hatshepsut records that she rebuilt temples at Hebenu, Hermopolis and Cusae. These works were supervised by the overseer of the treasury Djehuty which is recorded in his tomb. Apparently all of the new temples were dedicated to local gods, so religious cults were growing in the new economy of Egypt.

22 Speos Artemidos. *Photograph Wayne R. Frostick*

Most of her building works, however, were carried out at Karnak temple and the cult of Amun. She built the eighth pylon at Karnak which unfortunately is in a terrible state of disrepair at present.

During the first seven years of the co-regency, Hatshepsut filled all the positions of power with men who supported her cause so that when she declared herself king she would have little, if any, resistance from those in authority. Her support included the High Priest of Amun, Hapuseneb, who was responsible for building her tomb in the Valley of the Kings, as well as promoting the divinity of Hatshepsut. This meant she had the support of the Priesthood of Amun, which could explain her many building projects at Karnak. The royal 'Seal Bearer' Nehesi also supported her and was responsible for sealing royal documents and therefore held a lot of power over lesser officials. Both of their tombs were within viewing distance of Deir el Bahri, the site of her mortuary temple, with the facades of their tombs resembling the terraces of the temple, suggesting they had access to her architect. The position of these tombs ensured their loyalty even in death, and therefore eternally under her command.

The most powerful of her officials was her chief steward Senenmut. He had served the family throughout the reign of Thutmosis II, and served Hatshepsut during her reign. He came from humble origins but grew in favour, some say due to his intimate relations with Hatshepsut. He was tutor to her daughter, Neferure, as well as being the highest administrative official of the period. He was only matched in religious power by Hapuseneb the High Priest of Amun.

Senenmut had two tombs, one in the Valley of the Nobles, and one near the mortuary temple of Hatshepsut, which further sparked rumours of their affair. However this speculation regarding their affair is not a modern idea; as the ancient Egyptians also assumed they were involved intimately, and graffiti near Deir el Bahri is thought to represent Hatshepsut and her steward in a compromising position. It is suggested that it may not have been drawn until after the end of the reign of Hatshepsut when there was open hostility against the female pharaoh.

Senenmut was responsible for building her mortuary temple at Deir el Bahri (*23*), primarily dedicated to Amun, although there is a chapel dedicated to Hathor and Anubis. It is reported that there was a small cave shrine dedicated to Hathor on the site prior to the building of this temple although nothing of this has survived. In some of the niches in the top terrace Senenmut is actually shown worshipping Amun alongside Hatshepsut which for an official was unheard of. Senenmut was buried in the precinct of Deir el Bahri.

He was also responsible for the erection of the obelisks at Karnak in year 16 of the reign of Thutmosis III and Hatshepsut, which is recorded at the temple of Deir el Bahri. They were quarried at Aswan and shipped up the Nile on low rafts of 100m long by 30m wide. According to an inscription on the Red Chapel (*24*) in the Open Air Museum at Karnak, there was a public festival to celebrate the erection of these obelisks.

By year seven of the co-regency Hatshepsut was 21 years old and old enough and strong enough to take such a bold political stand. When she abandoned her queenly titles and took over the position of king, her daughter Neferure was given the title 'God's Wife'. Neferure was represented alongside Hatshepsut in her role as king, more often than any other princess, 'King's Daughter' or queen. It has been suggested that she was taking the place of the 'Principle Wife' of the king, because as a woman Hatshepsut could not have a 'Principle Wife'. In the absence of a 'Principle Wife' the role is often filled by the king's mother, but Ahmose at this stage was dead, so the only suitable person would be the 'King's Daughter', i.e. Neferure. In one inscription Neferure even shares regnal years with Hatshepsut and Thutmosis III. These titles could have announced that Neferure was the intended heir to the throne of Hatshepsut.

23 Deir el Bahri, Luxor. *Photograph Wayne R. Frostick*

24 Red Chapel of Hatshepsut, Karnak. *Photograph Wayne R. Frostick*

It has been suggested that Neferure was married at some point to Thutmosis III although she is never called 'King's Wife' so it is unlikely that she married him during Hatshepsut's lifetime. It is possible that Neferure also bore Thutmosis III his eldest son Amenhotep.

It was originally thought that Neferure died during the reign of her mother as some statues of her daughter were removed from Deir el Bahri during Hatshepsut's lifetime. However a stela dating from after year 22 of Thutmosis III, after he had regained sole rule, may have included Neferure. The name was changed to Satioh, Thutmosis III's 'Principle Wife' although the only title used on the stela is that of 'God's Wife' which was never used by Satioh, but was the main title of Neferure.

HATSHEPSUT AS GOD

In order to reinforce her claim to the throne Hatshepsut needed to prove that she was the daughter of a deity and therefore chosen by the god to become king after her father. At Deir el Bahri, in the middle terrace of her mortuary temple, she records her divine birth, where the god Amun-Ra impregnates her mother Ahmose. This is one of the few images showing a pregnant woman from ancient Egypt (*colour plate 10*).

Also at Deir el Bahri Hatshepsut records her coronation on New Year's Day, during the reign of her father Thutmosis I where he declares her co-ruler in order to make it clear that she was the designated heir to the throne. However, this coronation did not actually happen and was a propagandistic tool to reinforce her claim using the influence of her dead father who was still greatly revered. The real coronation of Hatshepsut is recorded on the Red Chapel in Karnak, and presents dancing girls and musicians from the procession to celebrate this event (*25*).

The inscriptions on the fallen obelisk suggest that she acts in the manner of a king i.e. a male, but is aware, proud and acknowledging of the simple fact that she is female.

The inscriptions on the obelisks (both the fallen and the one still standing) use both the masculine and feminine designations indicating that she is both son and daughter of Amun. She claims:

As I rule this Land like the son of Isis,
As I am mighty like the son of Nut.

Although she calls herself the daughter of Amun:

I am his daughter in very truth.

And she records that the people comment on her obelisks:

How like her it is, she is devoted to her father! [Who is Amun in this instance]

The scribes of her time were confused about whether she should be described as male or female and used both masculine and feminine pronouns and grammatical terms in her inscriptions. However, on monuments she had to be shown as a king in traditional kingly attire, as she was the incarnation of Horus on earth as was traditional for all the kings and in some inscriptions she is called the 'Female Horus' in order to associate herself to this myth and legitimise her claim to the throne. Obviously all of these propagandistic tools were employed after she became king, and were devised by the High Priest of Amun, solely to prove her legitimacy.

WARFARE

Hatshepsut's reign was seen as primarily peaceful with only one recorded campaign to Nubia. However it is recorded on a stela belonging to an official called Djehuty, that he saw Hatshepsut herself on the battlefield binding captives and collecting the spoils of war; as any warrior king should. There is a small ostracon that shows a queen, maybe Hatshepsut, in a military chariot and this may have been a cartoon of her part in this campaign (26).

Despite participating in this Nubian campaign there is little evidence of other battles, and Hatshepsut may have avoided military action unless absolutely necessary because.

- ✧ If she failed in any campaign it would be blamed on the fact that she was a woman rather than other factors that would be considered if she were male

- ✧ She needed to match the military prowess of her beloved father and she may have felt unable to do this

- ✧ If Egypt was involved in warfare, Thutmosis III would have become heavily involved in the army gaining support which could have threatened her throne

Hatshepsut would have needed to maintain her reputation of being a 'good king' and any warfare embarked upon would need to be carried out in the method and stamina of her father which perhaps is what she displayed on the Nubian battlefield.

25 Coronation of Hatshepsut, Red Chapel. *Photograph Wayne R. Frostick*

26 Ostracon of a queen (perhaps Hatshepsut) in a war chariot (after Partridge R. 2002 fig. 266). *Illustration by Charlotte Booth*

MORTUARY TEMPLE

The mortuary temple of Hatshepsut at Deir el Bahri was an innovation, and although based on the terraced temple of the Middle Kingdom king, Mentuhotep I, it is unique. The façade that is visible with the three terraces constituted the main temple, but from the lower terrace is a causeway that goes into the cliff, leading to the valley temple of Hatshepsut.

It would seem, however, that it was considered too modern for her contemporaries and no other temple was ever built in the same style. Her mortuary temple does not have the traditional scenes of smiting enemies or records of battles. Instead she records her expedition to Punt in year eight or nine where we see the bizarre imagery of the Queen of Punt. Hatshepsut took scribes, artists and soldiers on this expedition and the Queen of Punt would appear to have been particularly interesting to them. From this expedition Hatshepsut brought an abundance of exotic goods to Egypt including animals, ivory, wood, gold, apes, exotic animals and myrrh trees which lined the causeway to her temple. It is suggested that this expedition to Punt was devised to keep the idle army occupied to prevent any uprisings, as well as to fulfil her kingly role as the provider of exotic goods to Egypt. It has been suggested that she was attempting to cut out foreign trade that provided Egypt with myrrh by planting these trees at Deir el Bahri. This would have aided the Theban economy had it worked. However, although in theory a good idea there is no evidence that myrrh became native to Thebes, although tree pits at her mortuary temple indicate the trees were planted. In the booty list of the things brought back from Punt, there are remarkable comparisons between this and the Middle Kingdom literary tale of the *Shipwrecked Sailor*, where a sailor gets washed up on an amazing island and is greeted by a god who gives him many goods to bring back to Egypt. Although this text may have been up to 500 years old at the time of Hatshepsut she may have been reminding the audience that this was a modern miracle, and although she was a woman, in a man's role, they were in fact living in a golden age.

In addition to building this mortuary temple and the Speos Artemidos temple Hatshepsut also built the Red Chapel, in year 17 of her reign, the top made of red quartzite and the bottom layers made of black granite, and was intended to house the sacred bark of Amun. It was originally composed of two parts: a vestibule and a bark room, but as not all of the blocks have been discovered it has not been fully restored. The chapel was dismantled by Thutmosis III and was discovered in 300 blocks in and around the third pylon at Karnak, which was built by Amenhotep III some time after the Thutmosids. The decoration is not complete and it is possible that the temple was never actually constructed. The decoration is unusual as each block contains a complete scene and therefore could have been carved in a workshop and placed in situ when completed. The type of decoration was of important events in the life of Hatshepsut. They include her coronation, with a scene of Hatshepsut being crowned by Amun, each scene showing her with a different crown; in her *heb sed* she is shown running against the bull to show her strength as a ruler. There is also a scene showing the festivities that accompanied the *heb sed* including a procession with musicians and dancers.

The function of the chapel is also reflected in the decoration as Hatshepsut is shown making offerings at the bark shrines on the journey between Karnak and Luxor temple where the statue of Amun was carried in procession. She is also shown on a barge with the shrine of Amun on it, for the journey to the West Bank. Hatshepsut is shown standing in front of the shrine and Thutmosis III is shown behind the shrine rowing.

The Red Chapel may originally have been intended to be placed in the sanctuary of Karnak, although this is not certain. Thutmosis III after removing this chapel built his own there which was since replaced by that of Phillip Arridaeus (323-17 BC) which is still in place.

Both Hatshepsut and Thutmosis III built numerous monuments in Nubia, at Qasr Ibrim, Sai, Semna, Faras and Buhen where Hatshepsut built a temple dedicated to Horus. Originally the decoration showed images of herself and Thutmosis III but then he removed her name and added that of Thutmose II and I. The entire temple has since been moved to Khartoum Museum, to salvage it from the floods after the Aswan Dam was built.

DEATH?

By year 22 of the reign of Thutmosis III Hatshepsut had completely disappeared from inscriptions and monuments, indicating Thutmosis was reigning alone. However, whether she died naturally, was assassinated or forcibly removed is unknown. The last inscription concerning her was dated to the tenth day, sixth month of her twenty-second year, which would be early February 1476 BC. She was nearly 40 at this point, which was considered old for ancient Egypt. No body has been discovered, although she has been identified with a female mummy discovered in KV21 the tomb of Hatshepsut's nurse, although no conclusive evidence has been produced.

Hatshepsut took over the Valley of the King's tomb of her father Thutmosis I (KV20), enlarging it and placing the body of her father in a new burial chamber, where she intended her body to lie alongside his. For his reburial she used one of the sarcophagi that she had built for herself when she first became king, as she had since carved a bigger and more impressive one for herself. After her disappearance the body of her father was removed from this tomb and placed in another tomb built by Thutmosis III. Thutmosis III actually built his own tomb next to that built by Hatshepsut when she was queen. It would seem that the body of Hatshepsut remained in KV20, until at least the turn of the twentieth century although where her body is now, as discussed, is uncertain. In the Deir el Bahri cache they found a box bearing her name which contained the mummified remains of a liver and spleen indicating that she had been traditionally mummified.

She had already started to build her own Valley of the King's tomb at the start of her reign which is numbered KV42. Excavations here have uncovered the foundation deposits of the tomb inscribed for Hatshepsut clearly identifying the tomb as hers. This tomb had been decorated with scenes from the *Book of the Amduat*, which was a guide to the 12-hour journey into the afterlife which would eventually have led to the deceased being reborn.

Some of Hatshepsut's funerary equipment was discovered in a side room of the tomb of Ramses IX (KV6) and it has been suggested that robbers opened her tomb and took away the most valuable items and stored the less valuable items in the nearby, already open and violated tomb of Ramses IX, to be taken away at a more convenient time. The funerary equipment discovered is very scarce as most of her monuments and equipment were destroyed after her disappearance. Only one shabti has been discovered from KV20 belonging to Hatshepsut; other items include a signet ring, engraved in turquoise and set in gold and a lion-headed red-jasper game piece with the two cartouche names of Hatshepsut. A linen winding-sheet inscribed with the name of Hatshepsut was also discovered in the tomb of Maiherperi, a child of the royal nursery and fan bearer. His tomb is thought to date to the reign of Thutmosis IV and would therefore suggest that it was an heirloom that had been kept in the royal nursery, and was a prized possession of Maiherperi.

AFTERMATH

Although the destruction of her monuments started in the reign of Thutmosis III it was not until 20 years after Hatshepsut's disappearance (*27*). Images of her in temples were replaced by images of her father, or husband, or they were carved out leaving just an outline where she originally stood. Her obelisks at Karnak were not removed,

27 Destruction of Hatshepsut, Karnak. *Photograph Wayne R. Frostick*

but enclosed within a wall so they were not visible. This delayed reaction would suggest that Thutmosis III did not feel any resentment towards her but was forced to carry out the destruction due to political expectancy. If there was no resentment then it could be assumed that she died a natural death rather than assassination which is also supported by the mummification of her body.

It has also been suggested that the delay in the destruction of Hatshepsut's monuments could be due to her belated death. Her disappearance could have been due to her retirement from public life and she may have lived for another 20 years after this disappearance. Then after her death Thutmosis III wreaked his revenge. The monuments of Senenmut, Hatshepsut's vizier and advisor were also destroyed, indicating that he was believed to have been a driving force behind the ambition of Hatshepsut.

CONCLUSION

As we can see Hatshepsut led an interesting and innovative life and could even be said to be the very first feminist. She suffered trauma at an early age with the death of her father whom she was very close to and I believe that her ambition may have been a by-product of this devotion. Thutmosis I was a warrior king, and Hatshepsut may have wanted to emulate this, except culture meant that as a woman she was unable to be the same. Therefore she decided to rule a peaceful Egypt rather than being an aggressor and warrior like her father. In this manner she did reign successfully and if she had been a man she probably would not have been criticised for this type of reign. She never lost the devotion to her father as shown by her attempt to be buried with him. Although she did take over the throne as king she did not make many changes and showed as much devotion to Amun as any other king. She ruled as a king, concentrating on festivals and the economy. However the change was still too much for the officials of Egypt who were all male and may have been threatened by a powerful woman. In the past whenever a female regent had ruled alone it had caused the collapse of the royal line. The regent Nitocris brought about the end of the Old Kingdom and Sobekneferu ruled at the end of the Middle Kingdom so they may have feared that Hatshepsut would end the New Kingdom which had only been established for about a century.

As well as suffering the death of her father Hatshepsut also suffered the death of her own daughter, which could also explain the devotion she had for her remaining daughter Neferure. Her life was a constant battle against tradition, and she needed to display strength for most of her adult life. She looked for respite and pleasure in her relationship with her daughter and her lover Senenmut, who were the only people she could have trusted wholeheartedly. It would be nice to think that she retired after 22 years on the throne, but considering the effort it took to get to her position it seems unlikely that she would give it up without a struggle.

SIX

SENENMUT

LOVER OF AN EGYPTIAN QUEEN

INTRODUCTION

Senenmut was the vizier and architect of Hatshepsut, as well as her lover and greatest adviser. Through his hard work and dedication he rose through the ranks from humble origins to a position of great power and prestige.

FAMILY

Senenmut was born to an ordinary but educated family; the literate middle class. His father was called Ramose and his mother Hatnofer. They were a large family, and Senenmut had three brothers, Amenemhat, Minhotep, Pairy, two sisters, Ahhotep, and Nofret–Hor and a half-brother, Senumen, who succeeded him as tutor to the Princess Neferure. He is mentioned in Senenmut's tomb 71 but not in tomb 353 with the rest of his siblings.

Senenmut was probably born in a small town or village, away from the hustle and bustle of Thebes and therefore owed his career entirely to the favour of Hatshepsut. We do not have a year for his birth but we know he was an adult when she came to the throne in 1522 BC.

Beneath one of his tombs (TT353), Senenmut built a joint tomb for his parents. Ramose, his father, who was about 60 years old when he died; his mother died after his father. Ramose was originally buried in a humble tomb as his children did not at the time have the means for an elaborate burial. By the time Hatnofer died in year seven of Hatshepsut's reign, Senenmut had access to wealth, and buried her beneath his own tomb, providing an expensive mummification, a wooden anthropoid coffin, a gilded mask, canopic equipment and grave goods. Ramose at this point was rewrapped and put into a new anthropoid coffin and placed in the same tomb as his wife. Also in the burial chamber of Hatnofer were two further coffins, with three badly mummified anonymous women, and three children. If seven people of Senenmut's family truly died at the same time, there may have been an epidemic sweeping his village or it is probable that they had all been buried nearby and had received an upgrade when he was burying his mother. There is evidence of mud on some of the bandages which did not come from this tomb indicating they had originally been buried in poorer conditions.

Although Senenmut was a well-educated administrator, and powerful official, there is no evidence to suggest that he had been married and there is no record of any children. This was very rare in Egypt as most people married young and wanted children to look after them in old age. It is possible that he may have married at the beginning of his career, and was a widower but there is no mention of a wife in either tomb. It is more likely that if he had been married his involvement with Hatshepsut as lover and confidant prevented him from mentioning a wife, dead or alive.

CAREER

Senenmut began his administrative career by entering into temple or royal administration. He held numerous religious administration titles indicating this was the route he had chosen.

The titles include 'Overseer of Amun's Granaries', 'Overseer of Amun's Storehouses', 'Overseer of Amun's Fields', 'Overseer of Amun's Gardens', 'Overseer of Amun's Cattle', 'Overseer of Amun's Slaves', 'Overseer of the works of Amun' and 'Controller of the Hall of Amun' which suggest he began his career in the temple of Amun at Karnak. Many of these titles dealt with the control of revenue of the temple from taxes, and yield of land belonging to the cult of Amun. This position is likely to have been well paid.

As his career progressed he was given a number of extra titles, including 'Steward of the Estates of Amun', 'Overseer of all Royal Works', 'Tutor to the Royal Heiress Neferure' and 'Steward of Property of Hatshepsut and Neferure'. All of these were high ranking and powerful positions. These titles were given to Senenmut when Hatshepsut was queen, before year seven when she took over the throne as king, indicating that he may have worked at the palace for Thutmosis II and III.

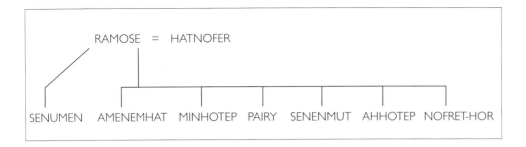

As 'Steward of the Estates of Amun' he was in control of revenue generated by the land belonging to the temple of Amun which in the New Kingdom was so wealthy it eventually rivalled the royal family.

The 'Overseer of all Royal Works' was a very powerful position supervising Hatshepsut's building works throughout Egypt. He is solely accredited for the design and building of Hatshepsut's mortuary temple, Deir el Bahri.

As 'Tutor to the Royal Heiress Neferure' Senenmut was in a prestigious position as it was unusual for a man of such a lowly birth to hold such a title. Although he was educated he has no noble ancestry, and achieved this position on merit alone. He is often shown in this role, cradling the child Neferure on his lap; again an unheard of privilege.

In ancient Egypt with the acquisition of powerful positions came a number of honorary titles, which held no responsibilities but represented the status of the title holder. The titles of Senenmut included 'Superintendent of the Private Apartments', 'Superintendent of the Bathroom' and 'Superintendent of the Royal Bedroom', indicating he had private access to the queen and her apartments, although whether he ever had need to go into them is not recorded. This huge number of titles, both practical and honorary, could suggest he was an elderly man by the later years of Hatshepsut's reign.

As he grew in the affections of Hatshepsut, Senenmut was mentioned on numerous shrine and temple walls in connection with the queen; a great honour for any official. At his shrine at Gebel el Silsila he uses the title of 'Steward of the Gods wife and Steward of the King's Daughter'. These women although not named are likely to be Hatshepsut and her daughter Neferure. The shrine led to a small square room with a seated statue of Senenmut carved directly from the rock. Rather than the traditional funerary and earthly feasts that normally decorate these shrines Senenmut had an image of Hatshepsut being embraced by Sobek and Nekhbet, reflecting his close relationship with Hatshepsut. Senenmut's rapid increase in titles, wealth and status is often attributed to his personal relationship with Hatshepsut.

We have many images of Senenmut, although to what extent these stylised images reflect his actual appearance is unknown. There are four surviving ink drawings of Senenmut which appear to be portraits. All four of these sketches show him in profile, sporting a round face, double chin and wrinkles and could represent him in later life rather than as a young man.

As well as these sketches of Senenmut there were 25 hard stone statues of him; more than any other official. Many of these statues may have been gifts from Hatshepsut or Thutmosis III. The majority of them were placed at the temple of Amun at Karnak, in ranks facing the sanctuary of the Red Chapel of Hatshepsut. This enabled the living Senenmut to benefit from the close proximity to the God, participating in ceremonies and being present for all the rituals via the presence of his *ka* in the statues. Senenmut also placed statues of himself in practically every other Theban temple. The statues show him in various positions each reflecting his importance and status; kneeling, presenting a religious symbol (shrine or sistrum) to a deity, or holding the Princess Neferure on his lap (*28*). He is even shown as a block statue, reflecting his noble status with the princess's head popping out of the top of the cloak wrapped around him.

As well as official art there is graffiti in an unfinished tomb, above the cliffs of Deir el Bahri used as a rest place for those working on Deir el Bahri. The graffiti is explicit in the representation of the physical relationship between Hatshepsut and Senenmut indicating this speculation is not a modern idea.

There is enough circumstantial evidence to suggest there was a relationship between them, but it is clear that Hatshepsut would never have been able to marry Senenmut. Firstly she was married to Thutmosis III who was a young healthy boy, unlikely to die naturally for a number of years. Even if she had been free it is unlikely that she could have married Senenmut as although he was of high rank at the height of her reign, he was of humble birth which may have compromised her tenuous claim to the throne. Though it was impossible for her to marry Senenmut, he did not appear to have been married to anyone else. Either his love for Hatshepsut was too much for him to commit to another woman or to save Hatshepsut's feelings he either did not marry or kept his relationships quiet.

It has been suggested that Hatshepsut trusted Senenmut with all the plans of state and it is likely she sought his support in everything she did. The most important thing that Senenmut is credited for is the building of her mortuary temple at Deir el Bahri, and the erection of the two obelisks at Karnak, recorded at Deir el Bahri. However his titles state he was overseer of all her works, although it is only human nature to have a favourite achievement, and Deir el Bahri was Senenmut's.

28 Senenmut and Neferure. *Copyright Robert Partridge: The Ancient Egypt Picture Library*

At Deir el Bahri there are over 60 representations of Senenmut, in various positions. Many of these images are on walls hidden by doors to niches and shrines, so they would not have been seen if the doors were open. He is even shown praising Hatshepsut and the god Amun, an honoured activity for a non-royal individual. Being represented in such close proximity to the god would have had unspecified benefits to the living Senenmut, whose *ka* was able to look upon the god and receive his blessings. As this type of imagery was a royal prerogative it is suggested that he may have carved these images of himself in secret. However he does claim to have permission for these images here, and in every temple, which is written on the doorway to the north-west Offering Hall of Deir el Bahri.

> Senenmut, in accordance with the favour of the King's bounty which was extended to his servant in letting his name be established on every wall in the following of the King, Dejeser-Djeseru (Deir el Bahri), and likewise in the temples of the gods of Upper and Lower Egypt. Thus spoke the King.

It is unlikely that Hatshepsut would be oblivious to what was depicted on the walls of her mortuary temple and therefore probably did give her permission.

It is suggested that Senenmut placed these images in the temple without her knowledge, and the disappearance of Senenmut and destruction of his monuments was caused by Hatshepsut herself after she found out his images had been placed in her temple. This, however, is unlikely. Senenmut was not the only official to be depicted on the walls of royal monuments as Nehesi, the viceroy of Kush also has his image in the temple dedicated to Horus, built by Hatshepsut and Thutmosis III, at Buhen. It was obviously considered a way to reward favourites by having them close for eternity.

TOMBS

During his lifetime Senenmut built two tombs, both of which were finely decorated and situated in Thebes. TT71 was at the top of Sheikh el Gourna Hill, near the Valley of the Nobles, and TT353 was beneath the precincts of Deir el Bahri. Tomb 353 has an astronomical ceiling (*29*), and TT71 has a variety of religious texts and ostraca, indicating that Senemut was cultured and educated.

As TT71 was near the Valley of the Nobles it would seem that as his career progressed Senenmut believed that he was too important to be buried here hence he started building his second tomb near the mortuary temple of his queen. TT71

29 Astronomical ceiling TT353. *Copyright Robert Partridge: The Ancient Egypt Picture Library*

was therefore used as a family tomb, and has a number of mummies within it. There is the body of an unknown woman in a cheap coffin with a scarab inscribed with 'God's Wife Neferure' indicating it may have been a reburial of a relative, and the scarab may have been a gift to her from Senenmut. There was also the body of an unknown male wrapped in reed matting which was a rare way to be buried. This indicates a reburial of a relative from a poorer grave to this elaborate tomb. There was also the body of a young boy, named Amenhotep, believed to be Senenmut's brother although he is not mentioned in the tombs alongside his other siblings. The mummy of a male singer, Hormose, was buried alongside his lute, and may have been a beloved servant of Senenmut or even another relative. There were also a further two anonymous mummies in anthropoid coffins. In addition to this collection of mummified humans there was also a mummified horse and a mummified ape, both of which were valuable and treasured pets in Senenmut's household.

The construction of TT71 started in the spring of year seven of Hatshepsut, just as she had taken over the role as king. The date is identified through wine labels on jars in the tomb burial chambers. He was obviously quite prominent at this stage to be financially able to build a rock-cut tomb in the Valley of the Nobles. He had the entrance carved directly into the cliff face, with an artificial terrace built over the descent of the cliff, to disguise the entrance. There was a narrow forecourt on top of the terrace and there are two deep pits cut into the forecourt, although the use of these is unspecified. Beneath the now collapsed terrace was the burial chamber of Senenmut's parents Ramose and Hatnofer.

In a niche at the end of the tomb chapel was a false door stela inscribed with chapter 148 of the *Book of the Dead* and the inscription 'May you give to the steward Senenmut, life, prosperity and endurance'. Above the false door stela was a niche for a statue of Senenmut. Offerings would have been left at the false door, so his *ka* could partake in them as it travelled through the door.

The whole of TT71 was originally decorated with painted plaster of which very little has survived. There are remnants of a Hathor-headed frieze, three of six Aegean men presenting vessels to Senenmut in his official capacity, indicate trade with Crete was continuing during this period.

This tomb contained a brown quartzite sarcophagus which was generally only supplied for royalty. The sarcophagus had been broken into over 1000 pieces, and some were scattered over 100m. Some of the larger pieces had been reused in antiquity as millstones. The sarcophagus was originally cartouche-shaped with a carved image of Isis and Nephthys kneeling at each end. Down each long side were carved images of the four sons of Horus and two Anubis figures. Inside the sarcophagus was an image of a standing Nut and on the sides were texts from the *Book of the Dead*. The carved decoration on the chest had been highlighted, with yellow and blue paint. This style of decoration, on a stone sarcophagus, including the shape, indicates it was originally intended for Hatshepsut, rejected by her and then adapted for use by Senenmut: her sarcophagus was practically the same in design. It was rare for royalty to give a royal sarcophagus to a non-royal official unless there was a special relationship between them.

It would appear that Senenmut intended to be buried in TT71 as this was where his sarcophagus was found, and it would seem very unlikely that he would want to be buried without it. This tomb was abandoned when it was close to completion; the burial chamber and the rock-cut shrine above still needed completing. Due to the poor-quality rock the ceiling had collapsed and the painted plaster had crumbled, although some of the damage was deliberate. There appears to have been a three-stage process of deliberate damage to this tomb. The names of Senenmut and

Hatshepsut were destroyed by Thutmosis III as part of his campaign to disassociate himself from Hatshepsut's reign. Amun, Mut and other gods' names were erased during the Amarna Period when there was a campaign against all gods. Damage to the face of Hathor had probably been done during the Christian Period when there was a campaign against pagan idols.

The collapse of TT71 encouraged a new tomb, TT353 to be built. Graffiti indicates it was started before year 16 of Hatshepsut's reign. This tomb was more secretive than that of TT71 and was built at Deir el Bahri, using rock from the quarry that provided the material for the mortuary temple of Deir el Bahri. There was a concealed entrance to the tomb, and three subterranean chambers linked by descending stepped passages. The chamber walls were smoothed and images were outlined ready to be carved and painted. Tomb 353 was built of good solid rock ideal for carved relief. This tomb was in the early stages of completion when it was abandoned, and the damage in this tomb was caused by natural salt seepage, and had been repaired with plaster at the time of building. However, there was later destruction in this tomb with deliberate random destruction of faces of people outlined on the walls. There was, however, no attempt to erase names and texts, indicating it may have been the Christians who would not have had knowledge of the language and would not have understood the relevance of the images and viewed them as idols.

The texts on the wall were religious and were designed to ease Senenmut's journey into the 'Field of Reeds', the nobleman's afterlife. There were images of Senenmut, with his brother Amenemhet and the text mentions other siblings. There are also images of Senenmut and Hatshepsut. The decorated ceiling in this tomb is the earliest astronomical ceiling in Egypt, including a calendar of lunar months, the northern constellation and illustrations of Mars, Venus, Jupiter and Saturn.

After TT353 had been started, Senenmut abruptly retired between year 16 and 20 of Hatshepsut's reign and was not buried in either tomb. By year 16 he was approximately 50 years old and may have died of old age, although that would not explain his lack of burial. It has been suggested that Senenmut was killed by supporters of Thutmosis III who saw him as the real power behind Hatshepsut. However, the recovery of a statue of Senenmut, engraved with the cartouche of Thutmose III, from the Deir el Bahri temple, indicates that the memory of Senenmut was not erased by Thutmoses III.

It is also possible that he may have died abroad, drowned or burned to death, all valid reasons why he did not have a burial. There is even the possibility that he had a third, even more impressive tomb not yet discovered, which may include another sarcophagus and canopic equipment.

CONCLUSION

It has been suggested that the death of the Princess Neferure, if she died before Hatshepsut, may have caused Senenmut to lose influence with the queen and therefore instigate his gradual decline from office. However there is no evidence that she pre-deceased her tutor or her mother.

Like the disappearance of Hatshepsut in year 22 the disappearance of Senenmut in year 20 has caused much speculation, amongst scholars and lay people alike. It is strange for someone who had such a powerful position to suddenly just disappear from public life and not even leave behind a body. Maybe the recovery of his body would be telling regarding his sudden demise or maybe it would simply add to the mystery.

SEVEN

REKHMIRE

THE VIZIER OF THUTMOSIS III AND AMENHOTEP II

INTRODUCTION

Rekhmire, an eighteenth-dynasty noble, held the position of mayor of Thebes and vizier in the last 19 years of the long reign of Thutmoses III and the beginning of the reign of Amenhotep II. All we have regarding this official is his tomb, although his body was not found here so we know nothing about the illnesses that he may have suffered from, or indeed how he died. Luckily the tomb of Rekhmire is extremely detailed regarding his work-life and can give us an insight into the busy role that a vizier in the eighteenth dynasty held.

TT100

Rekhmire's tomb in the Valley of the Nobles is unusual for three reasons. Firstly, it was carved into the lower slope of a cliff, and this has been incorporated into the design, with the walls at the end of the corridor of the tomb being a lot taller than the walls near the door. A niche at the end of the corridor was designed to house a statue of Rekhmire of up to 6ft tall, accentuating the height of this unusual tomb, but the statue has never been found. The second reason the tomb is so unusual is the detailed record of the installation of Rekhmire in the position of vizier as well as the role the vizier played within Egyptian society. There are only three other examples of this text, from the tomb of Amenuser, Amenenope and Paser, all viziers during the New Kingdom, but none written in such detail. The third unusual thing about this tomb is that there is no burial shaft, insinuating that this tomb was not intended for burial but was rather used as a funerary chapel, with his burial taking place elsewhere.

Due to what appears to be intentional damage on some of the images in his tomb it has been suggested that he may never have had a proper burial due to falling from royal favour. However, what could have disgraced the vizier in such a fashion will sadly remain a mystery. During the reign of Akhenaten further damage was caused to Rekhmire's tomb, when any reference to Amun, the gods and the images of the priests of Amun were erased, even in the highest corners of the tomb. When the tomb was discovered in 1833 further damage was caused as the outer hall was occupied by a family and the main passageway was being used as a cowshed, complete with resident cow.

FAMILY

The decoration chosen by Rekhmire for his tomb covered all aspects of his life. We learn that his father was called Neferweben, and was a priest of Amun at Karnak, and his mother was called Bet. His uncle, Woser, was a vizier, and he may have inherited the position from him. Rekhmire was married to the lady Meryt and they are shown seated together at offering tables receiving numerous goods, as well as enjoying an elaborate banquet. He also had numerous sons, one of which was given the role of high priest, and all are shown in the tomb bringing numerous offerings to Rekhmire for his use in the afterlife.

ROLE OF VIZIER

His main role as vizier would be to oversee all of the workshops commissioned by the palace. He reported on the progress and production directly to the king. These crafts are all depicted on the walls of his tomb as Rekhmire looks on. He was also in control of the army and the police, supervising the territorial limits between provinces, collection of taxes as well as the observation of the weather and the flood levels which influenced taxes.

The most important scene in this tomb is the installation of Rekhmire as vizier under the reign of Thutmosis III. Rekhmire is shown facing the king as he bestows the title and promotion on him. The full role is inscribed on the wall outlining the responsibility and also correct conduct of a vizier.

Regulation laid upon the vizier Rekhmire. The council was conducted into the audience hall of Pharaoh. One brought in the vizier Rekhmire, newly appointed.

His Majesty said to him: 'Look to the office of vizier; be watchful over all that is done therein.' Behold, it is the established support of the whole land.

Behold, as for the vizierate, it is not sweet; behold, it is bitter, as he is named [*i.e. everyone knows who he is*]. Behold, he is copper enclosing the gold of his lord's house. Behold, the vizierate is not to show respect of persons to princes and councillors; it is not to make for himself slaves of any people.

Behold, as for a man in the house of his lord, his conduct is good for his lord. But lo, he does not the same for another [*i.e. he must not be loyal to anyone but Pharaoh*].

Behold, when a petitioner comes from Upper or Lower Egypt, even the whole land, see to it that everything is done in accordance with law that everything is done according to the custom thereof, giving to every man his right. Behold, a prince [*i.e. hereditary prince*] is in a conspicuous place, water and wind report concerning all that he does. For behold, that which is done by him never remains unknown.

When he takes up a matter for a petitioner according to his case, he shall not proceed by the statement of a department officer. But the matter shall be known by the statement of one designated by him, the vizier, saying it himself in the presence of a department officer with the words: 'It is not that I raise my voice; but I send the petitioner according to his case to another court or prince.' Then that which has been done by him has not been misunderstood.

Behold, the refuge of a prince is to act according to the regulation, by doing what is said to him. A petitioner who had been adjudged shall not say: 'My right has not been given to me!'

Behold, it is a saying which was in the vizieral installation of Memphis in the utterance of the king in urging the vizier to moderation: Beware of that which is said of the vizier Kheti. It is said that he discriminated against some of the people of his own kin in favour of strangers, for fear lest it should be said of him that he favoured his kin dishonestly. When one of them appealed against the judgement which he thought to make him, he persisted in his discrimination. Now that is more than justice.

Forget not to judge justice. It is an abomination of the god to show partiality. This is the teaching. Therefore, do you accordingly. Look upon him who is known to you like him who is unknown to you; and him who is near the king like him who is far from his house. Behold, a prince who does this, he shall endure here in this place.

Pass not over a petitioner without regarding his speech. If there is a petitioner who shall appeal to you, being one whose speech is not what is said [i.e. who has spoken improperly], dismiss him after having let him hear that on account of which you dismiss him. Behold, it is said: 'A petitioner desires his saying be regarded rather than the hearing of that on account of which he has come.'

Be not angry against a man wrongfully; but be angry at that at which one should be angry.

Cause yourself to be feared. Let men be afraid of you. A prince is a prince of whom one is afraid. Behold, the dread of a prince is that he does justice. But indeed, if a man cause himself to be feared a multitude of times, there is something wrong in him in the opinion of the people. They do not say of him: 'He is a man indeed'. Behold, this fear of a prince deters the liar, when the prince proceeds according to the dread one has of him. Behold, this shall you attain by administering this office, doing justice.

Behold, men expect the doing of justice in the procedure of the vizier. Behold, that is its customary law since the god [i.e. since the beginning of time]. Behold, it is said according to the scribe of the vizier: 'A just scribe' is said of him. Now, as for the hall in which you hear, there is an audience hall for the announcement of judgements. Now, as for 'him who shall do justice before all the people,' it is the vizier.

Behold, when a man is in his office, he acts according to what is commanded him. Behold, the success of a man is that he act according to what is said to him. Make no delay at all in justice, the law of which you know. Behold, it becomes the arrogant that the king should love the timid more than the arrogant!

Now may you do according to this command that is given you – behold, it is the manner of success – besides giving your attention to the crown lands, and making the establishment thereof. If you happen to inspect, then shall you send to inspect the overseer of the land-measuring and the patrol of the overseer of land-measuring. If there shall be one who shall inspect before you, then shall you question him.

Behold the regulation that is laid upon you.

The inscription, as well as describing the conduct of the vizier, also describes the vizier's palace office, the type of reports he made to the king and the treasury and 30 separate activities that were part of the position.

It is very likely that at this stage in the career of Rekhmire he met the king personally, and throughout his role as vizier he may have worked very closely with Thutmosis III and then later with Amenhotep II. In the same scene Rekhmire resides over numerous foreign dignitaries who are bringing goods to the king. It is likely that in his role as vizier he would accept these tributary payments on behalf of the king, and would then report the inventory to the king. In order to be able to communicate with the foreign dignitaries it is possible that Rekhmire spoke numerous languages, even if just greetings and pleasantries.

People from Punt are shown bringing incense trees, lumps of gum carried in baskets and gum pressed into the shapes of obelisks, rings of gold, ivory tusks, ebony and ostrich feathers. Cretans are shown bringing jewellery, gold, silver and lapis vessels and jars of oil. They are shown with ingots of silver, baskets of lapis lazuli and ivory in the form of an elephant tusk. They are shown wearing national costumes of patterned fringed kilts and ankle length sandals, with long hair with waist-length curled tendrils. The people of Nubia are shown bringing gold, ebony, and exotic animals including giraffes, leopards, baboons and monkeys. A man at the end of the line is shown herding seven long-horned cows and seven large hounds. The Nubians are shown wearing animal skin kilts, and short curly wigs.

The parade of Syrians bring decorated vases, similar to those from Crete, glass vessels (one blue, white and red with a gold top), bundles of reeds, silver dishes, baskets of silver and gold rings, wood, semi-precious stones and copper. They also are shown bringing a horse and chariot, a bear and a small elephant. They are presented in the stereotypical way for this nation with pointed beards and long white robes with a red trim. The fifth register shows:

> Bringing forward the children of the chiefs of the southern lands, together with the children of the chiefs of the northern lands ... and to take the chiefs of the countries of the South at the same time, the best of the loot brought back by His Majesty the king of Upper and of Lower Egypt from all foreign countries – to fill the stores and to serve like servants of the divine offerings of his father Amen, Lord of the thrones of the Two Lands, depending on whether this one placed the gathering of the foreign countries in his fist, the chiefs falling under his sandals.

In other words this scene shows the prisoners from various countries; namely the children of the chiefs being brought to Egypt to be raised as Egyptians. These children, once grown would be sent back to their native country as vassal leaders who would be loyal to Egypt. There are seven Nubian men, twelve Nubian women, the first four leading or carrying children, seven Syrian women, the first four with children; and Egyptian guard with a throw stick stands at the back of the line, to encourage them to walk forward.

Rekhmire, as vizier, resided over the court of law (the *knbt*), listening to the cases, including the administration of punishment, shown in graphic detail in the tomb as a criminal found guilty is taken outside the court and given a beating. Other duties involve the collection of taxes in the form of gold, silver, animals and products from towns north and south of Thebes. The products of the north of Egypt are represented by rings of gold, livestock and honey and are all delivered to the vizier's representatives by the local farmers. The tax collecting scenes also include some agricultural scenes, wine making, fishing and hunting, indicating the sources of the taxes. It is however, unlikely, that Rekhmire himself visited the villages. He would have sent subordinates who would bring the taxes to him; for him to record and report to the king.

Many of the taxes were taken straight to the temple stores at Karnak, which during this period was extremely wealthy, and owned the majority of the farm land in Thebes and much of the surrounding area. The scribes under the vizier would record all goods before storing them and these records would then be passed on to Rekhmire so he could make his report to the treasury and the king.

As vizier Rekhmire would also have supervised, albeit in an administrative capacity, the building of royal monuments. The building of a great entrance pylon at Karnak was under his authority and there are scenes of Libyans making bricks for the ramp to be used for the construction of this pylon. Remains of the type of ramp being built can still be seen behind the first pylon at Karnak temple (*30*). The brick-making scene shows the men getting the mud out of the ground with a hoe, and putting it into buckets. Then other men put the mud into frames to dry in the sun; the same method is used today in Egypt for making mud bricks to build houses.

The carving of colossal statues, sphinxes, furniture and implements, vessels and precious objects were also under Rekhmire's supervision. The scene of the stonemason's workshop shows the manufacture of stone vessels using hammers and chisels. Behind the men in the top register making incense stands we see a table showing some of the completed objects, which include bowls and an incense burner in the shape of a hand that kings are seen using in many temple scenes. Another part of this scene shows the stone masons carving a colossal statue of the king out of quartzite, where six men are working on various levels of a scaffold.

30 Mud-brick ramp, Karnak. *Photograph Wayne R. Frostick*

The temple had a jewellery workshop attached to it and Rekhmire recorded their progress. The scene starts with the weighing of the gold, before being crafted into necklaces, beads and gold counterpoises. A further scene shows carpenters at work on a sacred shrine, where each inlaid symbol is carved by hand before being placed in the completed shrine.

It is unlikely that Rekhmire was present in the workshops on a daily basis but would have received reports from them that were then passed onto the king. It is possible, however, that he would make random inspections of the various workshops.

CORONATION OF AMENHOTEP II

One of the most interesting scenes in this tomb is the death of Thutmosis III and the rise to the throne of his son Amenhotep II. Rekhmire held an important part in both the funeral and coronation ceremonies. At the death of Thutmosis III, the newly enthroned Amenhotep II travelled from Memphis where the coronation took place, to the religious capital of Thebes. The mayor of Thebes and vizier, Rekhmire donned his best robes, anointed himself with perfumed oils, prepared a speech and went to meet the new king. Amenhotep II travelled to Thebes by boat and there is an image of two boats; one has 12 oars and the second boat is shown at the dock at Thebes with the sail lowered. Rekhmire travelled northwards to meet the king half-way to offer him a bouquet in welcome, and then accompanied him back to Thebes. After the arrival of the king, an elaborate banquet took place, organised by Rekhmire, to celebrate the new king's rise to the throne and also to show his continuing loyalty.

THE FUNERAL OF REKHMIRE

There is very little information in the tomb about what happened after Amenhotep II came to the throne, indicating that Rekhmire may have died shortly after his succession.

The west section of the tomb wall is filled with details of the burial rites and funeral of Rekhmire. There are registers showing the funerary procession including all of the funerary goods being brought into the tomb. On one of the boats the funerary bed with the coffin on top is steadied on the journey across the Nile to the west bank by three pall bearers. The women sat at each end are likely to represent Isis and Nephthys, but the names and inscriptions above their heads are damaged.

Near the false door at the end of the tomb are four registers showing servants bearing offerings so that the *ka* of Rekhmire would be sustained for eternity. The numerous goods shown in the funeral procession of Rekhmire indicate that as vizier he was extremely wealthy. It would be interesting to know exactly what was put into his tomb, and whether the wall scenes were more elaborate than reality.

The funeral procession then follows the offering bearers, with musicians, two women with castanets and a man carrying clapper-boards. A statue of Rekhmire is carried in a bark towards the sacred tent of Anubis. The lower registers record the sacred pilgrimage of Rekhmire to Abydos, the burial place of Osiris. Finally is the sarcophagus, drawn by two cattle, which arrives at the necropolis guarded by the goddess of the west.

These elaborate funeral rites and ceremonies may not have reflected the actual funeral of Rekhmire. Although Rekhmire was of high status it is possible that the images in his tomb were of an 'ideal' funeral, and could take the place of a real funeral of simpler means. If, as the deliberate damage suggests, Rekhmire fell out of favour he may not have had a funeral at all, and as he was never buried in TT100, doubt could be cast on whether this event ever actually took place.

CONCLUSION

The tomb of Rekhmire shows he held an important role, with numerous activities under his command. He would spend much time in his office, with various supervisors filing reports on the workshops,and tax collections. He would write a weekly or monthly report combining all of these shorter reports, which he would give to the king directly or to the treasurer. As vizier he would also be an advisor to the king, and may have had some influence over the king's decisions. Rekhmire clearly was a powerful man, and would have accumulated wealth, land and property over the 20 years of his vizierate. It is likely that before Thutmosis III promoted him to vizier and mayor he would already have held a position of power as an official and scribe. It is likely that he was literate, and as he did not follow his father into the Priesthood of Amun he was probably a gifted scribe. Through his early career he caught the eye of Thutmosis III and was promoted after proving himself to be trustworthy and capable. Maybe he betrayed this trust when he fell from favour, although how this happened is not known.

Like many people in ancient Egypt there are many gaps in Rekhmire's life story. We know the name of his wife and parents and also his children, indicating that he was a family man and would have shared his wealth and power with them, ensuring that they had decent burials and a privileged life. The image of his funeral procession hints at some of the wealth he accumulated and it could be very informative if his mummy and perhaps an even more elaborate tomb were to be discovered.

EIGHT

AKHENATEN
THE HERETIC KING

INTRODUCTION

The reign of the 'Heretic King' Akhenaten covered a short period of only 17 years in the eighteenth dynasty (1350-34 BC). Despite this short reign Akhenaten is one of the most studied and discussed pharaohs in ancient Egypt; the king who single-handedly changed the religion of Egypt to the worship of one god.

PARENTS AND CHILDHOOD

Akhenaten was the second son of Amenhotep III (*colour plate 11*) and Queen Tiye (*31*); born as Amenhotep he only later changed his name to Akhenaten. Tiye was of noble, not royal, birth and by marrying her, Amenhotep III had flouted tradition as it was traditional for a king to marry a royal princess.

It has been suggested that Tiye was a strong and domineering woman and may have had huge influence over the reign of both her husband and her son Amenhotep. She was regularly shown alongside her husband in a complementary rather than inferior position, and was represented in her own right without the king in many places.

Between year 16 and 27 of Amenhotep III's 38-year reign, his oldest son Thutmosis died leaving Prince Amenhotep as the heir to the throne. He was thought to have been a sickly youth and it has been suggested that the epithet he chose in later life 'Great in his Duration' meaning 'The Long Lived' may have been an expression of hope, as he may not have been expected to live long. It would appear that Prince Amenhotep may have had three sisters, Beketaten, Sitamun, and Isis; the latter two were married to their father Amenhotep III, suggesting they were older than Amenhotep and his brother Thutmosis. There has been some doubt expressed as to the parentage of Beketaten although scholars believe her to either be the sister or daughter of Akhenaten.

During their childhood the royal princes were raised at the palace at Memphis where they were trained in the athletic arts, like hunting lions, wild ass, gazelles, charioteering and archery. Amenhotep III himself was often shown participating in sports of this kind and it is natural that he would want his sons to also display skills in these areas. In later years Prince Amenhotep is rarely shown in reliefs performing these traditional acts of kingly prowess, and may indicate a lack of interest or a lack of skill.

Being raised at Memphis would, from an early age, expose the prince to the solar cults, more so than other deities. Near Memphis lay Heliopolis, the site of the creation myths, which saw the primeval mound raise from the primeval waters. At Heliopolis the whole cycle of the solar journey was favoured and Atum, Re, Khepri and Horakhty were worshipped here. There had been a rise in the power of the solar cults since the Middle Kingdom, and the solar cult had risen to such a level of popularity that most local deities were 'solarising' their names by adding Re to them. This new solar age also saw an introduction of new funerary texts including the *Book of what is in the Amduat*, and the *Litany of Re*, the latter of which introduces the name Aten in reference to the sun-disc. During the reign of Amenhotep III the Aten was mentioned more often in connection to the royal solar bark, the palace and some royal names than any other deity, indicating that during the childhood and early adulthood of Prince Amenhotep, the solar cult was very prominent, with increased importance of the sun in his form as the Aten, the sun-disc.

MARRIAGE

As Prince Amenhotep's sister Sitamun was already married to his father, he was unable to marry her as tradition would dictate. Instead he married Nefertiti (*33*), who is sometimes believed to be the daughter of Ay, the brother of Queen Tiye. During Akhenaten's reign his father-in-law Ay was promoted and became 'Master of the Horse' and also the 'King's Secretary' and was privy to the king's thoughts and plans. In his tomb at Amarna Ay writes: 'My Lord taught me, and I carry out his instructions'. Being this close to the king obviously helped Ay in later years when he himself became king. He has many of the same titles as Yuya, the father of Queen Tiye and came from the same small town and therefore it is likely that he was the son of Yuya and inherited his titles from him.

31 Queen Tiye, Berlin. *Copyright Robert Partridge: The Ancient Egypt Picture Library*

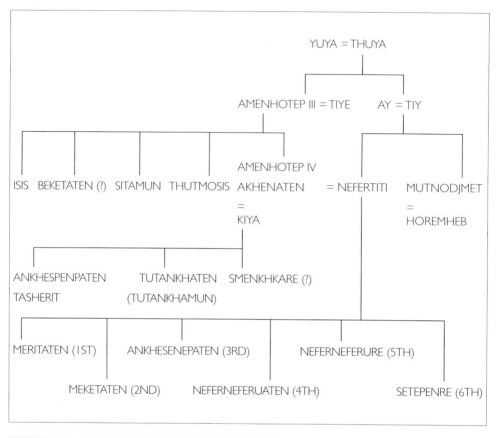

YUYA = THUYA

AMENHOTEP III = TIYE   AY = TIY

ISIS   BEKETATEN (?) SITAMUN   THUTMOSIS   AMENHOTEP IV
AKHENATEN   = NEFERTITI   MUTNODJMET

=   =

KIYA   HOREMHEB

ANKHESPENPATEN   TUTANKHATEN   SMENKHKARE (?)
TASHERIT   (TUTANKHAMUN)

MERITATEN (1ST)   ANKHESENEPATEN (3RD)   NEFERNEFERURE (5TH)

MEKETATEN (2ND)   NEFERNEFERUATEN (4TH)   SETEPENRE (6TH)

Left: 32 Amenhotep III worshipping the deified image of himself at the temple of Soleb in Nubia. *Illustration by the author*

Opposite: 33 Nefertiti bust, Berlin. *Copyright Robert Partridge: The Ancient Egypt Picture Library*

Akhenaten's marriage to Nefertiti happened before he became king and her parents' names are not mentioned. It has been suggested that she was the Mittannian princess, Tadukhipa, sent originally for marriage to Amenhotep III, but who married his son instead. Nefertiti's mother is completely unknown although Ay's wife Tiy was called the 'Wet Nurse' of Nefertiti and was probably her step mother (34).

Nefertiti and Akhenaten had six daughters; the oldest, Meritaten, was born at the start of Akhenaten's reign, Meketaten was born next and in year seven Ankhesenepaten, the future wife of Tutankhamun, was born. Neferneferuaten was born in year eight and Neferneferure in year nine. The youngest daughter was Setepenre and she died in childhood (35). There is no record of Akhenaten and Nefertiti having a son although Tutankhamun is called 'Son of the King' on blocks from Amarna, although his mother's name is also not mentioned.

CO-REGENCY

In year 26 of Amenhotep III, Prince Amenhotep was crowned as co-regent. His coronation took place at Memphis, where all coronation ceremonies had taken place since the time of Narmer (3100 BC). As well as this traditional coronation ceremony the new king Amenhotep IV was given traditional titles, reflecting the solar cult of the period including 'Neferkheperure Waenre' which means 'Fair of forms like Re, the only one of Re'. The practice of co-regency was traditional from the twelfth dynasty so an infirm king could delegate some responsibilities onto a younger individual as well as making it clear who the heir was to be. It is thought they divided the kingdom and Amenhotep III was believed to have ruled from Thebes and Amenhotep IV ruled from his new capital, Akhetaten (Tell el Amarna).

Amenhotep III died in year 12 of Akhenaten's reign or year 38 of his own, after a prolonged period of ill health. Amenhotep III would seem to have been a very superstitious individual and sculpted over 700 statues of Sekhmet, the lioness–headed goddess of epidemics, as a defence against whatever ailment he was suffering from. These were placed at Karnak in regimental rows in the precinct of Mut (36).

Two years later in year 14 of Akhenaten's reign, Queen Tiye died and was buried at Akhetaten, where she probably lived. It is thought however, that her body was later moved to her husband's tomb in the Western Valley of the Valley of the Kings. There has been some debate as to the identity of the body found in a side chamber of the tomb of Amenhotep II commonly known as the 'Elder Lady' although it has been suggested that it may be Tiye. Hair samples from the tomb of Tutankhamun labelled as belonging to Tiye have been analysed using ion etching and scanning electron

Above: 34 Ay and Tiy, Amarna. *Photograph Wayne R. Frostick*

Right: 35 Amarna princess. *Copyright: Petrie Museum of Egyptian Archaeology, University College London, UC 24317*

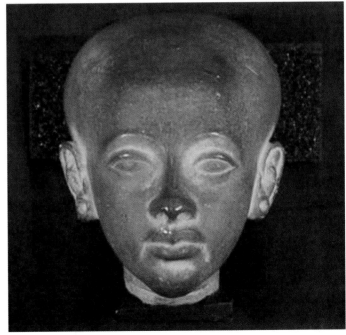

36 Precinct of Mut, Karnak. *Photograph Wayne R. Frostick*

microprobe analysis, and seem to match the hair on the Elder Lady. Also X-rays of the skull have shown a very close morphology to that of Thuya the known mother of Queen Tiye indicating that they are related. Marks on the face of the Elder Lady indicate that she may have died from small-pox, although it could also have been a reaction to the mummification process.

THE ATEN

The Aten is the key element to the reign of Akhenaten, but was not a new deity to the Egyptians at this time. The earliest record of the use of the name Aten is from the twelfth-dynasty *Coffin Texts*. The Aten traditionally was shown as a man with the head of a falcon surmounted by a sun-disc, rather similar to the iconography of Re-Horakhty. Amenhotep IV (Akhenaten) changed this imagery to a sun-disc with rays ending in hands holding an *ankh*. This, however, is also not a new image as it is shown on the stela at the Giza sphinx, dedicated by Amenhotep II showing the rays of the sun-disc embracing the cartouche. The *ankh* signs offered by the sun-disc during the Amarna Period are only ever offered to the king and queen, and occasionally to other members of the royal family (*37*).

The favouring of the Aten over other deities began in the reign of Amenhotep III, although he did not abandon the other gods, despite his campaign to limit the power of the Priesthood of Amun. At the start of Amenhotep III's reign the office of High Priest of Amun and that of Chief Minister were held by one man, Ptahmose, but by the end of his reign the two posts had been separated therefore diminishing the power held by one man. It was only in the early years of the co-regency with Amenhotep IV that the changes in the religion were more drastic.

AKHENATEN'S REIGN

Changes to the religion started early in the reign, although they were in small stages. The Aten's name was enclosed in two cartouches, in year three, as though part of a royal titulary. Although Amen-Ra had been called 'King of the Gods' this was the first time that there had been systemisation of the royalty of the god. Aten was also given regnal years that corresponded with those of Amenhotep IV ensuring that from this time on the king and the god were one and the cult of divine kingship was taken to extremes. They even celebrated their *heb sed* together as two gods/two kings. In year five Amenhotep IV changed his name to Akhenaten showing his increased support of the deity.

In the early years of the reign the numerous deities of the Egyptian pantheon co-existed alongside the Aten, and the first sanctuary dedicated by Amenhotep IV to the Aten was at Karnak temple. This Aten temple is thought to have been oriented towards the sunrise and contained colossal statues of the king. There was also a sanctuary dedicated entirely to the 'Great Royal Wife' Nefertiti, where the queen was shown either alone or with her daughters, performing cultic activities normally reserved for the king, including smiting enemies and wearing crowns normally reserved for kings. Nefertiti like Tiye before her, was represented in art as almost equal to the king and was also given a new name, similar to a throne name. Hence she became known as Neferneferuaten 'Aten is the most beautiful' Nefertiti. Although this was not officially a throne name, her name was also enclosed in two cartouches to give the appearance of a traditional titulary. It is suggested that this apparent equality between Akhenaten and Nefertiti could indicate there was a co-regency between them in the later years of the reign, although the evidence for this is inconclusive.

In year nine of the co-regency, Akhenaten closed all the other temples and redirected the revenue of those temples to his Aten temple at Amarna. In later years he also started destroying temples and statues of Amun in particular – the name Amun was chiselled out. In the earlier years he was probably more tolerant of the other temples as they were vital to the economy of Egypt.

37 Nefertiti, Ashmolean Museum. *Photograph Wayne R. Frostick*

AMARNA

In the early years of his reign Akhenaten decided to build a new capital city on ground that had previously been untouched by other religious cults. He chose the site at Tell el Amarna due to a dip in the cliffs that resembled the hieroglyphic sign for horizon, and even named the city 'Horizon of the Aten' (Akhetaten). Unlike traditional Egyptian settlements, everything in Akhetaten was in the east and oriented towards the east. On one of the earlier boundary stelae Akhenaten gives directions to be buried 'where the sun rises' not in the traditional Western realm of the dead, which was too closely tied up with the traditional religion.

By year four, work had begun on defining the boundaries of the site of Akhetaten and in year five three boundary stelae were set up around the city site to identify these boundaries, as well as to describe how Akhenaten chose the site and dedicated it to Aten. In year six, there were 14 boundary stelae, all of which show Akhenaten, Nefertiti and two of their daughters (Meritaten and Meketaten) worshipping the Aten.

In year nine the royal court moved to the new city, although it was not developed as a normal city but rather as a cult centre devoted to serving the Aten, Akhenaten and his family. The types of officials that lived here suggest the site was not designed as the administrative capital, but as a religious one with temple officials, a large abundance of artists, temple scribes and police officials, but only one vizier and no other civil administration. The archaeological evidence suggests the first buildings to be erected here were the palaces and temples in the Central City area in the centre of the plain on the east side of the Nile.

Between 50,000-100,000 people lived at Akhetaten during the height of Akhenaten's reign, 10 per cent of which were the elite. Although this city was not fortified it was closed off to all who did not have a function within it. All slaves and servants stayed with their masters and did not have homes of their own. It is unlikely that there was a poor underclass and the wealth of the home owners was reflected in size and grandeur of the houses. Some of the homesteads were large enough for a chariot with horses to pass through and it is thought the chariot was a general mode of transport rather than purely a military vehicle. The king and queen would travel down the 'Kings Road' in a chariot on a daily procession viewed by all of their favoured officials.

The city was planned around an official centre with palaces, temples and military barracks, although no evidence has been found for shops, taverns and schools. Workshops, however, were closely associated with private homes. The home and adjoining workshop of Thutmose from the sculptors' quarter has uncovered a large number of stone sculptures in various stages of completion. These were left behind when the city was abandoned at the end of Akhenaten's reign. Other workshops include those of glass and faience which Amarna has become particularly famous for.

In the workshop of Thutmose statues and votive objects of the traditional gods were also discovered indicating that the old religion was not abandoned completely by the people at Akhetaten. Several votive figures of this kind were also found in the house of the High Priest of the Aten, which is a little more surprising. From the workshop of Thutmose are numerous images of the royal family in various stages of completion, the most famous being the painted bust of Nefertiti. There were a number of unfinished heads of Akhenaten, and 20 of the royal family and non-royal individuals. Three quartzite heads of Amarna princesses show shaved, elongated skulls, which have prompted debate as to whether they are indicative of artificial head deformation, or hydrocephalus. These heads were carved for use on statues and would have been attached to a body of the same stone and the join covered with a necklace or wig.

Akhenaten also had a workman's village very similar to that at Deir el Medina in the Theban region. This worker's village at Akhetaten was walled and had 70-80 houses and it is thought that some of the workmen may have been transferred from Deir el Medina. The village was relatively self-sufficient although water needed to be brought from the outside either from the Nile (2 miles away) or from communal wells. Excavations have shown that pigs would also have been kept as extra support for the villagers. Although they were considered unclean, pigs were definitely used economically, and the Egyptians probably used them for waste disposal.

The workman's village like the rest of the city only appeared to show lip service to the new religion with the excavation of many houses uncovering amulets of Bes, Taweret and Hathor, and murals of Bes painted on the walls.

PALACES

Akhenaten built at least four palaces: the King's House, the Great Palace, the Northern Palace and the North Riverside Palace. The excavations at the Northern Palace (38) show that there was a huge stone structure built in the centre of the mud-brick screen wall which divided the Entrance Court from the sunken Central Court. The stone was removed in antiquity but the gypsum foundations showing the imprints of the stone blocks, setting-out lines, finger grooves along the edges of the courses and even footprints of the ancient builders which are still clearly visible. This stone building may have housed the 'Window of Appearances' that dominated Amarna art where the king and queen bestowed gold necklaces to their favoured courtiers.

38 Northern Palace, Amarna. *Photograph Wayne R. Frostick*

Near the gateway and door-jambs of this stone structure, gold leaf and paint fragments were found. In the Central Court there was a sunken garden with a small well or a shallow pool surrounded by chambers decorated with images of birds in papyrus thickets. One of the rooms clearly shows that the whole wall was painted with the bottom half representing water and the top half representing marsh land. The Northern Palace, however, seems to have been used only for the royal women and therefore would have housed the harem.

Ornamental gardens and pools are often represented in Amarna art, and the period is known for the realistic images of wildlife. The palaces and the pavements of the city were decorated with images from nature and it seems that Akhenaten may have had a zoological garden filled with wild desert animals at the Great Palace. In one of the palace halls Petrie discovered a floor of 250 square feet made of plaster decorated with a lake and reeds with pin tailed ducks flying in the air and calves kicking their heels on the ground. Petrie applied for a roof to be built over it to protect it, and whilst he was waiting for this he built a walkway for visitors to walk on so they could see it without damaging it. He also covered the whole floor with a hand-applied thin layer of tapioca and water to preserve it. Eventually a shed was erected over it. About 20 years later a farmer who was tired of the hordes of tourists walking over his field, to see the floor, destroyed it by hacking it to pieces. The fragmentary remains are currently in the Cairo Museum although heavily restored.

The necropolis at Amarna is to the east of the city and it would seem that Akhenaten was trying to start a new Valley of the Kings for himself and his family. His rock-cut tomb followed the standard eighteenth-dynasty style, although it was intended as a family tomb, and was unfinished. The sarcophagus inside the tomb was deliberately smashed after his reign had ended. On the corners of the sarcophagus instead of having winged figures of the godesses Isis, Nephthys, Neith and Selket, as was traditional, he had four winged figures of Nefertiti to protect him in death indicating that he may have considered her his personal goddess.

TEMPLES

There were numerous temples at Akhetaten all dedicated to the Aten and these were different in style and function to traditional Egyptian temples. The temples of the Aten were open-roofed and were not shadowy and dark like traditional temples. There was no need for a cult statue, and the processional way ended with an elevated altar rather than a sanctuary. With this open roof the king and priests were able to witness the god in every corner of the temple. There were dedicatory stela and many offering tables which were constantly filled with traditional offerings of bread, beer, fowl, oxen and geese. The temple had its own slaughterhouse so ritual sacrifices of geese and cattle could be carried out near-by. The rays of the sun would touch the offerings, absorbing nourishment from them and then they were distributed amongst the priests of the Aten.

Worshipping was different at Amarna as the Aten himself did not speak, so there was no 'Holy Book' or mythology surrounding this deity. This imagery was just a representation of the light radiating from the solar disc and therefore was merely an element of the iconography of the solar cult. Akhenaten received all his information and teachings directly from the Aten, but not as a prophet, rather as an element of the god himself. He then placed a 'Teaching' or 'Instruction' into the heart of his subjects through an oral tradition as there is no surviving written evidence of these teachings. The Great Hymn to the Aten is said to be written by Akhenaten himself, although the only copy is in Ay's tomb.

> Adoration of Re-Horakhty-who-rejoices-on-the-Horizon, In-his-name-Shu-who-is-Aten, living forever; the great living Aten who is in jubilee, lord of all that the Aten encircles, lord of the sky, lord of earth, lord of the House of Aten in Akhetaten; (and of) the King of Upper and Lower Egypt, who lives by Maat, the Lord of the Two Lands: Neferkheperure Waenre; the Son of Re, who lives by Maat, the Lord of Crowns:

Akhenaten, great in his lifetime; (and of) the Chief Wife of the King, his beloved, the Lady of the Two Lands: Neferneferuaten Nefertiti, who lives in health and youth forever; (by) the Vizier, Fan-Bearer on the Right Hand of the King , Ay. He says:

'Splendid you rise in heaven's lightland,
O living Aten, the creator of life!
When you have dawned in eastern lightland,
You have filled every land with your beauty.
You are beauteous, great, radiant, high over every land;
Your rays embrace the lands to the limit of all that you have made:
Being Re, you reach the limits;
You bend them for your beloved son.
Though you are far away, your rays are on earth;
Though one sees you, your strides are unseen.

When you set in the western lightland,
The land is in darkness, in the manner of death.
One sleeps in chambers, head covers,
One eye does not see the other.
Were they robbed of their goods, that are under their heads
People would not remark it,
Every lion is comes from his den;
All serpents, they bite.
Darkness hovers, and the earth is silent,
As their maker rests in lightland.

Earth brightens when you dawn in the lightland,
When you shine as the Aten of daytime,
As you dispel the dark, as you cast your rays
The Two Lands are in festivity,
Awake they stand upon their feet,
You have roused them;
Bodies cleansed, clothed,
Their arms adore your appearance.
The entire land sets out to work,
All beasts browse on their herbs;
Trees, herbs are sprouting,
Birds fly from their nests,
Their wings greeting your *ka*.
All flocks frisk on their feet,
All that fly up and alight,

They live when you dawn for them.
Ships fare north, fare south as well,
Roads lie open when you rise;
The fish in the river dart before you;
Your rays are in the midst of the sea.

Who make seed grow in women
Who creates people from sperm;
Who feeds the son in his mother's womb,
Who soothes him to still his tears
You nurse (even) in the womb,
Who gives breath to nourish all that he has made.
When he comes from the womb to breathe
On the day when he is born,
You open wide his mouth,
You supply his needs.
When the chick in the egg speaks within the shell,
You give him breath within it to sustain him.
When you have made him complete, to break out from the egg,
He comes out from the egg, to announce his completion,
Walking on his legs he comes from it.

How many are your deeds,
Though hidden from sight.
O sole god, beside whom there is none!
You made the world as you wished, you alone,
All people, herds and flocks;
All upon earth that walk on legs,
All on high that fly on wings,
The lands of Khor and Kush, the land of Egypt,
You set every man in his place,
You supply their needs:
Everyone has his food, and his lifetime is counted.
Their tongues differ in speech,
And their characters likewise;
Their skins are distinct,
For you distinguished the peoples.

You made Nile in the underworld,
You bring him when you will,
To nourish the people (of Egypt),

For you made them for yourself,
The Lord of all who toils for them,
Lord of all Lands who shines for them,
Aten of daytime, great in glory!
All distant lands, you make them live,
You have made a heavenly Nile descend for them,
He makes waves on the mountains like the sea,
To drench their fields and their towns.
How excellent are your plans, O lord of eternity!
A Nile from heaven, for the foreign peoples
And all lands' creatures that walk on legs,
For Egypt the Nile that comes from the Netherworld.

Your rays nurse all fields.
When you shine they live, they grow for you;
You made the seasons to foster all that you made,
Winter to cool them, heat that they taste you.
You made the far sky to shine therein,
To behold all that you made;
You alone, shining in your form of living Aten,
Risen, radiant, distant, near.
You have made millions of forms from yourself alone,
Towns, villages, fields, the river's course;
All eyes observe you upon them,
For you are the Aten of daytime on high....

You are in my heart,
There is no other that knows you,
Only your son Neferkheperure Waenre,
Whom you have taught your ways and your might,
Those on earth come from your hand as you made them,
When you have dawned they live,
When you set they die;
You yourself are lifetime, one lives by you,
All eyes are on your beauty until you set,
All labour ceases when you rest in the west;
When you rise you stir everyone for the king,
Every leg is on the move since you founded the earth
You rouse them for your son, who came from your body:
The King who lives by Maat.
The Lord of the Two Lands Neferkheperure Waenre.'

The temple, however, was still made up of pylons, courtyards and columned halls. Artistic representations show that the main temple of the Aten had 10 flagpoles, and Karnak only had eight indicating Akhenaten was trying to outshine Karnak with this Aten temple. Between the columns stood numerous colossi statues of the king and queen, which were the only statues housed in the temple.

Although the temples of all other deities were shut down in year nine there was little evidence of persecution during the first five years of Akhenaten's reign. In fact at the start of his reign he built temples to the Aten at the temple of Karnak (39).

In year four the 'High Priest of Amun' was sent 'into the desert' on a quarrying expedition and the High Priest of Ptah at Memphis reports that all was well at this temple showing that the worship of other deities was still tolerated at this point. When Akhenaten changed his name in year five he also stopped the worship of all other deities and then a few years later started to erase their names and images. The main persecution was against Amun and his consort Mut, to the point of erasing the name Amun from place names and personal names on monuments, scarabs and obelisks as far south as the fourth cataract. This included the destruction of his own name Amenhotep and that of his father. The erasure of gods' names had never happened before, and would no doubt have been met with horror by all. Only royal names had been erased in the past as a political tool and this persecution was probably a way of ensuring the Aten's superiority.

It would appear that there was some opposition to this new religion as there are numerous images of Asiatic and Nubian soldiers protecting Akhenaten as a personal bodyguard. Although his father and his grandfather were both military kings, Akhenaten is regarded as a pacifist so these soldiers were for his own protection and enforcement rather than for warfare. Akhenaten possessed all the power of the throne and the military, which he used to realise his ideals, no doubt ruthlessly when needed. This apparent opposition or threat of opposition caused Akhenaten to restrict himself to within the limits of Akhetaten, and the worship of the Aten also became restricted to within the boundary of the royal residence.

AKHENATEN'S APPEARANCE

The artistic representations of Akhenaten (*colour plate 12*) have caused much debate – it is suggested that he may have suffered from one of the following:

> ✧ Frolichs syndrome or dystrophia adiposogenitalis is a condition that leads to obesity and is used to explain Akhenaten's large hips and pendulous breasts.

39 Akhenaten, Karnak. *Photograph Wayne R. Frostick*

◇ Marfans syndrome is a hereditary disease where the sufferer grows very tall and thin which would explain the tall, thin appearance but there seems to be no evidence that Amenhotep III suffered from this, which raises the question of who Akhenaten inherited it from

◇ Klinefelters syndrome causes the male sufferer to develop breasts, small testes and very long legs with a high pitched voice and limited facial hair growth

One statue from Karnak shows Akhenaten naked, displaying no genitalia and it has been suggested he contracted a disease after he had fathered his six daughters or even that Nefertiti cuckolded him with a variety of partners including Horemheb. It is more likely that the sexless imagery indicated the androgynous characteristics of Akhenaten in order to associate him with the creator elements of the Aten. Creator gods are able to recreate by themselves with no need of a woman and Akhenaten presents himself as possessing both male and female fertility characteristics in these images. It has also been suggested that the grotesque image of Akhenaten would also have repulsed the Egyptians, and Akhenaten may have wanted to shock them by going completely against the traditional artistic style in the same manner in which he had retaliated against religion.

In addition to these physical representations the Amarna Period saw the introduction of the intimate family scenes which replaced images of the gods. The love that the royal family show each other was supposed to come from the Aten and therefore emanate all over the world. One image in the Louvre shows Nefertiti sitting on Akhenaten's lap, another shows Nefertiti leading her husband to her bed, and in some tombs the family are shown eating and drinking, which would not have been considered suitable for the pharaoh, in earlier or indeed later periods.

After year 13 the name of Nefertiti disappears from the monuments and it is thought that she may have died or that a disagreement about the Aten left her banished to the Northern Palace. It has also been suggested that she may have changed her name. In the tomb of Pere in the necropolis of Thebes, a draftsman drew a sketch and dated it to year three of the 'King of the Two Lands' Ankheperure Neferneferuaten. Neferneferuaten 'Beloved of Akhenaten', was a title always associated with Nefertiti and therefore identified this king with her. Ankheperure, however, is the throne name of King Smenkhkare. The draftsman may have confused the royal names or it has been suggested that Nefertiti was Ankheperure Neferneferuaten and ruled from Thebes whilst Akhenaten ruled from Amarna with Meritaten taking Nefertiti's place as 'Chief Royal Wife'. However, the discovery of the body in KV55 has now been identified as Smenkhkare. The body is a male in his 20s or 30s who was small boned and wide hipped, and clearly proves that he existed independently of Nefertiti. The tomb had undergone a number of different attacks over the years. The coffin had been crushed by falling masonry, severing the head. Much of the funerary goods in KV55 originally belonged to women and had been altered by the addition of a uraeus to the canopics and coffins, which were later removed when the tomb was destroyed. The names on the equipment were also hacked out and the gold removed from the coffin. The golden shrine of Tiye was also dismantled and an attempt had been made to remove it from the tomb, perhaps to remove the gold. This has been abandoned as it would not fit through the corridor. The tomb was then sealed and left.

In the tomb of Meyer, Smenkhkare and his wife, Meritaten, are together rewarding him, suggesting that Smenkhkare was married to Akhenaten's daughter even though Akhenaten himself was married to her. However, this scene could have been added after Akhenaten's death when the marriage is more likely to have taken place. The graffito in the tomb of Pere states that Smenkhkare's memorial temple was in Thebes indicating that he intended to be buried here in the traditional way; however, all the evidence suggests that he was buried initially at Amarna. He reigned for only three years and is thought to either be a younger son of Amenhotep III and Tiye or a son of Akhenaten. He possibly took over the throne before Tutankhamen because he was an adult and Tutankhamun was only a child.

In year 14, Meketaten died and was buried in the royal tomb of Akhenaten at Amarna. It is suggested that Meketaten may have either died in childbirth, or from an epidemic sweeping through Amarna. In the relief of the mourning there is a scene showing a nurse maid with a baby which is thought to have been Akhenaten's. He was married to his eldest daughter, Meritaten, and there has been speculation that this could be his child by her although she is considered too young at this point to have died in childbirth. Akhenaten did have a child with Meritaten, Meritaten-Tasherit (the younger), although it is not the child depicted here. It is further suggested and more commonly accepted that this child is Tutankhamun, and it is his mother Kiya, a secondary wife, on the funerary bier which further suggests this is the death and burial of Kiya instead. Kiya the secondary wife of Akhenaten, is also thought to have given birth to a daughter Ankhesenepaten-Tasherit (the younger).

THE END

The end of the reign of Akhenaten is vague and unrecorded, so we can only guess at the actual events. The collapse of the Amarna Period seems to have been the final event in a string of disasters in the personal life of the king. These disasters start from year 12 of his reign with the death of his father Amenhotep III, followed in year 14 by his mother Tiye. His daughter, Meketaten, appears to have died in year 12 possibly as a result of childbirth or disease. Soon after this, Nefertiti disappears from the inscriptions and is replaced as 'Great Royal Wife' by her daughter Meritaten. A number of inscriptions at the Sunshade Temple at Amarna show Nefertiti's name was erased and replaced with that of her daughter and it has been suggested that this was due to her falling out of favour, possibly due to a disagreement with Akhenaten over the Aten. However, a number of images and examples of Nefertiti's name still exist and were not destroyed, indicates that she was not disgraced, leaving death as the likely reason for her disappearance. Smenkhkare reigned for three years and died late in year 17 of Akhenaten's reign and may have ruled independently for a short time. The lack of records indicates that Meritaten had died prior to her husband Smenkhkare. In addition to these deaths Akhenaten had to deal with the death of the two younger daughters of Nefertiti, and Ankhesenepaten; all within a very short space of time. These deaths have often been attributed to a plague epidemic sweeping Amarna. This plague would no doubt have been viewed by the ordinary people as punishment for the abandonment of the traditional gods.

Akhenaten himself died after the grape harvest of year 17 of his reign, which was approximately July 1334 BC when he was in his 30s, and only five years after the death of his father. He left no known male heir. Nefertiti and Kiya only bore him daughters, although Tutankhamun may have been the son of Kiya. Nefertiti only appeared to have a sister, Mutnodjmet, who later married Horemheb legitimising his claim to the throne. After Akhenaten's death Amarna was abandoned, although not straight away, and much of the material used to build it was reused by Horemheb and Ramses II when they built their monuments over the river at Ashmunein (Hermopolis).

The collapse of the cult of the Aten was obviously going to happen as the main protagonists had all died, leaving only Tutankhaten, a young boy of about eight or nine, as the only possible male member of the family, and even his parentage is shrouded with doubt. He was surrounded by advisors, most of which were officials to the king prior to the move to Amarna and the rise of the Aten cult, resulting in a gradual change back to the traditional gods. The first thing he did as king was to change his name to Tutankhamun, and then to move the capital back to Thebes, re-establishing the cult of Amun. Once the king, the court and the power moved away from the city everyone else gradually followed leaving Amarna empty other than the faience factories which were in use throughout most of his reign. As Tutankhamun had no experience of anything other than the Aten cult and Amarna he would have been manipulated by his officials until he reached an age of manhood, where he could exert his own power. Then he mysteriously died; to this day the cause of which remains a hot topic of debate.

In reality the traditional religion of Egypt was never truly abandoned as religious paraphernalia found even at Amarna would suggest, so all Tutankhamun had to do was reinstate Amun and the pantheon, and this no doubt was supported by most people. The kings following Tutankhamun on the throne merely continued with this re-establishment of the old gods and the restoration of the temples in order to bring Egypt back to the glory of the reign of Amenhotep III.

NINE

TUTANKHAMUN
THE BOY KING

INTRODUCTION

Tutankhamun is one of the most famous kings of ancient Egypt due to the remarkable archaeological discovery of his un-plundered tomb in 1922 by Howard Carter. However, although his tomb has put his name in the history books Tutankhamun was a relatively unimportant king who ruled at the end of the eighteenth dynasty after the Amarna Period. He was only a child when he came to the throne and died before he had fully reached adulthood aged 18 or 19 years old.

FAMILY

Tutankhamun was born at Amarna, and a decorated tunic, wrapped around the statue of Anubis in his tomb may give the date of his birth. The tunic was plain except for red and blue stripes, giving the whole piece a purple appearance. On the bottom hem Akhenaten's cartouche is embroidered indicating it was produced during the reign of this king. The size of the tunic is suitable for a new-born baby, and the date under the cartouches could be the year of Tutankhamun's birth; seventh year of Akhenaten and suggests that Tutankhamun may have worn it during a ceremony in his early months. Perhaps even a naming ceremony.

Although Tutankhamun is thought to be the son of Akhenaten and Kiya, a secondary wife, there is no written evidence to prove it. There is an inscription from a talatat block found at Hermopolis that names Tutankhamun as 'King's bodily son, his beloved' but his mother is never named. There is also some doubt as to the true identity of Kiya, and it has been thought she may be Tadukhipa the Mittannian princess sent for marriage to Amenhotep III, who finally married Akhenaten instead.

It is suggested that the mourning scene in the royal tomb at Amarna may show the death of Kiya at the birth of Tutankhamun; a child is carried away by a servant, rather than Meketaten, or Meritaten. However it is also suggested that Smenkhkare may be his father and his wife Meritaten, his mother. Both theories are perfectly plausible although the former is the most accepted. Whoever his parents were it is clear that he was born between years seven to nine of the reign of Akhenaten as he was seven or eight years old when he came to the throne at the death of Akhenaten in year 17. At birth he was given the name Tutankhaten which he changed on his ascension to the throne to Tutankhamun.

It is often stated that the elusive king of only one year, Smenkhkare, was the brother of Tutankhamun and through analysis of Tutankhamun's skull and that in KV55, thought to be Smenkhkare, it would seem that they have the same morphology and are clearly related. Until clearer information regarding the origins of Smenkhkare are discovered the true familial relationship between Tutankhamun and Smenkhkare will remain uncertain.

Tutankhamun married Ankhesenepaten (40), who later changed her name to Ankhesenamun. Prior to this time she was married to her father Akhenaten, and was widowed upon his death. She may have been Tutankhamun's sister or half-sister, a traditional marriage custom, and she was possibly six to eight years older than him. The images of them together show a great deal of intimacy and affection, although this could have been part of the realistic style of Amarna art and may not reflect their true feelings.

Tutankhamun had no surviving children but buried in his tomb in a plain white wooden chest were two foetuses. They were buried in two small anthropoid coffins placed within this box, side by side and head to foot. One of the coffins had the feet sawn off in order to get the lid of the chest in place. Both of the foetuses appeared to be female but were never named; on their coffins they are simply referred to as 'Osiris'.

The smaller of the girls was mummified and had a gilded cartonnage mask that was several sizes too big and clearly not made for her. However, the larger of the girls did not have a mask at all. Perhaps there was only one child's mask in storage at the time.

The smaller girl was very premature and was only 25.75cm in length. It is likely that she was stillborn as she was only in the fifth month of gestation with the umbilical cord still attached. Her organs had not been removed for mummification and she had no jewellery or amulets amidst the wrappings.

Right: 1 Imhotep as a scribe, twenty-sixth dynasty. *Copyright: Petrie Museum of Egyptian Archaeology, University College London, UC 8229*

Below: 2 Cast of Tety's funerary mask, Egyptian Museum, Cairo. *Copyright Robert Partridge: The Ancient Egypt Picture Library*

8229

3 Copper statue of
Pepy I, son of Tety.
*Copyright Robert
Partridge: The Ancient
Egypt Picture Library*

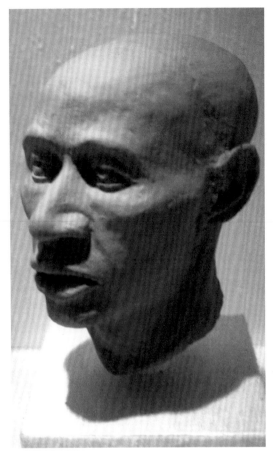

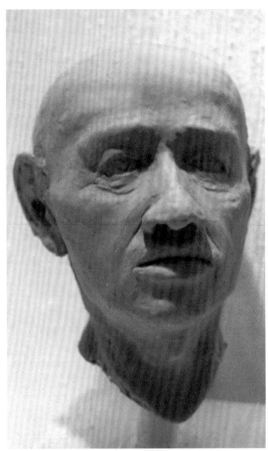

Above left: 4 Clay reconstruction of Khnumnakht,
Manchester. *Copyright Robert Partridge: The Ancient Egypt
Picture Library*

Above right: 5 Clay reconstruction of Nakhtankh,
Manchester. *Copyright Robert Partridge: The Ancient Egypt
Picture Library*

Right: 6 Ahmose-Nefertari. *Copyright: Petrie Museum
of Egyptian Archaeology, University College London,*
UC 15486

7 Ahmose-Nefertari, British Museum. *Copyright Robert Partridge: The Ancient Egypt Picture Library*

8 Thutmosis III, Luxor Museum. *Photograph Geoffrey Webb*

Left: 9 Hatshepsut Sphinx, Cairo
Museum. *Copyright Robert Partridge: The
Ancient Egypt Picture Library*

Below: 10 Pregnant Ahhotep, Deir el
Bahri. *Photograph Wayne R. Frostick*

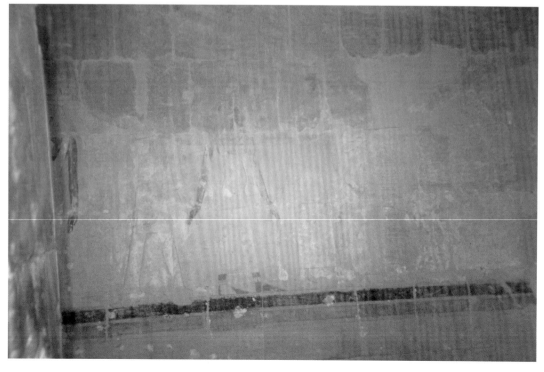

11 Amenhotep III, Luxor Museum. *Photograph Wayne R. Frostick*

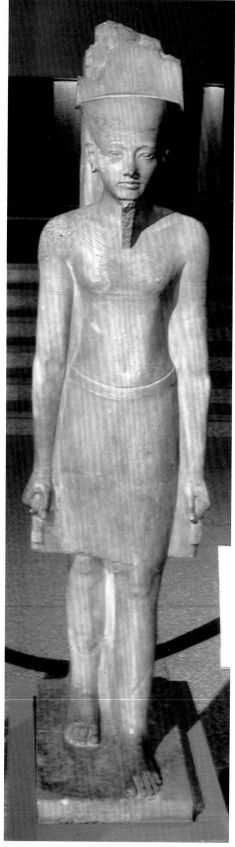

Above: 12 Akhenaten colossal statue, Luxor Museum.
Photograph Wayne R. Frostick

Right: 13 Amun with Tutankhamun's face, Luxor Museum.
Photograph Wayne R. Frostick

Opposite: 14 Door-jamb of Horemheb, British Museum.
*Photograph Clare V. Banks. Copyright: The Trustees of the British
Museum, London*

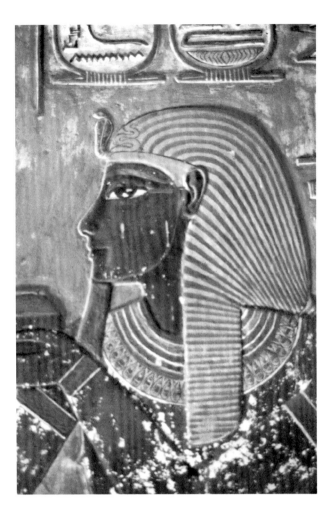

Left: 15 Horemheb, KV 57. *Copyright Robert Partridge: The Ancient Egypt Picture Library*

Below: 16 Ramses II colossal statue, Memphis. *Photograph Wayne R. Frostick*

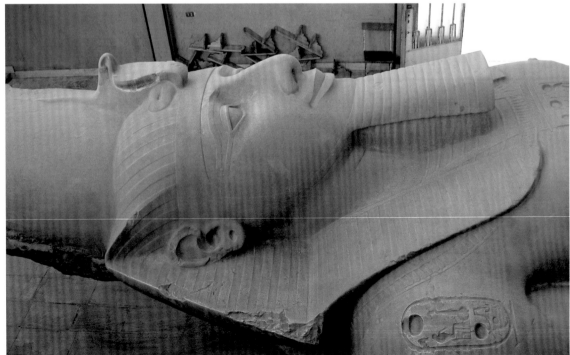

Right: 17 New Kingdom
scribal statue, Luxor Museum.
Photograph Wayne R. Frostick

Below: 18 Ramses III,
Medinet Habu. *Photograph
Wayne R. Frostick*

Left: 19 Mummy of
Natsefamun, Manchester.
Copyright Robert Partridge: The
Ancient Egypt Picture Library

Below: 20 Mummy of Asru,
Manchester. *Copyright Robert*
Partridge: The Ancient Egypt
Picture Library

Opposite: 21 Reconstruction
of Asru, Manchester.
Copyright Robert Partridge: The
Ancient Egypt Picture Library

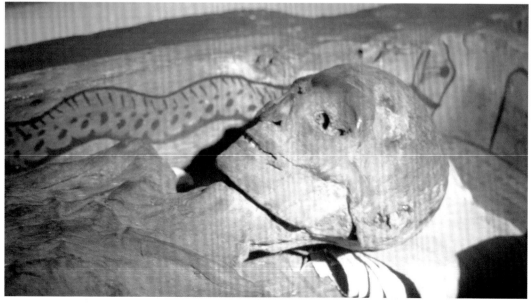

22 Cleopatra and Caesarion at Dendera. *Photograph Wayne R. Frostick*

23 Bust of Cleopatra, Allard Oierson Museum, Amsterdam. *Copyright Robert Partridge: The Ancient Egypt Picture Library*

24 Taimhotep, British Museum. *Photograph Clare V. Banks Copyright: The Trustees of the British Museum, London*

25 Ritual statue of Ptah, Egyptian Museum, Cairo. *Copyright Robert Partridge: The Ancient Egypt Picture Library*

40 Tutankhamun and Ankhesenamun, Luxor Temple. *Photograph Charlotte Booth*

The larger child was 36.1cm in length and was in the seventh month of gestation. There was no umbilical cord indicating that she had survived a premature birth but died shortly after. She had been traditionally mummified with her brain removed through the nose, and her internal organs removed through a slit in the left-hand side of her abdomen. Her head and chest had been packed with linen packages filled with natron to preserve the shape of her body and also to continue the drying process. She also did not possess any jewellery or amulets within the bandages. X-ray studies have indicated that this child may have suffered from sprengel's deformity which affects the shoulder by pushing the shoulder blade upwards; the x-ray shows that her left shoulder was affected by this. She also suffered from spina bifida, and scoliosis (curvature of the spine).

LIFE AT AMARNA

It is clear that Tutankhaten (Tutankhamun) spent at least the first nine years of his life at Amarna and it is thought that he lived in the Northern Palace with Nefertiti and the other royal women. He received a traditional royal education consisting of reading and writing as well as military skills. It is quite clear that Tutankhamun was literate, as in his tomb there are a number of scribal palettes. One was inscribed with the name of Meritaten that may have been a memento of his mother, should she be his mother, or his half-sister; and another inscribed with the name of his half-sister Meketaten. Meritaten's palette was obviously a special object of his as it was placed between the paws of the Anubis statue in the Treasury of his tomb. He may have lived at the Northern Palace with his half-sisters and therefore grew up alongside them. As he possessed a number of palettes, which display partly used inks in varying sizes it indicates he had received a basic education in reading and writing which probably took place in one of the palaces at Amarna.

As part of the traditional royal education Tutankhamun was probably trained in the art of warfare, and charioteering. These skills would have been used in what appears to have been his passion for hunting. In the tomb there were four hunting chariots, which were light Egyptian chariots, with six-spoke wheels, made of bent wood and leather. They seem to have been well used. There was also a golden fan, discovered between the third and fourth shrine in the burial chamber, bearing scenes of Tutankhamun hunting ostriches in the desert. He was obviously quite a talented hunter as he has already struck two of these birds with his arrows. An image from reused talatat blocks from the ninth pylon at Karnak shows Tutankhamun participating in a lion and bull hunt. These images were a typical tool for showing the prowess of the king, and indicating that he was able to control chaos. However, although his official images were stylised, there were a number of pairs of gloves and gauntlets in the tomb indicating that he needed them whilst hunting and riding. The gloves have five fingers whereas the gauntlets are separated into two fingers with the thumb left free and were used primarily for charioteering. There are varying sizes and he obviously owned some pairs when he was a child suggesting that he learnt to ride a chariot whilst still young. Gauntlets were more ceremonial than ordinary gloves and may have been worn in public displays. In the tomb of Tutankhamun there were also two ceremonial chariots which were covered with gold leaf decorated with embossed relief; one with the traditional images of bound captives. Perhaps Tutankhamun accompanied Akhenaten and Nefertiti on their daily parades through the 'Kings Road' at Amarna.

He was trained in the skills of warfare and a number of items in his tomb designed for children, including sling shots and scimitar swords, would indicate that the use of these weapons was part of his royal education. The skills he used in hunting would also have been useful in warfare and hunting traditionally was carried out with bows and arrows, spears or throwsticks; all of which were also used on a battlefield. He also was trained in survival skills as the presence of a fire drill in his tomb would suggest. This would ensure that when hunting he would be able to at least light a fire to keep warm in the cold desert evenings. There was also a walking stick made of reed which had been set into a golden handle inscribed with 'a reed which his majesty cut with his own hand' indicating that in his years at Amarna he was taught to carve using a sharp tool, either a copper or flint knife. He was obviously proud of this achievement, hence it had been set into a handle and placed into his tomb, albeit alongside 130 other sticks.

There is also evidence that Tutankhamun may have participated in, or at least been present during a *heb sed* of Akhenaten. A tunic from his tomb, decorated with embroidery, was designed for a child, with gold centres of embroidered rosettes and Maltese crosses. The collar has several rows of beads and the edge of the garment has an appliquéd Heb Sed design. As the festival was officially performed every 30 years Akhenaten may have performed one after year seven and the birth of Tutankhamun which was a great public celebration and could warrant the production of ceremonial clothes. Other ceremonial clothes discovered in the tomb indicate that Tutankhamun was meant to act as a *sem* priest for the burial of his predecessor, although whether this was for Akhenaten or Smenkhkare is uncertain. In his tomb there were three leopardskin cloaks, which are worn by the *sem* priests. Two were made of linen and were elaborately decorated with appliquéd circles in red and blue; golden stars were then stitched on top of the circles, surrounded by stitching to give the appearance of leopard spots in blue and red thread. The whole cloak is lined with a linen sheet. The third cloak was a real leopardskin and was decorated with gold rosettes, discs, stars and animal heads. Attached to all three cloaks were wooden leopard heads covered in gesso and overlaid with gold, with the eyes inlaid with blue glass and crystal and the markings just in blue glass. The cloaks also had four paws with silver claws at the top to attach to the cloak. These skins appeared to have been made for a small child and were probably designed for the 'Opening of the Mouth' ceremony. Whether he actually wore it during a funeral is unknown.

When Tutankhamun was not participating in ceremonial events he would pass the time playing *senet*, a game of strategy rather like chess, played with two players with seven game pieces each. Throwing the 'knuckle bones' or dice, which were sticks with a coloured and a plain side, determined how many squares the player should move. There were 30 squares on each board and the objective was to move all the pieces off the board. A number of *senet* boards were discovered in the tomb including a portable set indicating that he was a keen player. All of Tutankhamun's boards were double sided and all had drawers within which he could store the pieces.

In the later years of Tutankhamun's life it would appear that he had a liking for wine and there was a large supply in his tomb, some that was bottled in his own vineyard. Studies carried out on 6 of the 30 jars of wine from the tomb by a team from Barcelona in 2006, show that all of them contained tartaric acid, and one contained syringic acid; only found in red grapes suggesting that they all contained red wine made from grapes.

From the study of his body and other items in the tomb it is possible to get an impression of what Tutankhamun looked like (*colour plate 13*). He was 5ft 5in (167.5cm) in height which was average for ancient Egyptian men. He had a chest measurement of 80cm which was taken from the wooden mannequin found in his tomb and a waist of 75cm, taken from the measurements of sashes from the tomb. His hips were 108cm determined by measuring the adult-sized loincloths. He had a narrow waist and large rounded hips and it is possible that he suffered from bilharzia or other infestations causing bodily changes. There is also evidence that he suffered from a mild cleft palate and large frontal incisors giving him a substantial overbite which was characteristic of his family line. His mummy had shown signs of a scoliosis (curvature of the spine), although a CT scan in 2005 has arrived at the conclusion that this was due to the embalmers wrapping him whilst in an unnatural position. Tutankhamun also had pierced ears, which is supported by the number of earrings discovered in his tomb.

ASCENSION TO THE THRONE

After the death of Akhenaten in year 17 of his reign, his co-ruler Smenkhkare died shortly afterwards. Then Tutankhamun took the throne. The first major act was to change his name to Tutankhaten from Tutankhamun, before moving the city from Amarna to the traditional administrative capital of Memphis in year two or three of his reign. It is likely that initially the court moved to Memphis where the coronation of Tutankhamun took place as was traditional. However, the focus of his works at Thebes would indicate that he also resided here for part of his reign at the palace of Amenhotep III at Malkata. Although the royal family left the city of Amarna remained inhabited city until the reign of Horemheb, albeit with a fraction of the population. The people residing at Amarna were primarily concerned with the faience factories at the city which were still functioning throughout his reign.

At the same time as this royal move he reburied Smenkhkare in the Valley of the Kings in KV55, normally known as the 'Amarna cache'. It is possible that a funeral was carried out here with Tutankhamun officiating over it, wearing one of his leopardskin cloaks. It would seem that Smenkhkare may have been buried in a traditional royal burial in Amarna and when he was reburied his royal goods were removed and replaced by others that were in the Theban stores. The goods that originally belonged to Smenkhkare seem to have been used by Tutankhamun in his own burial suggesting that he had placed them in store for future use.

Smenkhkare's coffin seems to have originally been designed for a woman, and when it was used for his reburial a false beard was added to show his kingly status. His canopic jars may have originally been designed for up to three different individuals which may have been Akhenaten, Tiye, Kiya or Meritaten as they seem to be particularly feminine. A combination of burial goods have been found in KV55 including four magical bricks belonging to Akhenaten, a toiletry vessel belonging to Queen Tiye and also a shrine belonging to Queen Tiye. Even the tomb chosen for Smenkhkare was not a royal tomb and was therefore not designed for him. It was a rough-cut noble tomb which may have been intended for Ay as the vizier.

At the same time as the Smenkhkare reburial it is possible that Tutankhamun reburied his grandmother, or at least rescued some of her funerary goods to preserve her memory. A lock of her hair was found labelled in his tomb and in KV55 the golden shrine belonging to Tiye had been rescued, perhaps by Tutankhamun.

The move away from Amarna saw the start of the restoration of the traditional culture and religion of Egypt and the start of a campaign to destroy the monuments of Akhenaten. A number of talatat blocks have been discovered at Karnak in the second and ninth pylons which depict two battles of Tutankhamun. The blocks originally belonged in the temple of Akhenaten to the Aten at Karnak. Tutankhamun dismantled the temple and recarved the blocks and used them to build his mortuary temple on the west bank at Thebes. It was traditional for kings to reuse masonry from earlier temples to build their own, so this act in itself does not necessarily mean there was any animosity towards Akhenaten. However it is likely that Tutankhamun, as part of his campaign to restore Egypt back to its former glory, wanted to eliminate the existence of this king.

At Karnak temple Tutankhamun also erected the *The Restoration Stela* which outlined some of the plans he had to re-establish the cults and traditions of Egypt. As he was very young it is likely that Horemheb, the army general, or Ay, the vizier, contributed greatly with this text.

> He restored everything that was ruined, to be his monument forever and ever. He has vanquished chaos from the whole land and has restored Maat to her place. He has made lying a crime, the whole land being made as it was at the time of creation.

> Now when His Majesty was crowned King the temples and the estates of the gods and goddesses from Elephantine as far as the swamps of Lower Egypt had fallen into ruin. Their shrines had fallen down, turned into piles of rubble and overgrown with weeds. Their sanctuaries were as if they had never existed at all. Their temples had become footpaths. The world was in chaos and the gods had turned their backs on this land. If an army was sent to *Djahy* (Beth-Shan) to extend the boundaries of Egypt, it would have no success. If you asked a god for advice, he would not attend; and if one spoke to a goddess likewise she would not attend. Hearts were faint in bodies because everything that had been, was destroyed.

As well as re-establishing the temples and shrines of Egypt Tutankhamun also re-employed personnel to run these establishments:

> He allocated *wab*-priests, God's Servants and the heirs of the Chiefs of the Cities to be the sons of wise men whose reputation is established. He has enriched their tables with gold and silver, bronze and copper without limit. He has filled their storehouses with male and female workers and with His Majesty's booty. He has added to the wealth of every temple, doubling, trebling and quadrupling the silver, gold, lapis lazuli, turquoise and every noble precious stone, together with *byssus*, white linen, ordinary linen, oil, fat, resin, incense, perfumes and myrrh without limit.

He also reinstated traditional festivals and at Luxor temple he depicts the 'Beautiful Opet Festival' an annual Theban festival, when the statue of Amun from Karnak was removed and taken on procession to the temple of Amun at Luxor (2km away). It was held in the second month of the inundation and was a fertility festival. The journey between Karnak and Luxor started along the processional way or 'Sphinx Avenue' and the return journey was by water, with the divine boat being towed by small sail boats, on the Nile. The procession was accompanied by the Egyptian army running along the banks of the Nile, as well as singers, dancers and dignitaries. This festival also has connotations of rejuvenation of the king and may have been viewed by Tutankhamun as a reinstatement of traditional kingly values.

BUILDING WORKS

Tutankhamun, like many other kings, started a number of building projects including work at Luxor and Karnak temple which was dedicated to the god Amun. He actually commissioned so many monuments that an epithet on the stamp on his tomb door refers to him as he 'who spent his life in fashioning images of the gods'. The *Restoration Stela* also outlines the building works that Tutankhamun had initiated at the start of his reign:

> He made the holy statue out of genuine electrum, giving to it more than he had done before. He made his father Amun 13 poles long, the holy statue being made of electrum, lapis lazuli, turquoise and every noble and precious stone, although the majesty of this noble god had been only seven poles long before. His Majesty made monuments for the gods, making their statues from electrum from the tribute of the foreign lands. He renewed their sanctuaries as his monuments forever and ever, endowing them with offerings forever, laying aside for them divine offerings daily, laying aside bread from the earth. He added great wealth on top of that which existed before, doing more than his predecessors had ever done.

Tutankhamun focused most of his building works at Thebes. As he wanted to associate himself with Amenhotep III rather than Akhenaten, Tutankhamun continued the building works of this king. At Karnak the processional way from the tenth pylon to the complex of Mut, originally erected by this king, was completed by Tutankhamun and consists of ram-headed sphinxes. A sphinx bearing the face of Tutankhamun is still visible in the first court of the main temple at Karnak (*41*).

Tutankhamun also constructed a number of statues to Amun at Karnak all bearing his face and that of his wife Ankhesenamun (*42*). Additionally, he continued work at Luxor temple by completing the colonnade and the decoration in this temple.

41 Tutankhamun sphinx, Karnak temple. *Photograph Wayne R. Frostick*

42 Tutankhamun, Karnak. *Photograph Wayne R. Frostick*

He also travelled to the Nubian temples of Amenhotep III at Soleb and continued work on them. Tutankhamun built temples to his own divine cult, in the manner of Amenhotep III at Faras and Kawa in Nubia although the Faras temple has now been totally destroyed. This region of Nubia formed the centre of Nubian administration from where Tutankhamun and his newly appointed Viceroy of Kush, Huy, controlled the import of Nubian goods, in particular gold.

Tutankhamun did build a mortuary temple on the west bank of the Nile at Thebes, although the foundations of this have not been identified. It is thought that it was built under the temple of Ay and Horemheb as two colossal statues of Tutankhamun have been discovered at the site. It is also possible that part of the temple may have been usurped by Ay and Horemheb as the statues were usurped by both of these kings. One of these statues is now currently in the Cairo Musuem.

FOREIGN RELATIONS

During the reign of Akhenaten foreign relations initially were good as the numerous Amarna letters would indicate, but were somewhat neglected by the reign of Tutankhamun. During the reign of Tutankhamun he worked to re-establish these links. In his tomb there were numerous goods which appear to be gifts from foreign kings indicating that these relations may have been ongoing. A pair of leather sandals was sent, as a gift from Mittanni, and is actually mentioned in the Amarna letters (EA 22). These foreign shoes have a toe loop and are filled in at the back, totally different from other Egyptian shoes which are more like modern flip-flops. Several linen socks were also found in the tomb with two separate toes, and fastenings along the front, like shoelaces which are also probably of foreign origin. Socks would generally not have been worn in ancient Egypt due to the very hot climate. One of Tutankhamun's tunics was also sent to him from Mittanni when he was 12-14 years old, judging by the size of the garment. It was elaborately embroidered with his names and titles. Another item sent as a diplomatic gift from Mittanni was a silver dagger blade, which was considered very valuable as silver was not available in Egypt. There was also a matching dagger made of iron, which was also unavailable in Egypt and may have been a set. These relations with Mittanni could support the theory that his mother Kiya may have been of Mittannian origin.

Goods from the tomb were also imported from other foreign areas; for example, some of the collars on the tunics belonging to Tutankhamun are elaborately decorated and through the examination of the weave on some of these collars it is clear that they were not produced in Egypt but were imported from Ethiopia.

Tutankhamun also had a Syrian-style hip wrap which was 2.1m in length and trimmed with a red braid on the edges as well as having a further two bands down the centre of the fabric. It was wrapped one and a half times round the body and held in place with a sash. This may have been a diplomatic gift from a Syrian leader or may have been part of the booty captured during the Syrian military campaign.

BATTLES

The reused talatat clocks discovered at Karnak from the mortuary temple of Tutankhamun show two battles, which probably took place in the later years of his reign. Some of the blocks have a cartouche bearing Tutankhamun's name and one shows an image of the king with a humble image of Ay, the vizier, standing behind him. These battle scenes probably flanked a doorway of the mortuary temple of Tutankhamun, with the Nubian battle on the left and the Asiatic battle on the right. This displayed Tutankhamun's subjugation of both the northern and southern territories. It is thought that Tutankhamun may not have actually taken part in the battle itself due to his young age although he may have accompanied the army to the battlefield. Included in his tomb furniture were five beds including a folding or travelling bed, which folded into a Z-shape on copper hinges, which was probably used on military campaign. This is further supported by his body, armour which consists of a close-fitting bodice without sleeves which was Asiatic in origin and is actually a form of scale armour. The earliest depiction of this type of armour is on a chariot of Thutmosis IV. Bronze scale armour has also been found at the palace of Amenhotep III at Malkata indicating it was being worn during this period, and Tutankhamun may have worn it in the northern campaign or indeed purely for protection whilst hunting. A number of military weapons were also found in his tomb including swords, scimitars, slings, throwsticks and eight shields indicating that if he did not actually go to war then he was at least trained in the skills needed. Strangely enough, although there were six chariots in his tomb there were no war chariots, only ceremonial and hunting. This could indicate he did not go to war or that the war chariots were kept for the following king.

There were four different episodes from the battle recorded on the talatat, although the Asiatic battle is better preserved than the Nubian campaign. It is likely that both of these campaigns were led by the army general and 'Deputy King', Horemheb, who in his own tomb at Memphis depicts images of a northern and southern campaign which may be the same battles represented at Tutankhamun's mortuary temple.

The scenes start with an image of the battle itself which was carried out in chariots. The Egyptian chariots held two men and the Asiatic chariots held three. The Egyptian chariots were lighter than the Asiatics and they could therefore move quicker and were more manoeuvrable. The battle itself is quite graphic and there are a number of Asiatics who have fallen from their chariots with arrows and spears in their bodies, or are being dragged under the wheels of the Egyptian chariots. The Asiatics themselves are depicted as coming from two different groups: Canaanites with mushroom haircuts and beards, and Syrians with cropped hair and full beards.

The Asiatic chariots are being chased by the Egyptian army to a walled citadel. There are a number of Asiatic women at the bottom of the tower crying and throwing their arms up in fear of the Egyptian army. Scaling ladders are placed against the walls of the citadel and no doubt the Egyptian soldiers were preparing to climb them. Some of the Asiatics within the citadel have already been hit by the Egyptian arrows and are falling from the ramparts.

The end of battle shows the victory of the Egyptians, with a pile of Asiatic corpses having their hands cut off by the Egyptian soldiers as a means of counting the enemy dead. These hands after being counted are threaded onto the spears of the Egyptian soldiers who carry them in parade in front of the king in the next scene showing the prisoners and booty being presented to Tutankhamun (*43*). The soldiers are shown in parade carrying these spears and also tasselled helmets belonging to the enemy. The procession consisted of rows of chariots with the infantry marching alongside before Tutankhamun who is seated on a raised dais. Piles of booty are placed in front of the king who appears to be standing in a portable 'Window of Appearances' and the prisoners, bound together, are marched before him. The royal chariot is empty and standing behind the king on his balcony, almost as if he has just alighted from it.

After the procession before the king, the Egyptian army make a spectacular return to Thebes with a river procession. The king's royal barge is towed by four towboats with full sail on the Nile with rows of infantry running alongside the Nile on both banks. Hanging from the royal barge is a cage with a Syrian prisoner within, which is the first time this has appeared in artistic imagery although it has been mentioned in a Thutmosis III text regarding punishment of chieftains of enemy tribes.

Once they have arrived in Thebes the booty and prisoners then are offered to Amun. The king and Amun are both seated on a raised dais facing each other. At the base of the dais the Egyptian soldiers have four rows of bound prisoners behind them ready to present to Amun. The pile of booty is before the dais and contains a floral vase and pitcher.

43 Tutankhamun receiving booty after the Asiatic Battle (after Johnson W.R. 1992, fig. 20). *Illustration by Charlotte Booth*

It is possible that there were two further scenes that preceded these. There was possibly a scene of Amun handing the sword of victory to Tutankhamun, showing that he was supported by the god in his endeavours. Then the army travelled northwards to the site of the northern campaign and the citadel that appears in the battle scene.

DEATH

It has long been known that Tutankhamun died when he was young, only 18 or 19 years old, although how he died has interested scholars since 1922. The mummy has been X-rayed twice since the discovery, once in 1968 by R.G. Harrison and in 1978 by J.E. Harris. Since 1968 it was believed that Tutankhamun had been murdered by a blow to the head and this theory has dominated the theories regarding his death. This theory was based on a fragment of bone in his skull, which was thought to have been dislodged due to the blow to the head. The left leg and right knee cap were also broken just before death in addition to numerous other fractures both post- and pre-death. However since 1968 further studies have been carried out and the CT scan on his remains in 2005 has shown no evidence of a blow to the back of the head, and it is now believed that Tutankhamun may have died in a chariot accident. A large lesion on the left cheek of the mummy of Tutankhamun had started to heal and scab before the death of the king perhaps due to an accident which may have led to his death. The pieces of bone in the skull may have been caused by Carter's team when they were examining the body.

As Tutankhamun did not have a male heir, the succession to the throne after his death was unclear. Although he had named Horemheb as 'Deputy King', Ay took on the role as *sem* priest in the tomb of Tutankhamun and was clearly acting in the place of an elder son. The widow of Tutankhamun, being only a young girl did not want to relinquish her position as 'King's Wife' and is believed to have written a letter to the Hittite king Supplilumas, requesting his son to be sent to her, so she could marry him and he could become king of Egypt. She stated in particular that she did not want to 'marry a servant'. This request was very unusual and the king did not believe that it was genuine. Ankhesenamun assured him it was and he sent his son Zennanza to Egypt. Unfortunately he was murdered before he reached the Egyptian border. Ankhesenamun then married Ay, possibly the 'servant' referred to in her letter. It is surprising that the letter was ever actually sent, as Ay as the vizier had access to all messages leaving the palace. However, perhaps he felt that it was a harmless gesture as the Hittite king was certain not to believe the request. I am sure he was not intending to murder the prince as this would be detrimental to the relationship between the Egyptians and the Hittites.

TOMB

After the mummification process had been completed the embalmers cache was buried outside KV54 in the Valley of the Kings. Initially when it was discovered it was thought to be worthless. It consists of 12 jars containing floral collars made of dried leaves and flowers which were probably worn by the mourners at his funeral; a gilded cartonnage mask normally placed over small canopic coffins; broken pottery drinking cups; wine jars and two hand-brooms. Further floral collars were draped over the first and second coffin and it is thought these were placed here during the funeral by Tutankhamun's grieving widow Ankhesenamun. The funeral feast included mutton, fowl and game-bird bones and the remainder of this meal was also found in the jars of the embalmers cache. It would appear that there were eight people present at this feast and this jar was used as a means of cleaning up before leaving the tomb. The funeral procession consisted of 12 important dignitaries acting as pall bearers, pulling the funerary sledge to his tomb. Then Ay, as the *sem* priest, carried out the 'Opening of the Mouth' ceremony and recited the appropriate incantations before the burial took place.

Tutankhamun's death was obviously unexpected as many of his funerary items were not actually made for him. The second coffin, for example, had been miscalculated and the feet had to be sawn off in order to get the outermost lid in place. The

44 Tutankhamun KV62. *Photograph Charlotte Booth*

pieces that had been sawn off had been thrown in the bottom of the sarcophagus, so perhaps this had been carried out in the tomb itself. The face of the second coffin is also different from the first and third coffin and was made in a slightly different manner, indicating that it was made for someone else.

The statue of Tutankhamun standing on the panther clearly has breasts and is also not made for him. It is thought that it may have been made for Amenhotep IV (Akhenaten) at the start of his reign which was then abandoned when he changed the religion. As Tutankhamun had not commissioned a full set of funerary goods for himself he needed to use whatever was in store.

Luckily for Tutankhamun, at the time Horemheb started eradicating the names of the Amarna kings, including Akhenaten, Smenkhkare, Tutankhamun and Ay, it would appear that the entrance to this tomb may have been covered as it escaped any damage.

There were however at least three robberies in antiquity before tomb KV62 was opened by Howard Carter in November 1922 (*44*).

The first robbery happened shortly after the burial of Tutankhamun. The corridor had been filled with rubble before the doorway had been sealed, and the robbers had created a small crawl-space in the upper left-hand corner, only allowing one person through at a time. They passed rock and debris back through the hole for up to eight hours in what would have been a dark, hot and dusty space. Then they reached the second doorway which was easy to break through and entered into the tomb. The robbers were searching for solid gold which could be melted down and sold on. However, this was difficult to identify from the gilded wood in the dim light. They threw caskets into the centre of the antechamber, emptying them so they could search them in the brightest area lit by their torches. It is difficult to identify what was actually taken during this robbery, but it is clear that a small statue was stolen which would have been placed within a golden shrine which was still in the tomb. One of the thieves had knotted a handful of solid gold rings into a scarf which he then dropped on the way out. When the Valley guards entered the tomb the next day this scarf was thrown into one of the caskets in their attempt to tidy the mess left by the robbers.

After the robbers had searched the antechamber they broke into the annexe and emptied a number of precious oils into leather pouches which were then sold in the Theban region. In their rush to empty the oils one of these robbers left his fingerprint on the jars. Footprints of a second robber can clearly be seen on a white wooden box where he had scrambled over it in his search for further treasure.

The robbers then made their way through to the burial chamber and into the treasury, guarded by the figure of Anubis seated on his shrine. Many pieces of jewellery were taken, although how much and what, we will probably never know. However, there was a large amount of gold inlaid jewellery left in the treasury and it is thought that they may have been disturbed and left the tomb quickly. They also prised polished silver from some hand mirrors and an inventory list on one of the caskets makes it clear that they took a number of gold and silver cosmetic vessels.

The following morning the Valley guards noticed the robbers' hole and entered the tomb via the same route. They evaluated the damage and tried to tidy up by placing objects back in to boxes. They were obviously working quickly and many items were in the wrong boxes. They then resealed the doors and filled the tunnel with rubble.

BODY

The body of Tutankhamun was damaged greatly by the excavations of Howard Carter in a manner that no other mummy had to endure. The resin that had been poured over the mummy during the funeral had stuck the body firmly into the coffin, and the head firmly into the golden mask. They tried various methods to soften the resin including hot knives and even on two occasions leaving the mummy in the hot desert sun for many hours, in temperatures up to 149 degrees Fahrenheit, both methods of which accelerates the deterioration of the fragile mummified tissue. Temperatures such as these can cause mummified tissues to burst, and the hot knives actually scraped away the mummified tissues on his head. In their desperation to remove the mask they decapitated Tutankhamun. The torso was also cut at the iliac crest just above the pelvis in order to remove any objects in the resin beneath him. There were 35 objects found on the torso alone. To remove his bracelets the hands were cut off at the wrist and the arms were cut at the elbow. The legs were separated at the hips and the knees, and the feet were also cut off during the autopsy by Dr Derry. The feet were later reattached along with the hands using resin before being rewrapped and returned to the tomb in 1926. They placed the body in a tray of sand and also crossed Tutankhamun's arms across his pelvis which hid the terrible state of the mummy from the eye of the public.

Even after the terrible damage caused at the time of discovery further damage was caused in the following years. Between 1926 when the photographs were taken and 1968 when further studies were made the penis went missing, and the right ear had gone, which may have been taken as souvenirs by tourists and could be languishing in a private collection. However, the CT scan of the body in 2005 indicates that the penis may have been in the sand around the king's body, alongside other body parts such as a thumb, and vertebrae fragments; the ear never materialised.

Strangely enough his sternum and rib-cage had also been removed, and initially they were thought to have been removed by the embalmers, perhaps due to damage caused in a crushing accident, in an attempt to ease the mummification process. Yet the CT scan suggests that they were actually removed by Carter's team in an attempt to remove artefacts within the chest cavity. The ribs have been cut with a sharp knife and there is no evidence on the body to indicate there had been a crushing of the chest pre-death. Carter's team do not mention in their reports that the ribs and sternum were missing, although they also do not record removing them. Regardless of who removed them, these items are now missing.

The skin tissue was originally a grey colour whereas now the skin has turned black as it is still slowly decomposing in the humid conditions of KV62. However, in 2005 an international team did a CT scan of the mummy to discover as much as possible about this elusive king. Despite his early death there were no signs on his bones of malnutrition or infectious disease during his childhood and he therefore would appear to have had a privileged upbringing and a well-fed healthy adulthood.

CONCLUSION

Although Tutankhamun was a relatively unimportant king, albeit with an elaborate tomb, there is an amazing amount of information that can be learnt about this elusive teenager. With the constantly improving scientific techniques there is no doubt that further light will be shed on the life and personality of this king. Although he seems to have been dominated before and after death by Horemheb and Ay it is clear that Tutankhamun made the initial changes that began the restoration of Egypt after the rule of Akhenaten. These initial changes were continued by Ay and after him Horemheb.

TEN

HOREMHEB
THE RESTORER OF EGYPT

INTRODUCTION

Horemheb was an important general in the army of Akhenaten, Tutankhamun and Ay before becoming the last king of the Amarna Period. Although in reality he was the founder of the nineteenth dynasty, and the new empire-building dynasty of the Ramses, he is placed at the end of the eighteenth.

EARLY LIFE

There is very little information available about Horemheb prior to the reign of Tutankhamun, but it is thought he was born in a small town called Hansu, close to the Faiyum, to a local middle-class family. However, no monuments were found dedicated to, or dedicated by Horemheb in this area. Although there are no known links between his family and the court officials, Horemheb was educated and was able to read and write hence his rise through the ranks of officialdom, to the role of king.

Horemheb entered one of the few avenues open to him, the army, and worked his way through military and political administration. Although this gradual rise is not well documented in the early years, by the reign of Tutankhamun, Horemheb had risen to the status of 'Deputy King'. He could not have risen to this rank from obscurity and was therefore clearly from the higher ranks of the palace officials.

It is believed that his early career, especially whilst at Amarna, was under the name of Paatenemheb, meaning 'Aten is in Festival'. Horemheb and Paatenemheb have similar military titles and he may have later changed his name from Paatenemheb to Horemheb 'Horus is in Festival' to assert his religious beliefs and to also distance himself from the Aten cult and Akhenaten.

At some point in his early life Horemheb married a woman called Amenia (45). It is unknown when they actually got married but she was buried in Horemheb's Memphite tomb along with his second wife and queen, Mutnodjmet.

MILITARY CAREER

Horemheb's military career is recorded in his tomb at Memphis, built when he was the 'Great Commander of the Army' during the reign of Akhenaten. Although Akhenaten is reputed to be a pacifist he was surrounded by bodyguards and the high positions at court were filled by military men, including the young Horemheb. During the reign of Akhenaten, the primary function of the army was the personal protection of the king.

Horemheb would have held an administrative role in the army during peace time, in control of the rotas, dossiers and military records. As he remained in military office for so long he was clearly not seen as a threat to Akhenaten, Tutankhamun or indeed Ay, regardless of their very different ideas surrounding kingship and religion. In year 12 of Akhenaten's reign there appears to have been a Hittite rebellion and a small military campaign. It is the only military campaign of Akhenaten's reign and he did not lead it himself, whereas every other pharaoh was always seen at the head of the army. This campaign was led instead by the general, Horemheb.

Many of the early statues of Horemheb show him in the traditional position of a scribe, indicating he probably held a scribal position, or that at least was literate. In later inscriptions he stresses his devotion to Thoth, the patron deity of knowledge and writing. His devotion to Thoth may have held further significance in the god's role as a lunar god, further drawing away from the Aten cult.

When Horemheb became king, he is often shown in group statues with Re-Horakhty, Thoth and Maat, indicating that cosmic balance (*maat*) is achieved by the sun (Re-Horakhty) and the moon (Thoth). This may have been retaliation against the Aten cult, which focused purely on the sun-disc.

The Memphite tomb shows Horemheb worshipping (*colour plate 14*) a number of deities including Osiris, with a unique hymn to this deity in his role as the nocturnal version of Re. The theme of Osiris as a nocturnal entity is introduced in the *Coffin Texts,* although as a hymn, but is first recorded in Horemheb's tomb. During the Amarna Period when the Aten set at dusk the world was thought to fall into the chaotic darkness of the primeval time until dawn, so Horemheb reintroduced the idea of the nocturnal journey of the sun god.

45 Horemheb and Amenia, Luxor Museum. *Photograph Wayne R. Frostick*

Horemheb's dedication to Thoth is still present throughout the reign of Tutankhamun, when he wrote this inscription raising Thoth to the status of Creator:

> Praise to you Thoth, Lord of Hermopolis, who came into being by his own accord and was not born. Unique god, lord of the netherworld … who distinguishes the tongues of foreign lands … may you set the scribe Horemheb firmly by the side of the Lord of the Universe, in the way that you gave him life when he came forth from the womb.

During the reign of Tutankhamun, Horemheb was the 'Commander' of the Egyptian army although this was probably still mostly an administrative position. He was high up within the palace officialdom and many inscriptions describe him as 'Deputy King' to Tutankhamun. On one occasion it was recorded that he was called to calm down the king when he 'had fallen into a rage', indicating his influence over the boy king. Horemheb clearly had a positive influence over the young king but he had to swallow his pride when called to deal with the tantrums of a small child.

Horemheb was very wealthy and was given the land and the materials to build his tomb in a prominent part of the Memphite cemetery. The king also provided him with workmen, in reward for this work at the palace. Despite holding this prestigious title, after Tutankhamun's death Horemheb does not become king. The 'High Priest of Amun', brother of Queen Tiye, Ay, becomes king instead. Horemheb did not fight this succession even though he had the backing of the army and already held a high-status position in the palace administration. It is possible that Ay and Horemheb had an arrangement where Ay would declare him as his heir to the throne. Ay was elderly when he became king, and he may have known he was not likely to rule for long.

When Horemheb took over the throne from Ay it appeared to be quite difficult for him to give up his tomb at Memphis which was almost completed at this time. Protocol stated as king he had to build a tomb in the Valley of the Kings, which was never completed, although this was where he was finally buried.

THE MEMPHITE TOMB

The Memphite tomb of Horemheb was a new type of tomb known as a temple tomb, because it was laid out like a traditional temple. A typical temple tomb has a pylon gateway, forecourt, open courts, store rooms and chapels. These tombs were difficult to protect from robbers and the natural elements as they were primarily above ground and open to the sky. Whilst the temple funerary cult was still in practice, the clearing of the windblown sand was relatively easy and was part of the cult practices. However, once these funerary rites stopped being performed the temple filled with sand and became buried.

The tomb of Horemheb was a medium-sized temple (above ground), with a number of shafts and burial chambers for him and his family (below ground), including a shaft for the burials of his wives with a separate burial chamber for his first wife Amenia, and another for his second wife Mutnodjmet.

The tomb was built on the site of two Old Kingdom mastabas. They were dismantled although the shafts and burial chambers were reused for the burial of Horemheb's wives. In the north-west corner of the temple courtyard a deep shaft (shaft i) gives access to burial chambers on two levels. The lower belonged to the original mastaba owner, a judge called Khuyer, from the fifth/sixth dynasty, and his body was left in situ. Some of the stone used to build Horemheb's tomb was also removed from the pyramid enclosure of Djoser nearby.

The pylon was originally 7m high, and unlike traditional temple pylons these were left undecorated. The exterior of the pylon was cased with smooth limestone blocks although within the enclosure walls of the temple tombs the limestone was smoothed and decorated with carved and painted relief. Just behind the pylon was a courtyard, open to the sky with a columned colonnade surrounding it. The floor in the centre was slightly lower than the colonnade to aid drainage. The columns stood 3m high and were rectangular in shape. They were decorated with scenes of Horemheb worshipping various traditional gods including Re-Horakhty, Osiris, Isis, Nephthys, Ptah, Sekhmet, Atum, Nefertum and Maat. The images were all facing the inner temple so as the sun moves from east (pylon entrance) to west the images appeared to be following its progress. The inclusion of these traditional deities would firmly suggest that the Aten cult had been abandoned before he started the decoration in his tomb. Horemheb seemed to particularly favour Re-Horakhty in this tomb, as in addition to the images in the first courtyard he had two stelae erected near the entrance of the statue room dedicated to him.

This courtyard was also decorated with scenes of the military life of Horemheb. One scene shows Horemheb acting as the regent for the young Tutankhamun. A senior colleague of Horemheb has been awarded numerous gold collars of valour for services to the state and it is suggested that this official could be Prameses who later became Ramses I. Horemheb is officiating over the ceremony, normally the role of king, and perhaps Tutankhamun was too young for such ceremonies at this time. This scene indicates the importance of Horemheb in the court of Tutankhamun.

On the door-jambs to the statue room Horemheb's elevated status is confirmed:

> Greater than the great ones, mightier than the mighty ones, great chieftain of the subjects
> … who follows the king on his journeys in the southern and northern foreign land …
> chief of the most important courtiers, who listens to the confidences of the unique ones
> … master of the secrets of the Palace.

It further indicates Horemheb participated in reasserting Egypt's dominance over Western Asia and Nubia during this reign. There would appear to have been two short campaigns during the reign of Tutankhamun, against the Libyans, Syrians and Nubians, and the captives depicted in this tomb are clearly identified and may represent the northern and southern campaigns represented at the mortuary temple of Tutankhamun. In the second courtyard the reliefs show many foreign captives presented before Horemheb and Tutankhamun, probably as a result of these campaigns. Horemheb is standing towards the right of the scene, and a Nubian chieftain is about to be pushed over in order to kneel to him. Another Nubian is being led away after kneeling and pledging allegiance to Horemheb, as the Egyptian soldier punches the Nubian in the face; a snapshot of military life. There are long lines of Libyans, Western Asians and Nubians representing captives guarded by the Egyptian soldiers. The Egyptian soldiers are smaller than the captives indicating they were either young recruits or that the prisoners were particularly burly making the Egyptians appear stronger. All of the personal details of the captives are recorded by army scribes and this event may have happened on the battlefield, to be later recorded more permanently.

Another scene shows Horemheb wearing numerous gold collars, given to him by Tutankhamun for his services to Egypt. He has attendants ensuring they are comfortable around his neck and behind him are rows of bound captives, men, women and children, from the Western Asian city-states, which he has probably just brought to Egypt. The exact fate of these prisoners is unknown but the men were probably sent to be labourers or bricklayers for the newly reinstated cult of Amun.

The prisoners are shown begging for clemency from Tutankhamun, clemency for what would appear to be uprisings against Egyptian rule. They appeal to the king and queen, but as they do not speak Egyptian they need an interpreter who translates to Horemheb who in turn repeats it to the royal couple. The supporting text is fragmentary and is difficult to decipher, although it tells us that Egypt's might was reasserted. The fate of the appealing foreigners is not known.

The booty from the enemy camp is also displayed before Horemheb including felines on leads, popular at the royal court as pets. Lions in particular were set loose in the royal grounds so they could be hunted in safety, or they were tamed and kept by the king as pets, showing how he was able to tame the chaotic force of nature.

There are also scenes of a military camp, which is unique to this tomb and may represent the army whilst on campaign. One scene shows the cleaning of a military tent; an officer dashes off, probably in answer to a request of Horemheb, and his batsman stands at the door of the tent in a respectful manner. The officer passes a naked boy carrying a water skin to fill the jars in the tent. A servant within the tent is sweeping the floor, whilst another servant pours water to get rid of the dust.

In the register above is a larger tent, which may belong to Horemheb. There are supplies of food and drink, flowers and furniture in the tent including a chair and matching footstool. Outside the tent the servants are carrying the possessions of Horemheb, including an animal hide used as a coverlet or groundsheet and water skins. They are followed by another naked boy carrying extra provisions. These small children are probably offspring of the camp followers responsible for the odd-jobs around the camp.

A scene also shows the camp on the move and the rolled-up tent is being carried on the shoulders of soldiers, all of whom are wearing openwork leather loincloths with a square patch at the back for added strength when sitting down. These scenes of military life were chosen by Horemheb for inclusion in his tomb possibly as an accurate representation of the life that he was very fond of.

A scene on the south wall shows Horemheb was present at the coronation of King Ay and represents a group of foreign dignitaries, including Libyans, Western Asians, Nubians and Aegeans who may have come to Egypt to pledge allegiance to the new pharaoh. There is also a scene of the 'Window of Appearances', which when complete would have shown the new King Ay giving tokens of achievement to the most favoured of his officials; no doubt one of them was Horemheb.

Other scenes in the tomb show the funerary rituals of Horemheb with a number of booths or kiosks containing drink and food, complete with mourners. The 'Breaking of the Red Pot' ceremony appears to have been carried out which was an Old Kingdom tradition. The ritual took place after the funerary feast and the pots were broken and then placed inside the tomb. The exact beliefs behind this ceremony are however uncertain. Sacrificial bulls are also shown being slaughtered at the same time and it is thought the two ceremonies may be connected. As the pots are red and the bull's blood is red it is thought there was some association between the two. The ritualistic destruction of the pots could represent the destruction of enemies of Horemheb. As Horemheb was not buried in this tomb, these funerary rituals were not carried out for him in this manner. He would have had a royal funeral where the rituals may have been slightly different.

There were numerous burial shafts in the Memphite tomb, some belonging to earlier mastaba tombs, others from the reign of Horemheb and some from later periods. Each of the shafts contained remains of burials.

Shaft i contained numerous nineteenth-dynasty mummies. There was a shabti of Binetanath, a daughter of Ramses II, and a heart scarab naming two unknown people. Foreign imported pottery fragments were also found here, and Coptic pottery indicates the reuse of this shaft in later periods. This shaft also contained the burial of the original owner of the mastaba that stood on the site of this tomb.

Shaft iv was Horemheb's intended burial chamber, although as king his burial took place in the Valley of the Kings.

The burial of Amenia, Horemheb's first wife, is in shaft iv which is sealed with the cartouche of Ay. As he only reigned for four years it means the date of her death was between 1325 and 1321 BC. The tomb had been robbed in antiquity and the mummy ransacked, although scarabs were found with Horemheb's name and his titles of royal scribe. The coffin was wooden but due to high humidity all that was left were fragments.

This shaft was also used for the burial of his second wife Mutnodjmet, his consort for nearly 15 years of his reign. After her burial the chamber was filled with limestone chips and the exterior was plastered over and stamped whilst still wet with the royal seal. This did not prevent tomb robbers who broke through the entrance. The bones found in the chamber were of an adult female who had given birth many times, and she was buried with a foetus. It is thought she died in childbirth. She had also lost all of her teeth in her early years and was virtually on a liquid diet until she died in her mid-40s. Both the bodies had been dragged to the pillared chamber above by the ancient robbers.

In Horemheb's intended burial chamber the walls were carved with the palace façade design, in order to make the entire chamber into a giant sarcophagus, therefore providing him with extra protection for the afterlife.

RULE AS KING

Despite Horemheb's loyal service to Tutankhamun, and Akhenaten prior to that, Ay was still chosen to be the king on the death of Tutankhamun. At the time Horemheb was a higher rank than Ay in the army, and already held the title 'Deputy King' and it is generally thought that Horemheb and Ay may have had some kind of arrangement, as Horemheb was clearly a better choice as king than the elderly Ay. Perhaps Ay promised that Horemheb would be named as heir and it is recorded that Ay accompanied

46 Horemheb and Amun, Luxor Museum. *Photograph Wayne R. Frostick*

Horemheb to Karnak during his short reign, for the 'Opet Festival' where the oracle of Amun confirmed that Horemheb would be the next in line to the throne.

To choose Horemheb as successor of Ay may have been a military decision to ensure Egypt's power was reinstated in the Near East. During the Amarna Period the Asiatic Empire had all but been abandoned by the Egyptians as Akhenaten concentrated more on religion than politics. This allowed Egypt to come under threat from the growing power of the Hittites.

When Horemheb became king he married his second wife Mutnodjmet to legitimise his accession to the throne as she is believed to be Nefertiti's sister, and therefore a link to the royal family of Akhenaten.

A statue of Horemheb and Mutnodjmet describes his coronation. It tells of the divine process of choosing the new king; the local god of Horemheb's hometown, 'Horus of Hansu' chose Horemheb as king before he was even born and placed him under special protection, until he was ready to rule. 'Horus of Hansu' then travelled to Karnak and Luxor temple and introduced Horemheb to Amun as the rightful heir. Amun then crowned him, firmly sealing his right to rule (*46*).

In the early years of his reign, Horemheb is recorded as travelling north to renovate temples which were 'wrecked from an earlier time'. He restored images, replenished the temples and filled them with priests and officials chosen from the army. The reinstatement of the Priesthood of Amun was one of the more important tasks that he fulfilled, although again the positions were filled with army officials. This ensured the priesthood would not gain too much power and potentially threaten the throne. During his reign he concentrated on the restoration of the traditional religion and rebuilding of the temples. At the beginning of the reign he appeared to be restrained in his building works, but by the middle of the reign he started more monumental works at Thebes especially Karnak. His increased work for the cult of Amun started at the same time as the death of his second wife Mutnodjmet in year 15, which cut all his ties with the Amarna dynasty. This was also the time he started erasing any reference to the Amarna kings, including Akhenaten, Smenkhkare, Tutankhamun and even Ay, as well as the name and image of the Aten. In the tomb of Ay all that escaped destruction was the image of the *ka* of Ay, all other people and inscriptions were intentionally damaged. The tomb of Tutankhamun escaped this desecration as the entrance may have been lost.

Prior to this there had been limited damage to Amarna monuments, but nothing on the destructive scale that started after year 15. It could be suggested that Horemheb believed that if he did not erase the existence of the Amarna kings then he would be seen as a collaborator and then his name may be erased by future kings. Horemheb even recorded his reign as starting at the end of the reign of Amenhotep III therefore obliterating the reigns of Akhenaten, Smenkhkare, Tutankhamun and Ay from the records. A nineteenth-dynasty tomb at Thebes (TT19) belonging to an official called Amenmosi contained a row of royal statutes, with Horemheb seated between Amenhotep III and Ramses I with no sign of the Amarna kings. However, rather than destroying inscriptions from the reigns of Tutankhamun and Ay, Horemheb often replaced their names with his own.

Horemheb designed the hypostyle hall at Karnak, although it was built by Sety I and Ramses II, and he also built the second and ninth pylon, and completed the tenth pylon started by Amenhotep III. These pylons were built to assert royal authority and also to show his increased dedication to Amun. He also used pylon II and IX as a means of destroying the Aten temples built by Akhenaten at Karnak by dismantling the talatat blocks and using them to fill the interior of the pylon. Unfortunately he did not realise that by placing them in the pylon he had preserved them for eternity. When archaeologists started to restore the ninth pylon they discovered over 10,000 of these blocks which could be removed from the pylon in the same order that they were dismantled from the temple. Over 100,000 of the blocks have been discovered and it is a mammoth task to try and reconstruct the images. Although placing them in the ninth pylon was designed to erase Akhenaten from history, the action instead preserved the blocks for thousands of years.

As Horemheb was no longer a military commander he needed to ensure complete control over the army. He divided the control into two divisions, the North and the South with a military commander for each, which limited the amount of power one man could hold. Despite this restructure there is very little evidence that Horemheb went on any military manoeuvres during his reign, other than a small expedition to Kush which may have been an inspection or royal progress expedition, and a small trading expedition to the south.

On a damaged stela at Karnak, known as the *Edict,* he describes the essence of his reign:

> As long as my life on earth remains, it shall be spent making monuments for the gods. I shall be renewed increasingly, like the moon … one whose limbs shed light on the ends of the earth like the disc of the sun god.

The reference to the moon, further reasserts his devotion to the god Thoth. Later in the inscription he takes credit for the reforms that Tutankhamun carried out, although as the 'Deputy King' he may have advised the pharaoh on his activities.

The ninth pylon at Karnak records the social reform that Horemheb began during his reign. This inscription lists particular abuses which he denounces and declares a punishment. This reflected the chaotic state of Egypt and Horemheb's role in re-establishing order. No one was immune from this social reform and the crimes included the requisition of supplies from local mayors by royal officials under false pretences. Soldiers who wrongly confiscated boats whilst on government service had their nose amputated and then were exiled to the Sinai:

> Then His Majesty took counsel with his heart … in order to expel sin and destroy lying …. Now if there is the man who wants to deliver dues for the breweries and abattoirs of Pharaoh on behalf of the two deputies of the army, and there is anyone who interferes and he takes away the craft of any military man or of any other person in any part of the country, the law shall be applied against him by cutting off his nose, he being sent to Sile.

This shows that even his former military colleagues were not immune from punishment. This displayed to the population that Horemheb was fair and just, and that he would protect them from corrupt officials. Any soldiers caught stealing hides from farmers would be severely punished as the hides were required to account for any deaths in the annual audit by the tax department:

The two divisions of the army … are taking away hides throughout the land, without stopping for a single year so as to grant a respite to the peasants … and seize those hides among them which are branded, while they are going from house to house beating and maltreating, without hides being left for the peasants, and if the one who … of Pharaoh goes to carry out the census of his cattle and he interviews them but the hides are not found with them, so that they are virtually in debt and they gain their confidence saying 'They have been taken away from us' seeing that this, too, is a wretched case, it shall be done accordingly. Now if the overseer of the cattle of pharaoh goes to carry out the cattle-census throughout the land – for it is he alone who shall collect the hides of the dead animals which … My Majesty has commanded that the peasant shall be left alone because of his honest intention. But as for any military man concerning whom one shall hear 'He goes about and also takes hides away' starting from today, the law shall be applied against him by inflicting upon him a hundred blows, causing five open wounds, and taking from him the hide which he has seized as being something that has been unlawfully acquired.

Any theft carried out by either a military man or a peasant was to be treated equally by Horemheb and would both be punished in the same manner.

Furthermore, those who take away herbs from the breweries … of the commoners, taking away their herbs daily, saying 'They are for the revenue of pharaoh' … and there is no success for the commoners in their labours – seeing that this too is a bad case … if one shall hear that they take away the property of any military man or any other person in any part of the country – the law shall be applied against them – for they are people who have disobeyed orders.

Horemheb also describes in the *Edict* how he managed to uphold the new laws and how to ensure that justice was done:

I have set this entire land in order – I have travelled through it thoroughly as far as the south; I have surveyed it entirely. I have learned its whole condition, having first toured its interior. I have sought out people … discreet of good character, knowing how to judge thought, listening to the words of the palace and to the laws of the Throne hall. I have appointed them to judge the two Lands and to satisfy their inhabitants – I have set them in the great cities of Upper and Lower Egypt, every one of them without exception, enjoying the benefit of a stipend. I have given the precepts and recorded laws in their journal … I have taught them the right course of life by guiding them to justice. I have instructed them saying 'Do not associate with other people. Do not take a bribe from another. What shall one think of men in your station, appointed to replace others, as long as there is one among you who violates justice?'

This makes it clear that justice will be carried out throughout Egypt which may have been reassuring after the focus of Akhenaten purely on the new city of Akhetaten. He also wants to make it clear that justice will be done, by non-corruptible officials. He clearly presents himself as a king for the people. Through the *Edict* Horemheb became a popular king and one who was to be emulated by the kings that followed.

Although he was married twice Horemheb had no male heirs, or at least none that survived into adulthood. The body of what is thought to be Mutnodjmet, appeared to have died in childbirth and the pelvis suggests that she had given birth many times. This would suggest that they had only had girls, or that they had all died in infancy. It appears that Horemheb, in his days as a military commander, adopted the army scribe Sementawy, as an heir to his military titles as was traditional for those without children. In his tomb at Memphis there are representations of Sementawy, which show even if he had not adopted him, he held Sementawy in great esteem. At some point Sementawy had died and his names were replaced to those of Ramose, and the titles were changed to 'Documents Scribe' or 'Private Secretary'. Horemheb does not appear to have adopted this scribe as his son, and he may have just been a favoured employee.

Before his death Horemheb named his royal heir – his army general Prameses, who was born in the Delta region and had no connections with the Amarna Period kings. He also had a son, ensuring that the new royal line would continue. Prameses became the vizier and then a 'Deputy King' to Horemheb. When Horemheb died this army general became king and called himself Ramses (I). Historians like to think of him as the first king of the nineteenth dynasty and of the line of Ramesside kings although Horemheb really started the changes that could be seen as the beginnings of a new era. The Ramesside family did not forget the opportunity that Horemheb gave to Ramses I and the Memphite tomb of Horemheb became quite important to them. Ramses II actually reinstated a cult for his ancestor Horemheb and he erected two plinths with figures of Anubis on them acting as guardians to the most western and intimate part of the tomb.

The exact length of reign of Horemheb has been questioned. An inscription of Mose from the reign of Ramses II claimed that Horemheb ruled for 59 years although this may have included the regnal years of Amenhotep III. A piece of graffiti in Horemheb's mortuary temple refers to year 27 of his reign and it is generally agreed that he ruled for 28 years between 1321 and 1293 BC. During these 28 years he managed to restore the polytheistic religion, rebuild the temples and restore Egypt's power in the Near East; no mean feat for someone of such humble origins (*47*).

47 Horemheb, Luxor Museum.
Photograph Wayne R. Frostick

ROYAL TOMB

As king, Horemheb was buried in the Valley of the Kings despite the near completion of his tomb in Memphis (*48*). Initially he changed some of the images in his Memphite tomb by adding a uraeus to his headdress, to indicate his new royal status, but it was not enough, and he had to arrange a new burial. His tomb, KV57, opposite the tomb of Ramses III, was the first full-size tomb to be built in the Valley of the Kings since Amenhotep III, although sadly it was not complete (*colour plate 15*).

The burial chamber had six pillars, all crumbling due to shifting rock over the centuries but the rest of the burial chamber is unfinished. The sculptors and workmen were interrupted by the royal burial and the chambers were still filled with limestone chips which had not been removed by the workmen. The outlines of the illustrations were drawn on the walls but not yet painted or carved. Leading from the burial chamber were a series of elaborate storerooms, which were designed to hold the funerary equipment.

KV 57 was the first tomb in the Valley of the Kings to have carved relief as prior to this painted murals were favoured. As the tomb is unfinished it is possible to see the working progress of these reliefs, which went through the following stages:

◇ Grid squares were outlined on the polished limestone walls of the tomb

◇ The outlines were then freely sketched in red ink

◇ The overseer would come and correct the drawings with black ink

◇ The preliminary carving would begin

◇ The carved reliefs would be painted in bright colours

The decoration had only been started in the well shaft, the ante chamber and the burial chamber, with a blue-grey background with multi-coloured hieroglyphs. The artwork is a transitional style between the Amarna Period and the Ramesside Period. The paunchy stomach is still apparent with slightly short legs, but with a more formal style than Amarna art.

The valley tomb of Horemheb has the first use of the *Book of Gates* describing the nocturnal journey of the Sun God Ra, and was an alternative to the *Book of the Amduat* which was very popular throughout the New Kingdom.

His funerary equipment included a pink granite sarcophagus with a skull and a few bones still inside, although whether they were his, is unknown. In antiquity the lid was broken by robbers as they threw it aside. The remains of four other bodies were found in the burial chamber and these are likely to be members of his family. It has even been suggested that the body of Ay may have been brought here for protection. There is some graffiti in the tomb which says that Horemheb's body had been taken to the nearby tomb of Twoseret and Setnakht for restoration although his body has not been identified in either of the royal caches.

There were other unusual funerary objects, in the form of various deities made of resin-coated wood, all discovered in the burial chamber (49). These were uncommon and depicted deities of the underworld, the most unusual one being the turtle-headed deity which is currently in the British Museum. The canopic equipment was made of alabaster, with portrait lids of Horemheb, which were damaged in antiquity. Alongside the canopic equipment were four miniature lion-headed embalming tables, also smashed. These tables were used for the embalming of the internal organs, and may have been broken to prevent any harm coming to the organs in the afterlife.

48 Door-jamb,
Memphite tomb of
Horemheb. *Photograph
Clare V. Banks.
Copyright: The Trustees
of the British Museum,
London*

49 Wooden deity, British Museum.
Photograph Charlotte Booth

Many other things were found in the burial chamber including life-size guardian figures, a hippo-headed couch and Anubis figures, which when in mint condition were identical to those found in the tomb of Tutankhamun, indicating that they may have been traditional goods for royal burials of this period. There was also an Osiris bed (planted with grain, symbolising rebirth as the grain grew), magical birth bricks (which helped with the king's rebirth in the afterlife) and model boats for the pilgrimage to Memphis.

As king, Horemheb also required a mortuary temple for the cult of his *ka*. Horemheb usurped the temple of Ay which was situated very close to the later temple of Ramses III at Medinet Habu. Ay had already usurped this temple from Tutankhamun. The temple was substantial in size, and the pylon seems to have been 60m long, only 5m shorter than Medinet Habu. However the pylon was not built of stone but of mud brick and retained some of the cartouches of Ay stamped on them. Due to being used in later periods as a quarry there is not much left of this mortuary temple, other than a few statue fragments and inscriptions. It would appear that all the cartouches were replaced with that of Horemheb, and wine jars in the temple magazines state it was 'wine for the temple of Horemheb'.

Horemheb's mortuary temple was still standing during the reign of Ramses III, as when he built Medinet Habu he built his enclosure wall around the enclosure wall of Horemheb's temple. Ramses III also seems to have copied some of the battle scenes that appeared in the temple of Horemheb onto his mortuary temple. A number of reused blocks from the temple of Horemheb have been found in the temple of Khonsu at Karnak, mostly in the pylon staircase. They include a battle against the Libyans as well as a chariot siege of an Asiatic citadel with Canaanite and Syrian soldiers in the surrounding battlefield.

CONCLUSION

Horemheb is clearly an interesting character with great diplomatic skills as he managed to pacify Akhenaten, Tutankhamun and Ay despite their very different ideas. As he was a traditional individual, rather than forcibly taking the throne after the death of Tutankhamun, he stepped back and let Ay rule in his place. If he had used military force then his reign may have been tainted and erased by later kings, alongside those of the Amarna kings.

The general of Horemheb's army, Ramses I, took over the throne of Egypt at the death of the king. He was elderly but when he came to the throne he already had an elder son who became Sety I, the father of Ramses II. Ramses I only ruled for two years and therefore did not make a mark on history, although he did start the tradition of burying his wife in the Valley of the Queens. Previously the queen was buried alongside her husband. After his death Sety I came to the throne and ruled for 13 years, firmly establishing the nineteenth dynasty.

Considering that Horemheb was one of the most important kings of the eighteenth dynasty, who instigated major changes and reforms in what was essentially a country of chaos after the Amarna Period, there is very little evidence of his life and times. There is more evidence of the 17-year reign of Akhenaten than the 27-year reign of Horemheb.

ELEVEN

RAMSES II

THE GREATEST KING OF THE NEW KINGDOM

INTRODUCTION

The most famous king of the New Kingdom is Ramses II of the nineteenth dynasty, who had a reputation for being egotistical and a megalomaniac. However, his life was a difficult one and to a certain extent a lonely one. He ruled for over 65 years and this fact alone could account for the sheer extent of his monumental works.

FAMILY LIFE

Ramses was born in 1304 BC to Sety I and Muttuya the daughter of the 'Lieutenant of Chariotry' Raia. Ramses had at least two sisters Tia and Hunetmire, and a brother although his name has been sadly lost. In later years Ramses was married to at least one of his sisters, Hunetmire, who was only ever a secondary queen. She bore him no children and she was buried in the Valley of the Queens (QV75) in year 40 of his reign. Ramses's sister Tia was a singer of Hathor-of-the-Sycamore, Re of Heliopolis, and Amun-Great-of-Victories, and she married a man called Tia, a high-ranking civil servant, who later obtained titles in Thebes including 'Superintendent of Treasury' and 'Superintendent of Cattle of the Temple of Usermaatsetepenra in the estate of Amun' (Ramesseum). Both Tia and her husband Tia are buried in Saqqara in a tomb adjoining Horemheb's temple tomb.

Ramses's mother is represented on the main temple at Abu Simbel (50), as the same size as the other royal women alongside the second and fourth colossi.

In the Ramesseum (51) she is again shown in colossal form beside a larger figure of Ramses in the first courtyard. There is also a chapel dedicated to her here although it was dismantled and reused at Medinet Habu by Ramses III. This monumental display by Ramses reflects his love and respect for his mother.

Despite the evident pride in his parents, Ramses made a claim of divine birth in order to secure his place on the throne. He was born before Sety I became king so his mother was not royal at this point. He set about proving he was born of Amun. The 'Divine Birth' story is presented in the Ramesseum in the chapel dedicated to his mother. The image shows the queen seated un-chaperoned on the bed, facing Amun, who is holding an *ankh* sign in his right hand and is reaching for Muttuya

50 Abu Simbel. *Photograph Charlotte Booth*

with his left hand representing the divine conception of Ramses. At Karnak this scene is expanded upon; Ramses the child is suckled by a goddess and a pre-birth Ramses is being moulded on the potters' wheel of the creator god Khnum. This is also repeated in the Sety Temple at Abydos. This was a typical act of Egyptian kings primarily from turbulent reigns, to prove their divinity and their right to rule.

At 10 years old Ramses was named 'First King's Son' (i.e. crown prince); when he proved himself worthy, he was crowned as co-regent to Sety I. Upon this co-regency he adopted the name Usermaatra (Strong-in-Truth-is-Re) and then later he added Setepenra (Chosen-of-Re), reflecting his growing interest in the solar cult of Re of Heliopolis. Throughout his reign he was affectionately known as 'Sese' by his friends and loyal subjects. This co-regency allowed Sety to semi-retire as Ramses gained more power. Ramses, however, did not start counting his regnal years until Sety I had died, leaving him as sole ruler. After four years of co-regency Sety died, at the Delta site of Avaris when Ramses was only 14 years old. Ramses became sole ruler of Upper and Lower Egypt on day 27 of the third month of Shemu (23 June 1279 BC) (*52*). Ramses was also in the Delta at this point and travelled south with his father's body and buried him in the Valley of the Kings (KV17).

51 Ramesseum from the air. *Photograph Wayne R. Frostick*

KV17 is the longest tomb in the Valley of the Kings and the corridor reached down to natural ground water. Ramses II's valley tomb also reaches the same level so perhaps they were going to join the two tombs to enable them to spend their eternity together. Both tombs were similar to Sety's Abydos cenotaph so it is probably a representation of the tomb of Osiris and his watery death and burial.

Sety had marked the co-regency between Ramses and himself by presenting his young son with his own harem of beautiful women 'female royal attendants, who were like the great beauties of the palace' which I imagine was an exciting, yet daunting gift for a young boy. The royal harem provided segregation for those chosen as wives for pharaoh and a secure home for the single women of the court, unwanted wives and their retinue, and any secondary wives or children. The harem given to Ramses would have consisted of the eligible unmarried women of the court that were potential royal wives and concubines.

However, whether Nefertari his chosen 'Great Royal Wife' came from this harem is unrecorded. They married young and had their first son before the death of Sety, when they both were in their early teens. Nefertari had as many as 10 children including the eldest son Amenhirwenemef, the third son Prehirwenemef, and the favourite daughter Meritamun. None of these children outlived Ramses.

A queen was generally only as divine as her husband and in the case of Nefertari she was greatly exalted by Ramses and played a complementary role in rituals connected with the divine kingship ideology. She held the titles of 'Hand of Atum', and 'Wife of Amun' representing her religious role. Ramses revered his wife greatly and she is in fact worshipped in her own temple at Abu Simbel.

Although the name of Nefertari is very well known there is very little personal information about her other than details from her tomb. Nefertari does not hold the title 'King's Daughter' so she was probably of non-royal descent, although unfortunately her parentage is unrecorded. Speculation regarding her father arose after a head of a cane bearing the cartouche of Ay was discovered in her tomb. It has been suggested that she may have been his daughter although this would have made her about 60 by the time she married Ramses and therefore rather unlikely. If she was related to Ay she was probably a granddaughter, niece or great niece. There is evidence that she had a brother, Amenmose, who was 'Mayor of Thebes' although his parentage is also unrecorded. Although she was of non-royal blood, she was born to an elite family and therefore a suitable wife for a prince.

52 Coronation of Ramses II, Karnak. *Photograph Wayne R. Frostick*

A list of Ramses children is recorded at Karnak, in birth order rather than status order as Nefertari's sons would be closer to the throne than those of secondary wives, but her children are not all listed first. In the early years of his reign there were two important wives; Nefertari and Isetnofret bearing children for the king, the first four sons and first seven daughters. After this he may have acquired more wives to produce children.

He had a maximum of 46 sons and 55 daughters, although he records having more. It is likely that no more than two thirds of these children would have lived longer than 15 years; therefore only 30 sons and 36 daughters would reach child-bearing age. Some of the high-ranking daughters remained unmarried as they could not marry anyone lower than a prince, and it was not acceptable for them to marry a foreign prince. Some would have been married Ramses rather than remain single and open to ambitious suitors. Ramses and Nefertari had numerous children, at least 10 have been recorded, although they all died before Ramses. She had at least six sons, whose names and occupations are recorded.

1. Amenhirwenemef (first son) known as Sethhirwenemef in the north of Egypt which means 'Amen/Seth is at the right hand'. He later changed his name to Amenhirkhopshef. He was in the army, and held the title of 'General in Chief'. In year 20 he was named as crown prince under the name Sethhirkhepshef but he died between years 25-40, without having the opportunity to rule.

2. Prehirwenemef (third son) was a teenage veteran of the battle of Kadesh and was rewarded with the titles 'First Charioteer of his Majesty' and 'First Brave of the Army'. He died before year 20.

3. Meriamun (sixteenth son).

4. Meritamun (second daughter) was the consort to the king by year 24 and acted as deputy for her sick mother. She is buried in QV68 and was a favourite daughter of Ramses.

5. Baketmut (third daughter) is believed to have died young although her tomb has not been discovered.

6. Nefertari II (fourth daughter) is presented on the façade of the main Abu Simbel temple.

7. Nebettawi (fifth daughter) was the consort successor to Meritamun after she died. She is buried in QV60, which was reused in the Christian Period as a chapel.

8. Henoutawi (seventh daughter) is represented on Nefertari's temple at Abu Simbel indicating that she was one of her daughters, although she was dead before the temple was dedicated; indicating she died before year 24 and is buried in QV73.

The throne was eventually passed on to Merenptah, Ramses's thirteenth son born of a secondary wife, Isetnofret. It must have been heartbreaking for both Ramses and Nefertari to watch their children die one by one, as no one feels they should outlive their children.

Nefertari appears alongside Ramses from the very start of his reign and is shown as the dutiful wife, accompanying him in ceremonies, and it is even suggested that she may have accompanied him on the long march to Kadesh. If this were true it would seem that she wanted to be by his side at all times; it is generally thought that Ramses II had great respect and love for Nefertari due to the number of reliefs and monuments that bear her image. However from a more cynical view everything beautiful dedicated to the queen reflects the power of the king and this is especially apparent in the Nefertari's temple at Abu Simbel as throughout the temple, images of the queen outnumber those of the king until you reach the back of the temple where Nefertari is replaced by Ramses in making offerings to Hathor.

In year 24 the temples at Abu Simbel were dedicated to the gods and a procession would have taken place from Thebes. Ramses was accompanied by Nefertari, their eldest daughter, Meritamun, and the Viceroy Heqanakht. However, a stela on the site recording the dedication shows Meritamun with her father performing the rituals, and it is thought that Nefertari may have been too ill to participate. After this date we see no more of Nefertari. Instead Isetnofret, a secondary wife, is represented on monuments as 'Principle Wife' although she also appears to have died before year 34 and was then replaced by her daughter Bintanath. The death was difficult for Ramses, as he had lost many of his sons by this date and then both his wives, whom he had grown up with.

Ramses's reverence of Nefertari is reflected in her tomb which is the most beautiful in the Valley of the Queens despite the poor-quality stone. The only human remains that have been found in the Valley of the Queens were in the tomb of Nefertari itself, and consisted of a mummified leg and foot, which may or may not belong to her. It is possible that like the Valley of the Kings the mummies here were moved to a royal cache for safe keeping which if discovered would hopefully reveal her cause of death.

Isetnofret, who upon the death of Nefertari became the 'Principal Wife', also does not possess the title 'King's Daughter' indicating she was also of non-royal descent. The name of her eldest daughter Bintanath 'Daughter of Anath,' could suggest she had Asiatic origins. However, as none of her other children have foreign names it could suggest that it was a popular girls' name at the time rather than proof of genealogy.

It would, however, appear that there were Asiatic women in the royal harem as two of Ramses's other children were named Meher-anath (Child of Anath) and Astarteherwenemef (Astarte is on his right) both Asiatic names.

Isetnofret had at least six children, one of whom, Merenptah, became king after Ramses.

✧ Ramses (second son) was a general in the army and crowned prince after the death of Amenhirkhepshef. In year 30 he was a judge on the trial of a Theban treasury officer and his wife who were stealing from royal stores. He died in year 52-53

✧ Bintanath (first daughter) was married to her father

✧ Khaemwaset (fourth son) was the '*sem* priest of Ptah' and died in year 55. He was crown prince after his brother, Ramses, had died. He is the most documented of Ramses's children. At 5-6 years old he went with his father and half-brother, Amenhirwenemef, to fight in a Nubian campaign. Ramses believed exposing his young sons to battle was a positive experience although Khaemwaset was not suited to it. Khaemwaset then became a priest of Ptah particularly associated with the funerary cults. He started as a deputy to the High Priest of Ptah; he built the Serapeum due to the increasing devotion to the Apis Bull and he was also associated with the *heb sed* of Ramses in year 30, 33, 36, 40, 42, 45, 48, 51, 54, 57, 60, 63 and 66.

✧ Merenptah (thirteenth son) succeeded Ramses to the throne. In the last 12 years of Ramses's reign Merenptah ruled Egypt as a co-ruler and then became king after his death

✧ Isetnofret II married her brother Merenptah

Other children of Ramses are recorded although their mother's names have not been identified; it can be assumed they were born of minor wives or concubines.

✧ Amenemwia (eighth son) changed his name to Sethemwia to represent the dual nature of Egypt and the family's worship of the deity Seth

✧ Sety (ninth son) was dead by year 20

✧ Merire the elder (eleventh son) was dead by year 20

✧ Prince Simontu (twenty-third son) was 'Administrator of the Royal Vineyard' at Memphis. He married Iryet a daughter of a Syrian sailor

✧ Ramses Meriamun (forty-sixth son) was a hunchback who died in his 30s. No coffin would fit so they used an abandoned outer coffin of Sety I when he was the vizier and he is buried at the bottom of a shaft at Medinet Habu

Isetnofret's daughters are depicted at Abu Simbel but as princesses, they would have outranked her whilst Nefertari was still alive, as she was only a secondary wife. After Nefertari's death, Isetnofret became more prominent within the public life of Ramses and she is recorded as royal consort in years 24-30 on a stela of Khaemwaset at Aswan and also year 33-4 in the temple of Horemheb at Gebel el Silsila. In the Aswan stela she is still alive, holding a floral sceptre but in the Gebel el Silsila stela she is holding an ankh and Bintanath holds a papyrus which suggests she is dead, indicating she died before year 34.

Ramses married four of his daughters Bintanath (who had a least one child), Meritamun, Nebettawi and Hentmire. The colossal Ramses statues at Karnak show Bintanath as 'King's Wife', and she is shown presenting a daughter twice in her tomb (QV71). This daughter, also called Bintanath, outlived her father and died during the reign of Merenptah, who she married after the death of Ramses. Most of the sons were intended to be buried in KV5, the largest tomb in the Valley of the Kings. The tomb was designed for the sons of Ramses and over 120 chambers have been discovered, including a number of burials and canopic equipment.

Isetnofret's tomb has not been found yet although a map was discovered in the Valley of the Kings giving directions to it. Unfortunately the landmarks used in the map are unidentified, so the tomb remains lost.

Although throughout his reign Ramses did not appoint a co-regent, at all times the heir was clearly defined. The lower ranking sons led relatively normal lives, whereas the eldest sons were trained all their lives for being the king; educated and serving as soldiers, priests or scribes.

After the death of Nefertari and Isetnofret, Ramses no doubt felt very lonely as he was outliving his children and the great loves of his life. However, as king he had a duty to perform and therefore he married further wives. The marriage stela of Ramses II records a diplomatic marriage in year 35 between Ramses II and the daughter of the recently defeated Hittite king. This Hittite princess was treated by Ramses as 'Great Royal Wife' which was uncommon for a foreign princess. Whilst waiting for her and her dowry to arrive there were long delays and Ramses wrote querying her absence even pleading poverty. Queen Padukhepa, the bride's mother, was not impressed and sent a letter of rebuke to Ramses 'that you my brother should wish to enrich yourself from me … is neither friendly nor honourable'.

The princess, accompanied by her dowry, entourage and her mother, eventually travelled to southern Syria where they were to be met by the Egyptian authorities. Ramses made an offering to Seth in the Delta to prevent snow from delaying his bride any further. The Levant then had an unusually warm spell and the entourage arrived safely to Egypt. The bride appeared 'beautiful in the heart of his majesty and he loved her more than anything'. She was given the Egyptian name Maat–hor–neferura, and she appears on royal monuments as an Egyptian queen, although Bintanath, Meritamun and Nebettawi filled the ceremonial role of the queen instead of her.

Ramses celebrated the wedding with a long inscription which gives the impression that he viewed the marriage as nothing more than tribute offered by a lesser king to his master: 'Then he caused his oldest daughter to be brought, the costly tribute before her consisting of gold, silver, ores, countless horses, cattle, sheep and goats'. This marriage text was recorded at Karnak, Elephantine, Amara and Abu Simbel. This text, however, reflects the official nature of diplomatic marriages rather than the opinion of Ramses himself. He housed her in the harem, at Pi-Rameses for a while and then at Merwer, the harem in the Faiyum, as a papyrus from here, containing her laundry list has been found. She had at least one daughter by Ramses. However she soon disappeared from the records and it is likely that she died young. The eagerness for her arrival could indicate his excitement at the prospect of having a new woman in his life after the death of his two 'Great Wives'. He probably was looking forward to a group of new exciting people coming to the court, as well as the exotic objects they brought with them.

Ten years after the first marriage, the Hittite king agreed to send another daughter and large dowry to Ramses indicating the first daughter had died and the alliance needed to be re-sealed. Although the marriage was recorded, the girl's name has not survived. Her fate is also unknown. This marriage inscription is also displayed at Karnak, in addition to Elephantine, Amara and Abu Simbel.

PI RAMESES

During his long reign Ramses did many things and one of these things was to change the capital of Egypt from Thebes and Memphis, to Pi-Rameses in the Delta, situated very close to the earlier Hyksos capital of Avaris. Pi-Rameses was originally built by Sety I as a harbour town; due to the prime position. It controlled transportation of goods from the Mediterranean into the Nile Valley. The site was also used as a store for barley and emmer, which were used for trading purposes. Ramses II turned this major harbour town into the royal residence. He wanted to build a city to rival Memphis or Thebes, which were, at the time, the main administrative and religious capitals of Egypt. He maintained a residence there as well as at the other capitals and would travel regularly between the three.

Ramses may have succeeded in the short term with this capital city, but by the end of the twenty-first dynasty Pi-Rameses had been abandoned and the monuments usurped and moved to Tanis, further north. Numerous monuments of Ramses II were discovered at Tanis in such quantity that it was originally thought by archaeologists to be the site of Pi-Rameses.

BATTLE OF KADESH

Ramses is particularly famous for his battle at Kadesh against the Hittites, a conflict started by his father Sety I, and continued by himself. The battle reports record Ramses II and Egypt as the victors, although further examination indicates that Ramses was not a talented general as he was very trusting of human nature to the detriment of his military judgment.

The Battle of Kadesh inscriptions form two overlapping reports, commonly known as the bulletin and the poem. The bulletin was copied seven times and the poem was copied eight times at the temples of Abydos, Luxor, Karnak, Abu Simbel (poem only) and the Ramesseum. The poem has also been discovered at Deir el Medina on two hieratic papyri, which suggest it was designed to be read out to the people of Deir el Medina, or was at least popular enough that the owners of the papyri decided to record it for posterity. Ramses commissioned the numerous copies of this record to display his magnificent bravery and military prowess.

The bulletin, which is much shorter than the poem, confines itself to the actual record of the day of battle, when Ramses is close to, or actually at, Kadesh, whereas the poem records activities from a month prior to the battle and describes the Egyptian's journey northwards. The pictorial record which accompanies the text completes the details excluded from the textual records with images of the dismembered hands of the fallen enemy, used to count the number of enemy soldiers slain. It is generally believed that the bulletin and the pictorial record note the events of the battle more accurately than the poem although all three records need to be examined to get a complete picture. There are many more references in the poem to Ramses being god-like and therefore it could be seen as being more propagandistic, written to reinforce the divinity of the king. The basic outline of the battle, was that Ramses and the Egyptian army were marching northwards in order to attack the Hittites. Ramses is approached by two men who claim that they have abandoned the enemy in order to join the Egyptian army. They tell of the Hittite location, stating it to be some miles northwards. However, they were not telling the truth. Two further Hittite scouts (53) were picked up and beaten, until they revealed the Hittite army were behind the next hill. The Egyptians received this information too late and they were attacked by the Hittite army. The Egyptian army were afraid and fled leaving Ramses to face the enemy on his own. He calls to Amun for help, and then manages to defeat the Hittite army single-handed, although in reality a back-up corps of the Egyptian army probably arrived and fought off the enemy.

DIVINITY OF RAMSES

There are regular references to Ramses in the Kadesh battle reports, in connection with various deities. In the moment of battle Ramses is described as Seth or Baa'l (the Canaanite storm god, worshipped in the Delta by the Hyksos and the closest Canaanite god to Seth). Even the Hittites are in awe of his god-like skills. The Hittite soldiers are recorded as saying:

> No man is he who is among us, it is Seth, Great-of-Strength, Baal in person. Not deeds of man are these his doings.

Even Ramses describes his actions as god-like: 'I was after them like Baa'l in his moment of power, I slew them without pause.' The text goes on to explain how Ramses attacked the Hittite army, alone, six times and killed thousands of men, chariotry and infantry all by himself.

Even the appearance of Ramses was god-like. He was a natural redhead, although it had gone white before he died. Red hair was unusual in dynastic Egypt and was closely associated with the desert, chaos and Seth. It is interesting

53 Capture of the scouts, Ramesseum.
Photograph Wayne R. Frostick

to think that Ramses's father Sety was named after this god also because of the fact that he had red hair. This family originated in the Delta which was the cult centre of the god Seth, and therefore it is not unusual that they worshipped this deity.

However, regardless of the god-like characteristics that appear when Ramses is in battle, he calls on Amun to help him.

> What is this, father Amun? Is it right for a father to ignore his son? Are my deeds a matter
> for you to ignore? Do I not walk and stand at your word?

Ramses also calls Amun his 'Protector' indicating that if anything happened to Ramses in battle it would be the will of the god and would possibly affect his popularity with the Egyptian people. The battle was seen by Ramses to be the will of the god, and therefore he felt it was Amun's responsibility to help him win it.

Ramses describes all the pious things he has done for Amun and explains if they are not rewarded it will reflect badly for Amun.

Have I not made for you many great monuments,
Filled your temple with my booty,
Built for you my Mansion-of-Millions-of-Years
Given you all my wealth as endowment?
I bought you all the lands to supply your altars
I slaughtered for you 10,000 cattle
And all kinds of sweet-scented herbs.
I did not abstain from any good deed,
So as not to perform it in your court,
I built great pylons for you,
Myself I erected their flagstaffs:
I brought you obelisks from Elephantine
It was I who fetched their stones
I conveyed to you ships from the sea,
To haul the land's produce to you

He further pushes the issue by stating that the Hittites are 'godless', namely that they do not recognise Amun as the king of the Gods and wonders how helping them would benefit Amun:

What are these Asiatics to you, O Amun, the wretches ignorant of god?

However, regardless of all the piousness of Ramses, the only help he receives from Amun in battle is acknowledgement that he is his son.

He gave me his hand and I rejoiced. He called from behind as if near by; …. Forward I am with you, I your father, my hand is with you

This was enough to give Ramses the strength of the god and enable him to beat the Hittite army single-handedly. However, as was traditional in battle reports, the Battle of Kadesh records emphasise the cowardice of the foreigners.

Not one of them found his hand to fight … their hearts failed in their body through fear of me.

The Hittites were so afraid of the Egyptian king that they refused to fight him and cowered in the safety of their palaces. In the bulletin, Ramses is told by the spies that the king of the Hittites had fled and was too afraid to face him. Ramses appears to believe his own publicity in reference to his greatness:

> Then came two Shosu of the Shosu tribes to say to his Majesty 'Our brothers who are headmen of tribes with the Fallen One of Khatti have sent to His Majesty to say that we will be servants of pharaoh and will separate ourselves from the Chief of Khatti'. Then said his majesty unto them, 'Where are they your brothers who sent you to say this matter to His Majesty?' and they said to His Majesty 'They are where the wretched Chief of Khatti is, for the Fallen One of Khatti is in the Land of Khaleb to the north of Tunip, and he feared Pharaoh too much to come southward when he heard that Pharaoh had come northward.' But the two Shosu who said these words to his majesty said them falsely.

Ramses believed these two spies, as to him the fact that the Hittite king was too afraid to face him seemed perfectly reasonable. However, this was to nearly prove his downfall, as shortly after this they were ambushed by the Hittite army.

The Battle of Kadesh reports have only been found in Egypt, and therefore we have a biased opinion of the outcome. According to this report, Egypt won and the Hittites were completely dominated. However, this is unlikely, and it is widely accepted that there was a peaceful draw between the two nations, due to both armies suffering huge loses without gaining any ground. Egypt at this time was the more formidable force in the Near East and therefore may have only held the upper hand in this instance on a very marginal basis.

There would no doubt have been an enquiry into the Kadesh battle, and the soldiers who deserted Ramses were punished, and those who stayed rewarded with the 'golden fly' or other military award for bravery. A boyhood friend of Ramses, Amenemiont, who was the 'Royal Charioteer and Superintendent of the Horses' upon the death of Sety I, was promoted to 'Royal Foreign Envoy' after the battle of Kadesh indicating that he had remained to fight.

The battle reports indicate Ramses was not a good general, as he was impatient, inexperienced and too trusting to make tactical decisions. This trusting nature may have been brought on through arrogance or naivety as he may have believed that he was divine and could not understand the concept of others having no fear of him.

RAMSES THE MAN

Ramses was a dutiful son who repaired and finished his father's monuments after Sety's death, and also tried to rule Egypt in the manner of his father, who had a reputation for being a good, just ruler, and a warrior king.

Ramses also had a pet lion so it could be suggested that he may have been an animal lover; however, it is possible that this animal, rather than a cat or dog, was chosen to prove his might and power. Imagine the awe of the Egyptians and enemies when they saw him in processions accompanied by a tamed lion walking at his heels.

As we have also seen, Ramses (54) was a loving husband and father although it is possible that he did not meet all of his children, or if he did, may not have known them very well, especially if they were born of lower wives. His devotion to his first two wives indicates some of the loyalty that he had, despite the custom of polygamy. Although he maintained this custom he remained loyal to these wives in turn. We also need to remember that he had to watch both of his great loves die in the first half of his reign and then rule for another 30 years without them.

DEATH AND AFTERMATH

Ramses II died in August 1213 BC in his sixty-seventh regnal year and it is suggested it may have been the result of dental infection leading to septicaemia. Marine sand was found amongst the mummy wrappings of Ramses indicating he was not mummified in the Theban area, suggesting he was embalmed in the House of Embalming at his new capital of Pi-Rameses and then taken to Thebes and the Valley of the Kings by his son Merenptah to be buried. The funeral was problematic as there was no official funerary record and as over half a century had passed since the last royal funeral, people had forgotten what to do. Despite his lengthy reign, very little of his funerary equipment survived; what has been found includes shabtis of varying materials (two wooden, a rare bronze and stone) and fragments of a canopic chest. The tomb has four storage rooms leading from the burial chamber, all of which were full to bursting with treasure.

Fragments of his calcite anthropoid coffin have been discovered, decorated with the *Book of Gates*, and may have been similar to that of his father Sety I, which is currently in the Sir John Soames Museum, London. No stone sarcophagus or fragments have been found so it is possible that Ramses was not provided with one, although this would seem unlikely.

His mummified remains arrived in Thebes in late October and were dragged on a wooden sledge in procession to the Ramesseum, his funerary temple, and then to the Valley of the Kings for burial. At the tomb door the procession was greeted by ritual dancers and a jackal priest, who performed the last rites. Merenptah acted as a *sem* priest and performed the 'Opening of the Mouth' ceremony on the mummy of his father, which confirmed his own right to rule Egypt as the heir to the throne.

Ramses was buried in KV7 near the entrance to the Valley of the Kings. Work started here on the thirteenth day of the second month of winter, year two of his reign, when a

54 Ramses, Luxor Temple. *Photograph Wayne R. Frostick*

silver tool was used to make the first ritual cut on the rock. The real work was completed with copper or bronze tools. Waste from the tomb was dumped a small distance away from the tomb entrance. The rock was of an inferior quality and it was not a good site; it was very low in the Valley, so was vulnerable to thieves and flash floods. Floods have filled the tomb at least 12 times since it was cut, tearing the illustrations from the wall, making the ceiling unstable and filling the passages with concrete-type rubble. The tomb has therefore been exposed since the end of the dynastic age. It is only now that a French team are in the process of restoring the tomb. Ramses did little to hide the entrance to the tomb being too trusting of the belief in the sanctity of burial, as well as in his own divinity. There was a wooden door bolted and sealed but not plastered over.

Ramses's body rested in the tomb for 200 years before being moved to the Deir el Bahri cache, where he laid for a further 2000 years before being moved again to his new home in the Cairo Museum (55). The mummy of Ramses shows he suffered from severe arthritis in his hips and arterioclerosis in his lower limbs which prevented comfortable walking. He also had badly decayed teeth, and abscesses which would have caused him much pain in later life. As his health deteriorated, although he never officially appointed a co-regent, he gradually let his son Merenptah take over the day-to-day responsibilities of ruling. Merenptah was in his 60s when he eventually took over the throne after the death of his father.

The reputation of Ramses lived long after him and numerous New Kingdom kings named themselves after him in an attempt to emulate his reign. Ramses III was

55 Mummy of Ramses II. *Photograph from Elliot Smith 1912*

the only one who came close. The Tanis dynasties were very fond of Ramses–abilia and they built Tanis from the remains of Pi-Rameses.

Although his military abilities were limited, Ramses ruled Egypt for over 60 years in relative peace. He was a loving father, husband and son who slowly watched his friends and family die in a civilisation where the average age of death was 40 years old. He therefore focused on building works as a means of expelling energy. Any other king ruling for as long, over such an economically affluent society, would no doubt have acted in a similar way to him, building vast and numerous monuments. However, this is often viewed as a sign of egotism and megalomania rather than the actions of a man with little else to do.

In modern times Ramses still maintained this reputation, and is further immortalised as Ozymandias in the poem written by Shelley. Ozymandias was a distortion of Ramses's throne name Usermaatsetepenra used from 60 BC onwards. The poem itself is inspired by the colossal statue from his mortuary temple, the Ramesseum.

> I met a traveller from an antique land
> Who said 'two vast and trunkless legs of stone
> Stand in the desert. Near them on the sand,
> Half sunk, a shattered visage lies, whose frown,
> And wrinkled lip, and sneer of cold command
> Tell that it's sculptor well those passions read
> Which yet survive, stamped on these lifeless things,
> The hand that mocked them, and the hand that fed:
> And in the pedestal these words appear
> "My name is Ozymandias,
> king of kings, look on my work ye mighty and despair."
> Nothing besides remains. Round the decay
> Of that colossal wreck, boundless and bare
> The lone and level sands stretch far away.'

TWELVE

RAMOSE

AN HONEST SCRIBE

INTRODUCTION

Our next character comes from the workmen's village of Deir el Medina (56), an exceptional settlement on the west bank of the Nile at Thebes, designed to house the workmen and artisans who built the royal tombs of the New Kingdom. Ramose lived in the village during the long reign of Ramses II.

The ancient Egyptians called Deir el Medina *Set-Maat* or 'Place of Truth' and in some texts it is referred to simply as 'The Village'. It was built during the reign of Thutmose I of the eighteenth dynasty, although most of the evidence that has survived is from the nineteenth and twentieth dynasties. The main source of evidence from Deir el Medina are hundreds and hundreds of limestone ostraca (limestone chips) used by the villagers and scribes as notepaper to write letters, draw sketches, and record absences from work.

During the reign of Ramses II the village was in its prime with 70 houses within the enclosure wall and 40-50 outside. The 'Servants of the Tomb' lived in the houses outside the village and included wood-cutters, water-carriers, fishermen, gardeners, washer-men and potters; those who had nothing to do with the actual building of the royal tombs.

The village had one main street, which ran north to south with smaller narrow alleyways running between the houses. These alleys may have originally been covered creating a cool shaded area between the houses. Just outside the North Gate was a communal well which was filled by the water carriers who lived outside the enclosure walls.

The houses opened onto the street and were one storey high with a staircase leading to a flat roof. There were also cellars beneath the houses for storage and in some instances the burial of infants. The outside of the houses were whitewashed, doors were painted red and the wooden door frames have the name of the family inhabiting the house painted on them in red ink. Some of these have survived today, giving an indication of who lived in which house.

The houses in Deir el Medina were quite small but each one may have accommodated up to 15 children, and numerous adults, including parents, grandparents and unmarried female relatives. However, as the workmen would be away during the week in the Valley of the Kings, the houses were primarily inhabited by the female members of the village, retired workers, invalids, children and servants.

The foremen and scribes were wealthier than the workmen, although there is evidence to show that they still lived within the village albeit in slightly larger houses. Our individual. Ramose was a scribe at Deir el Medina, and a rich one at that.

The freedom of the inhabitants of the village has often been questioned. The purpose of having the village cut off from the rest of Theban society was to prevent tomb robberies. However, this did not work as the *Tomb Robbery Papyrus* and the actual tombs would tell us. People were sometimes employed in the village from outside, so birth in the village was not a requirement to live and work there. Also the extensive families meant that when all the children grew up there would not be enough work for them within the village and they would leave to work in Thebes. There are also a few letters from Deir el Medina suggesting contact with relatives outside the village.

There is evidence of a market place on the east bank of the Nile, which was frequented by the villagers of Deir el Medina where they could trade grain for other goods. Some villagers were such frequent visitors that they had huts on the east bank so that they could stay overnight. Although this would suggest that they were free to leave the village and visit relatives, the village authorities would no doubt have monitored these visits and trips. There is evidence of five gateways or guard posts to which the villagers and visitors would need to report when entering or leaving the village.

Ramose is one of the best-documented scribes of Deir el Medina and has left more stelae and statue fragments than any other occupant in the village. He is reputed to be one of the richest inhabitants, although he seemed to be quite a private individual and information about his private life is difficult to come by (*colour plate 17*).

56 Deir el Medina. *Photograph Wayne R. Frostick*

FAMILY

Ramose was not born in the village and neither of his parents worked there. His father was the 'retainer' Amenemhab responsible for carrying written and verbal messages between numerous officials in the Theban area. Ramose's mother was the Lady Kakaia. Ramose was born in approximately 1314 BC.

As a young child Ramose may have accompanied his father on his daily errands and would have met many officials. Ramose was noticed by one of the scribes, who recommended him to a scribal school where he learnt to read and write (57). In his scribal training he learnt through copying traditional texts and also through dictation, as some of the errors from school texts would suggest. He also learnt the prayers that all scribes recited before they started work and the ritual of sprinkling water for the spirits of scribal patrons.

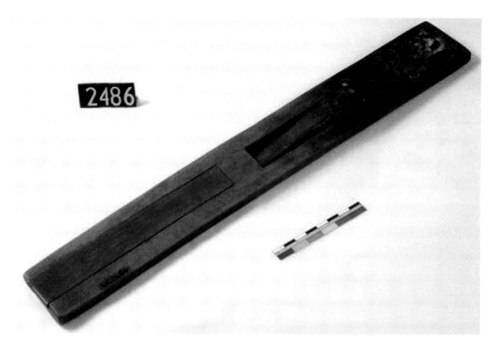

57 Scribal palette, eighteenth dynasty. *Copyright: Petrie Museum of Egyptian Archaeology, University College London,* UC 2486

Ramose was married to the lady Mutemwia, who held the epithet 'the lady of the house whom he loves'; she was a priestess of Taweret and was a resident of the village. He married her after he had moved to the village, and throughout their marriage he affectionately called her Wia. Unfortunately they were unable to have children which would have been very distressing, as children ensured the parents had someone to care for them in old age. Wia and Ramose actively petitioned various deities for children but it appeared not to have worked. There are two surviving stelae to deities of childbirth and fertility and a further stela dedicated to Qudshu the Asiatic goddess of love; Reshef the Asiatic thunder god; Taweret, hippopotamus goddess of childbirth; Min, the fertility god; and Shed the saviour and helper of mankind. This indicates they were a pious couple, but also a very desperate couple.

Ramose also dedicated numerous statues to Hathor of the Western Mountain and a stone phallus to the goddess Hathor with an inscription saying:

> O Hathor, remember the man at his burial. Grant duration in your house as a rewarded one to the scribe Ramose. O Golden One, who loves when you desire the praised one, Your desired one, cause me to receive a compensation of your house as a rewarded one.

This was a plea for fertility and was perhaps a final act of desperation.

Despite these dedications Ramose and Wia did not conceive a child. In this situation it was common to adopt an apprentice who would take the role of the eldest son, who would perform the burial rites and take over the father's profession. Ramose honoured this system and adopted another new arrival to the village, a scribe called Kenhirkhepshef. Although no legal documentation of this adoption have survived, there are texts belonging to Ramose that refer to Kenhirkhepshef as 'my son', indicating it was an informal affair to adopt an individual. Kenhirkhepshef was either adopted initially as a pupil or as a son.

EARLY CAREER

Ramose started his career outside of the village in the Theban area as 'Assistant Scribe of the Hereditary Prince' (mayor) before promotion in his early 20s to 'Scribe of the Treasury of the Funerary Temple of Thutmose IV'. His titles here included:

⬦ 'Scribe of the temple treasury'

⬦ 'Scribe Accountant of the cattle of the god Amun', where he would have kept account of all the cattle of the estates of Amun throughout Egypt

⬦ 'Chief of the Administration in the house of the seal-bearer'

⬦ 'Scribe of the Funerary Temple of Amenhotep, Son of Hapu' (the deified vizier of Amenhotep III) which formed part of the temple of Amenhotep III

Whilst working at these temples, during the reign of Sety I, Ramose was noticed for his scribal talent and called away from his religious duties and sent to Deir el Medina as the new 'Administrator' on the work of the royal tomb. This new role included writing many lists, inventories of the stores, checking rations of food and supplies, and recording all deliveries into the village. These would then have been reported back to the vizier, Paser. It is recorded that:

> The wages of the necropolis have been delivered being absolutely complete, without any arrears.

He was to live and work at Deir el Medina for 40 years. Ramose:

> Was made scribe in the place of truth in year five, third month of the season of inundation, day 10 [13 September] of the King of Upper and Lower Egypt Usermaatrasetepenre, Son of Re, Ramses II, beloved of Amun.

He held the post until year 38 (1274–1241 BC). Ramose was probably appointed this position by the vizier, Paser, and there is evidence suggesting they later became good friends. Ramose is thought to have been about 35 years old when he entered the village.

He seems to have been popular within the Deir el Medina community, and his wife Wia and himself are included on the wall reliefs of other people's tombs showing continuing respect of the tomb owner into the afterlife.

In the tomb of the sculptor Neferenpet (TT36) the tomb owner is shown receiving offerings from Ramose and Wia. In the tombs of the sculptor Qen (TT4) and the workmen Penbuy and Kasa (TT10) Ramose is shown alongside Ramses II, the vizier Paser and the tomb owners, worshipping various deities including Ptah and Hathor. In a lower register Penbuy and his brother Penshenabu are offering to Amenhotep I, Ahmose Nefertari, Sety I, Ramses I and Horemheb. The close association with Ramose, Paser and Ramses II shows that as well as being popular Ramose also held a very senior position, with influential acquaintances.

Ramose and his wife also seem to have been 'adopted' by the Scribe Huy and his wife Nofertkhe, who themselves were childless. In their tomb (TT336) the owners are offered perfume and pastries by Ramose and Wia, and they are referred to as 'son and daughter' by the tomb owners. In this position they were carrying out the role of the eldest son.

This adoption would not have been for the same reason as Ramose's adoption of Kenhirkhepshef, but more a patronage born out of respect. Huy's family commissioned Ramose to decorate some of their funerary furniture including the shabti box of Huy's brother and wife, which housed their servant figures; he was paid the equivalent goods of a week's grain for this work.

Despite these honours, Ramose was very modest and always referred to himself as an 'Honest Scribe', even in the inscription of his funerary monument where people are often prone to boasting and pomposity.

Ramose was probably the richest man that ever lived in the village and as he held one of the highest positions in the village, his monthly grain ration (or wages), was a third more than the ordinary workmen. This amount of grain could support 12-14 people.

In addition to this higher salary he owned cultivated land outside the village, which he probably purchased before he came to Deir el Medina. This land was tended by his servant Ptahsaankh (TT212), who is shown in one of Ramose's tomb chapel paintings as ploughing with 'West' and 'Beautiful Flood' his two cows. Ptahsaankh is one of the few peasants' names that have survived through the millennia. As he was named it indicates he was a real person rather than an idealised servant for the afterlife. Ptahsaankh states in this scene 'the fields are in a good state and their grain will be excellent'. The lands reported may have been part of the great temple estates of Amun, which may have been managed by Ramose, giving him an income from renting, and yield of the land. Ptahsaankh is also depicted on a stela dedicated to Hathor by Ramose and is titled 'servitor of Amun' further supporting the connection between him and the estates of Amun.

Ramose also could have earned extra income by working as the village scribe, writing letters, accounts and reports for the inhabitants of the village who were unable to read and write. Also, as mentioned briefly, he made extra income through the decoration of the villagers' funerary equipment with accurately written religious texts. Ramose built a large house which was in the oldest part of the village reflecting the wealth he had accumulated.

RAMOSE'S PIOUSNESS

As the stela appealing for a child would suggest, Ramose was a very religious man, which may have developed due to starting his early career within a temple environment.

Ramose was close friends with the vizier Paser and they commissioned a sanctuary together at Deir el Medina honouring Ramses II, known as the *khenw* and near the south wall of the temple of Hathor. The cult of the deified king was practised within this shrine. Within the *khenw* Ramose had installed stelaphorus statues of himself recording an endowment given by Ramses II for the temple of Hathor.

> His Majesty … ordered the endowment of god's offerings for this statue in the temple
> of Hathor, Chief in Thebes, in the restricted royal necropolis, the sacred offerings coming
> from the temple of Usermaatrasetepenre (Ramesseum) which is in west Thebes … the
> one who established their endowment is the scribe in the Place of Truth, Ramose who
> came concerning it together with the royal scribe, the city governor and vizier, Paser.

One statue of Ramose describes his role in the building of this sanctuary: 'I made a sanctuary for the god and this statue of my lord (Ramses II) rests in it'. There were a large number of stelae and statues of Ramose and Paser at the nearby temple of Hathor so there is no doubt that they built that temple too. The temple currently at Deir el Medina is Ptolemaic in date but may be on the site of this earlier example.

Evidence also suggests that the finance for the building and decoration of the temple of Hathor came from the personal fortune of Ramose.

Ramose was particularly devoted to Amun-Re, the local Amun of Thebes, and he set up a stela dedicated to him with a text that was a hundred years old, and was probably seen as classical. It may have been something that Ramose learnt during scribal training, or it may have still been an active prayer in the temples of Thebes.

> Adoration of Amun-Re – the chief of all the gods, the good god, beloved one, who gives life to all warm blooded creatures and all beautiful animals. Hail to you Amun-Re, Lord of the Thrones of the Two Lands, foremost in Thebes, bull of his mother, foremost of his fields, wide of stride, foremost in Nubia, Lord of the Medjay, Ruler of Punt, most ancient in heaven and eldest in all the world who dwells in all things.

Unlike some of the villagers, Ramose only ever worked on the tomb of Ramses II during his time at Deir el Medina. However, in the later years he may have been involved in the tombs in the Valley of the Queens, for the burials of the queens and children of Ramses II, including possibly the building of KV5, and the tomb of Nefertari. His involvement would not have been practical, but rather just record keeping and administration.

TOMBS

Ramose had three tombs at Deir el Medina, clearly a sign of great affluence. He started to build his first tomb and chapel before he married Wia, when he first arrived in the village. This tomb was at the top end of the Western Cemetery at Deir el Medina. When he married Wia this first tomb was abandoned and he built a bigger tomb chapel for both himself and Wia quite close to the first tomb. The third tomb was at the south end of the Western Cemetery and was closer to the village.

The first tomb (TT212) has Ramose described as 'Scribe of the Tomb', with no mention of his wife or adopted son Kenhirkhepshef. This tomb was therefore probably built before he was married, when he had just arrived at the village. It has been suggested that this tomb may have later been used for the burial of his male servants as TT250 was for the burial of the female servants. There would not have been many male members of the household other than servants, as men moved away to start their own homes and families, leaving Ramose responsible for unmarried female relatives, of his own and and his wife.

The tomb built for Ramose and Wia, (TT7), is thought to be Ramose's final resting place, as he is shown here in relief with his friend the vizier Paser and Ramses II, as well as his wife Wia and her parents. Images of the revered Thutmosis IV and Horemheb are also depicted near the door, indicating Ramose held a high-status position that enabled him to be in the company of royalty for eternity. Unfortunately no bodies were found in this tomb so whether Ramose and Wia were buried here is unknown. It is always possible that he built a bigger, more secretive tomb that has yet to be uncovered.

Tomb TT250 would appear to have been built for nine women of Ramose and Wia's household. This tomb had three separate chapels with burial vaults beneath them and the wall reliefs show the funeral of nine female mummies. One of these mummies is named Henutmehyt and is shown in another register accompanied by Wia. In the images the mummies of the women are all upended outside the tomb chapel whilst the priests perform the sacred funerary rites. A scribe checks that Ramose has made the correct number of offerings, as it was important that he provided well for their afterlife. Five of these women are Wia's relatives who probably all lived in Ramose's house, and the other four women were servants and concubines of Ramose. The servants in this tomb may be associated with the female servants of the foreman Neferhotep, who probably worked alongside Ramose, and it is generally thought that the tomb may be a resting place of the female servants of both Ramose and Neferhotep, as well as the female relatives of Ramose's wife Mutemwia. It is possible that as senior members of the village hierarchy Ramose and Neferhotep may have shared servants. The decoration in the central chapel shows the nine dead women at a funerary feast being served by the living guests, as a sign of respect and honour.

Although very little was found in these tombs it is believed that the funerary equipment of Ramose and Wia would have been as rich as their life in the village, including fine coffins, brightly decorated tomb furniture, elaborate shabtis and beautiful copies of the *Book of the Dead*. It must be remembered that the people living at Deir el Medina produced the tomb decoration and some of the funerary equipment of royalty, and for extra income would produce equipment of the same quality for those in the village. As a scribe Ramose could have ensured that he had the most elaborately decorated and accurate funerary texts, rendering them more effective than badly copied examples. All in all, his afterlife was every bit as affluent as his life at Deir el Medina.

DEATH

Ramose disappears from the records after year 38 of Ramses II when he was about 70 years old. People in Deir el Medina seemed to live longer than the national average, no doubt due to good food and readily available medical care provided by the state to ensure the healthiest people were available for the royal building works.

When Ramose died he was succeeded as 'Scribe of the Tomb' by his adopted son Kenhirkhepshef.

THIRTEEN

KENHIRKHEPSHEF & NAUNAKHTE

AN EARLY HISTORIAN AND HIS WIFE

INTRODUCTION

We were introduced to Kenhirkhepshef as the adopted son of Ramose 'The Honest Scribe'. Kenhirkhepshef led an interesting life both whilst Ramose was alive and afterwards when he took over the title of 'Chief Scribe' at Deir el Medina.

FAMILY

Ramose and his wife Wia adopted Kenhirkhepshef when he was only 15 years old, in the fourth decade of the reign of Ramses II. Kenhirkhepshef's natural father was called Panakht and was not a resident at the village, suggesting that Kenhirkhepshef was not born there; indeed we have no evidence of him prior to year 40 of Ramses II when he was appointed to the position of 'Scribe'. The name of Kenhirkhepshef's mother, Senetnefer, is recorded in a magical spell written on a piece of papyrus which Kenhirkhepshef wore folded as an amulet. It would seem that Kenhirkhepshef did not come from a family of scribes, and may have been the only literate person in his family.

The adoption by Ramose and Wia would provide an apprentice in the first place to inherit the role from Ramose; and then as a son to perform all the funerary rites that the eldest son would normally perform. Ramose does use the term 'my son' in reference to Kenhirkhepshef, although this is also used as a standard term of endearment.

Kenhirkhepshef was married to a village woman, Naunakhte, but they are not recorded as having any children together; it is thought that Kenhirkhepshef died childless. Naunakhte was approximately 12 years old when she married Kenhirkhepshef, who was much older than her, aged between 54 and 70. She outlived him by 51 years. There is no record of Kenhirkhepshef being married prior to Naunakhte despite his advanced age, but as he came to the village as an outsider perhaps the records of a first marriage are lost. It has been suggested that he may have adopted Naunakhte so she would be his undisputed heir and then to further secure this he made her his wife which also ensured care in his old age. Her particularly young age could account for their childlessness.

CAREER

Kenhirkhepshef is first recorded as 'Scribe' in year 40 of Ramses II (1239 BC) and it is thought that he kept the position until year one of Siptah (1193 BC), or year six of Sety II, which is between 46 and 54 years in the village. The first evidence we have of him is from the record of absentee workmen where he is recorded as having several men 'carry stones' for him on more than one occasion, over a period of time. In year three of Amenmesses (1199 BC), several workmen were absent due to carrying 'stones for the scribe Kenhirkhepshef'. The workman Iny was in fact absent twice in year 40 of Ramses II for this task suggesting he started abusing his position from the very beginning.

Further evidence of his abuse of power comes from an undated ostracon which has a 'list of people who were with the Scribe Kenhirkhepshef, he having taken leave from the work of Pharaoh and put them on carrying stones upon the hills at noon in the presence of the people who were in *msk'* (part of Theban necropolis). This 'free' labour helped Kenhirkhepshef become a wealthy man, although we are unsure which of the houses at Deir el Medina belonged to him and his family.

For the first 10 years after his adoption Kenhirkhepshef and Ramose worked together in an apprentice scheme until Kenhirkhepshef was ready to take over the role as Scribe. A few years later Ramose died after 40 years in the village, and Kenhirkhepshef took over as 'Chief Scribe'.

Kenhirkhepshef's first responsibility in his new position would be to bury his adoptive father, Ramose. He would have taken the place of the eldest son, following the funerary sled to the chapel. It was uncertain whether Wia had died before Ramose but both were buried together in the same tomb, although we do not know which of the three tombs, if any, they were buried in.

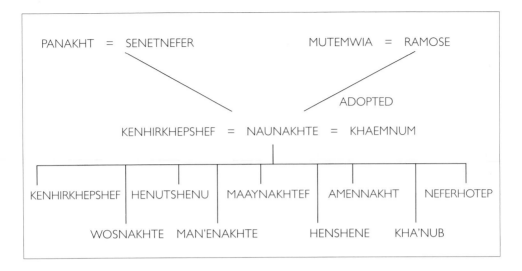

When work in the village started again after the funeral, Kenhirkhepshef would have taken all of his adoptive father's records and continued where he had left off. A lower grade scribe, called Anupemheb, took over all of the routine tasks, such as receiving and distributing rations of grain, fish and wood, and repairing the chisels, leaving the more important tasks to Kenhirkhepshef.

Kenhirkhepshef was friends with the foreman Neferhotep who was promoted to his position at approximately the same time and by the end of their careers they had worked together for about 40 years. The foreman's role was to control all of the work that occurred in the royal tomb, and the scribe's role would be to record and report on the progress. They were so close that Kenhirkhepshef included Neferhotep in a scene in his tomb chapel and this is the only tomb the foreman appears in other than his own.

At the start of Ramses II's reign the workmen of Deir el Medina had built a crude settlement on the cliffs between the Valley of the Kings and the village, situated just above the 'Amenhotep I Temple of the Garden'. These crude huts were inadequate for the cold winter nights and hot days but shortened their working day, as they did not have to walk back to the village. They later rebuilt this settlement with sturdier, more adequate huts. From here they could look over the Nile and see Karnak temple. The huts consisted of two rooms, a bedroom and the room at the front which had u-shaped stone seats so the workmen could get together and chat. Strangely enough, although they stayed up here for up to eight days at a time during their working week, there is no evidence of cooking.

It seems that meals were cooked for them and brought up from the village. This prevented fires being lit and signalling to potential tomb robbers the location of the Valley of the Kings. One note has survived from Deir el Medina where a workman asks his daughter to bring extra bread and beans as her two brothers had arrived to help him. Their arrival must have been unexpected or they would have been included in the rations. There were large stores at Deir el Medina that held the rations of all the men who worked in the tombs, and their families. The hut Kenhirkhepshef owned in this makeshift settlement was centrally placed and was bigger than all the others; instead of the standard two rooms his had three, each paved with limestone slabs. One room had been specially adapted to be used as an office where he could conduct business meetings and entertain visiting dignitaries, which does not appear to be a provision given to other scribes in the village.

Kenhirkhepshef's stone seat in his clifftop hut was inscribed with his father's titles: 'King's Scribe in the Place of Truth, Ramose, his son who makes his name live, Kenhirkhepshef'. By inscribing his father's name on his chair ensured that his father's name was remembered for eternity.

Kenhirkhepshef would not have supervised the work in the Valley of the Kings from this hut, but from a niche in the shade above the Valley, inscribed with 'The sitting place of the scribe Kenhirkhepshef'. There are also many examples of graffiti bearing his name, all over the rocks of the Theban hills.

To pass time in the evenings in this makeshift settlement the workmen made shabti figures which they would then sell to other inhabitants of the village. An ostracon was found with a sketch of a shabti and the text that was to be inscribed on it, was probably used as a guide.

Whilst the workmen were building the tomb of Ramses II, the Valley of the Kings suffered a flash flood, caused by brief bursts of rain resulting in water flooding down the gullies in the Valley. The floods filled tombs with rubble, damaging the decoration and funerary goods. Some tombs remained full of water for up to three years until it had evaporated. The houses of Deir el Medina were waterlogged and reverted back to the mud that the bricks were made of. People and all of their belongings were dragged away with the churning waters.

Ramses II's tomb was filled with water and the workmen were responsible for clearing and repairing it before they could continue to build. At the present time the tomb has been damaged by 12 or so flash floods leaving it full of a concrete substance. KV5, the tomb built for the sons of Ramses's sons, is also in the same condition. All of this would have been recorded by Kenhirkhepshef in his day-to-day journal.

After the death of Ramses in his sixty-seventh year of rule, the tomb builders started building the tomb of his successor, Merenptah, almost immediately. Kenhirkhepshef was in charge of the daily journal of work for the new tomb. It took 13 years to build Merenptah's tomb which Kenhirkhepshef started working on at 51 years of age. Above the tomb door Kenhirkhepshef built a niche so he could sit out of the sun and watch what was going on and this is inscribed with 'sitting place of the scribe Kenhirkhepshef'.

By year two of Merenptah the progress in the tomb was good and Kenhirkhepshef sent a report to the vizier entitled 'A summary of the work done in the Great Place of Pharaoh'. The entrance stairway was complete. In the upper corridors the scenes and texts were engraved and painted, although the burial chamber was still being excavated.

In the seventh year of Merenptah (1204 BC) statues of the gods to be placed in his tomb were brought to Deir el Medina. This was accompanied by a great festival to celebrate the progress. There would have been good food and drink, which were distributed to the workmen and they would have celebrated with singing and dancing.

In Merenptah's eighth year the vizier ordered special rations for the tomb makers in reward for their work 'Pharaoh let the workmen be rewarded for the tasks which they have excavated' recorded Anupemheb, Kenhirkhepshef's assistant. These extra rations were recorded by Anupemheb; there were 150 donkey loads of provisions brought to the village. These consisted of 9000 fish, with a large amount of salt for drying. Fish were filleted and salted and left on the roof to dry in the sun. Deir el Medina probably smelt quite bad at this period in time. Everyone in the village would also have had a salt block for seasoning food which they would crumble as needed. Also included in the rations were 10 oxen ready for slaughter (enough for a few meals per person; the blood would also have been used for food), four donkey-loads of beans and sweet oils; eight donkey-loads of barley malt which is enough for four pints of beer each; 9000 loaves of bread enough for 150 per household; and eight-donkey loads of natron used as soap. The whole village probably held a public feast in open land around the village as the houses would not have been big enough for the roasting of an entire ox. These festivities went on long into the night, with much dancing and singing.

The workmen from Deir el Medina would also have been responsible for ensuring the coffins would fit inside the tomb and would help to bring in the funerary equipment. Merenptah's sarcophagus was cut from alabaster and inside there would be two pine anthropoid coffins. Two granite lids were brought by barge from Aswan, and were to be laid over a hole cut in the burial chamber floor, designed to hold the alabaster coffin. Merenptah died in his thirteenth year when he was in his 60s. When he was being mummified the workmen quickly finished the tomb. The burial chamber was quickly plastered and painted.

There was however one major error. The huge black granite cover for the sarcophagus would not fit through the doors so they had to remove the painted door-jambs in order to manoeuvre it in. They got the cover through the doors but abandoned it at the narrower end of the tomb. The king's body was brought in around the block. The two other coffin lids were placed over the coffin as planned, the funerary goods were then placed in the tomb and the footprints swept away.

In the following years, Kenhirkhepshef's surviving records are mainly about the issuing of lamp wicks. They were made of twisted rags soaked in tallow and laid on the sloping side of the oil-filled lamp. He also wrote a letter to the vizier Panhesi regarding the absence of supplies. The absence of the court from Thebes had delayed administration so neither the royal warehouses or storekeepers at Deir el Medina were distributing the stocks they held. Kenhirkhepshef asks for chisels, plaster and leather baskets for carrying quarried stone from the tomb. They were clearly friends, and at the end of the letter he comments that Panhesi's sister's baskets were being woven, and that he would deliver a bed and some special tools that had been ordered from the tomb workers.

AN ANCIENT HISTORIAN

One of the most interesting things about Kenhirkhepshef was his fascination with the past. He had quite a substantial library consisting of a variety of texts including medical texts, spells, hymns, letters, poetry, household hints and also dream interpretations. His handwriting was large and functional and he did not always take time to refresh his pen with ink indicating a quick mind. Kenhirkhepshef particularly liked lists and made lists of Ramses II's sons and daughters, and a list of all the titles associated with 'Chief' and 'Overseers'.

In his library there was an ostracon with lists of kings recorded on them. One starts with the name of Ramses II and the names of 10 kings of the eighteenth and nineteenth dynasty in chronological order. The kings recorded were those whose funerary temples were at Thebes, so could have been compiled as part of a religious cult. All these kings images were carried to Deir el Medina in the 'Beautiful Festival of the Valley' and some of the kings had cult chapels in the village, with the villagers acting as cult priests, and may even have received some form of income from it. Kenhirkhepshef also had a copy in his library of the *Rituals of Amenhotep I* which was a list of spells to be recited in the cult of this king and could suggest some religious necessity that Kenhirkhepshef possesses this information, or it could even be something that was passed down to him from his adopted father Ramose, who worked in temples before entering the village. As well as showing an interest in history it also shows an interest in lexicography.

One thing he had in his library was a text about how to recognise a follower of Seth, the god of chaos, primarily from their red faces and hair, their violent nature and their enjoyment of being drunk. He records:

The god in him is Seth … he is a man of the people …. He is one dissolute of heart on the day of judgment … discontent in his heart. If he drinks beer he drinks it to engender strife and turmoil. The redness of the white in his eyes is this god. He is one who drinks what he detests. He is beloved of women through the greatness – the greatness of his loving them. Though he is a royal kinsman he has the personality of a man of the people … he will descend unto the west, but is placed on the desert as a prey to rapacious birds … he drinks beer so as to engender turmoil and disputes … he will take up weapons of warfare – he will not distinguish the married woman from … as to any man who opposes him he pushes … massacre arises in him and he is placed in the Netherworld.

He also had a further text that said:

Do not indulge in drinking beer for fear of uttering evil speech. If you fall no-one will hold out a hand to you. Your companions will say 'out with the drunk', you lie on the ground like a little child.

Kenhirkhepshef obviously detested alcohol and drunkenness.

On one papyrus, now known as the *Chester Beatty III Papyrus* he recorded the Battle of Kadesh of year five of Ramses II; a number of years before Kenhirkhepshef's time. He copied the poem during the reign of Merenptah, 60 years after the event. It is unknown whether he copied the poem from the temple walls, a draft copy or a book roll which was being circulated. On the reverse of the *Chester Beatty Papyrus*, he has recorded a *Book of Dream Interpretations* which can give an insight into the private concerns of the villagers. It is possible that the villagers approached Kenhirkhepshef with their dreams and asked him for guidance, and he felt he should keep a record of them, perhaps for further reference.

There were 108 dreams recorded, covering 78 activities and emotions including sailing, weaving, brewing, painting, pickling, copulation, plastering, sightseeing, stealing, and carving. Seventeen per cent cover seeing something, 15 per cent covered each of eating and drinking, five percent covered each of receiving something and copulation, 35 per cent concerns a dreamer's direct gain or loss (e.g. receiving a new house, wife or inheritance) or robbery, taxation, becoming an orphan, eating too much or starving, being in pain or having an illness and being cured. One fifth were concerned with giving and receiving of gifts, an essential part of the village economy.

The text was laid out in columns making it easier to consult. The Good or Bad interpretation was always written in red ink.

> If a man sees himself in a dream …. Dead …. Good: it means long life in front of him.

> If a man sees himself in a dream …. Uncovering his own backside …. Bad: he will be an orphan later.

> If a man sees himself in a dream …. Writing …. Bad: reckoning up of his misdeeds by his god.

In the interpretations clever linguistics were employed with the use of rhyming couplets and linguistic puns. Sometimes the dream interpretations were just reversed to get the meaning (death means long life). Modern dreams are believed to be the working of the subconscious, whereas in ancient Egypt they were seen as divine signals to predict the future.

The dream interpretation papyrus also includes a spell to be recited upon waking that would dispel all dreams and demons. This had to be recited accompanied by eating fresh bread and green herbs moistened with beer.

> Come to me, come to me my mother, Isis behold, I am seeing what is far from my city.

It would be interesting to know who came to Kenhirkhepshef asking for help with sleeplessness or troublesome dreams, or indeed whether Kenhirkhepshef suffered himself from either of these.

As this spell would suggest, Kenhirkhepshef was quite superstitious and religious and this is further attested from his monuments and letters. An offering table, now in Marseilles, shows Kenhirkhepshef adoring 18 kings and queens dating back to the seventeenth dynasty, even including the little-known king Seqenenre Tao I. As this king probably did not have a funerary cult that Kenhirkhepshef would have been familiar with he knew enough about history to record this king, and place him in the correct chronological order.

On the back of an old letter from the vizier, Kenhirkhepshef had written a spell against demons that 'fed on excrement – and lived on dung'.

> Scribe Kenhirkhepshef, born of Senetnefer. Turn back *Sh3kk*, which came forth from heaven and earth, whose eyes are on his pate, and whose tongue is in his buttocks; he eats of the bread which is under him. His right arm is far from him; his left arm is within sight.

The stars ... when they see how he lives on repelling dirt [in the southern sky]. Those who are within the Netherworld fear him. *Ndrhsmm* is the name of your mother; *Dwbst* is the name of your father. If you come upon the scribe Kenhirkhepshef, born of Senetnefer, I shall come forth to ... thee, my two arms being far away. You shall not come upon me. I am *Trws* behind his shrine. To be recited four times over flax made into arrows tied together, while two of the arrows stick out.

He folded this papyrus, tied it with flax and hung it around his neck. He was very superstitious and named his real mother and not Wia, Ramose's wife, which is the only attestation of his mother Senetnefer.

This spell was a popular one from this period and two other examples have been found. The demon *Sh3kk* was troublesome and could only be dispelled by the person doing the incantation taking the place of an obscure deity *Trws*, who should fire an arrow and take the demon away with it.

One could maybe understand the man's fear when we see some of the accusations against him by his workmen. He was not a very popular man and there were at least two accusations of bribery against him. Both are recorded in *Papyrus Salt*.

Apparently 'Paneb gave something to the scribe Kenhirkhepshef and he saved him'. From what Paneb was saved from is unknown, but it is clear that this was viewed as bribery.

Another accusation dated to year nine of Merenptah claims:

The workman Rahotep [who] shaved the hair of the scribe Kenhirkhepshef [.........] he gave a loincloth of 15 cubits and he gave him nine balls of yarn after his (Kenhirkhepshef's) concealment of his (Rahotep's) misdeeds.

It would be intriguing to know what these 'misdeeds' were, not just for interest's sake but also to see what kind of power Kenhirkhepshef actually held. Further complaints against Kenhirkhepshef involve his misuse and abuse of his position by using the workmen for his own purpose presumably without paying them.

The Draftsman Prahotep salutes his superior, the Scribe in the Place of Truth Kenhirkhepshef: What does this bad way mean in which you behave to me? I am to you like a donkey. If there is some work, bring the donkey, and if there is some food, bring the ox. If there is some beer, you do not look for me, but if there is work, you do look for me. It is good if you have listened, in the House of Amun-Re, King of the gods. I am a man who has no beer in his house. I try to fill my belly by writing to you.

This workman is bitterly complaining here about a ration of beer that he feels rightfully belonged to him. As beer was a staple rather than an alcoholic luxury this accusation indicates Kenhirkhepshef was neglecting the welfare of his subordinates.

Kenhirkhepshef appears to have had a close friendship with the foreman Nebnefer and his son Neferhotep, as on the left-hand wall of the inner chapel of TT216 we see Neferhotep, the tomb owner, followed by his father Nebnefer, his grandfather Neferhotep and the 'Royal Scribe of the Place of Truth Kenhirkhepshef', all making offerings to Osiris and Anubis.

Kenhirkhepshef was over 70 years old when he started work on his third royal tomb, that of King Amenmesse, possibly a son of Ramses II. His friend Neferhotep was almost the same age. After one year working on the tomb of Amenmesse, he died and Sety II took over the throne; 25 days later they started cutting his tomb, the fourth one that Kenhirkhepshef had worked as scribe for.

TOMB

The tomb of Kenhirkhepshef has not been clearly identified, but is thought to be at the southern end of the cemetery at Deir el Medina, as a double-seated statue of him and his wife Naunakhte was found in the chapel near the door to the inner room. This tomb was undecorated, but it was very spacious with a chapel and a large staircase.

DEATH

There was no retirement age in Egypt so Kenhirkhepshef kept working into his 70s, but in the later years he had long periods of illness. When he was at work he probably sat quietly observing whilst in the shade as his assistants Anupemheb and Paser did the actual work.

At the end of the reign of Merenptah, Kenhirkhepshef's handwriting had changed to an illegible, uneven size, indicating he could not see as well as he had when he was younger. The walk over the cliffs would eventually have been too much for him even with a stick, which prevented him from going to work at all. It may have been just before this that he started carving his name in the cliffs and remembering his real father 'Scribe of the Place of Truth, Kenhirkhepshef, his father Panakht' as he became aware of his own mortality. He died at about 86 years of age; how and where is unknown although it is thought to have been in year one of Siptah.

LIFE AFTER KENHIRKHEPSHEF

Eventually Kenhirkhepshef's widow Naunakhte married a workman, Khaemnum and they remained together for 30 years. Her oldest son was called Kenhirkhepshef after her first husband, and considering the age difference it is likely that she thought of her first husband as a father figure. Her oldest son Kenhirkhepshef had inherited affection for the dead scribe and even added his name and children to an inscription of Kenhirkhepshef I, where he shows his own descent from Panakht, giving him descendants that he did not have naturally.

When Kenhirkhepshef died Naunakhte would only have been in her 20s at the most. From her second marriage she had eight children: four sons who were all workmen, Kenhirkhepshef, Maaynakhtef, Amennakht and Neferhotep and four girls Wosnakhte, Man'enakhte, Henshene and Kha'nub.

We actually know very little from the life of Naunakhte from either of her marriages, but four papyri concerned with her will have survived. In the will it tells of how she disinherits four of her children, Neferhotep, Man'enakhte, Henshene, Kha'nub, so they would only get their father's two thirds of wealth and not her third which she inherited from her first husband including his extensive library:

> As for any property of the scribe Kenhirkhepshef, my husband, and also his landed property and this storeroom of my father and also this *oipe* of emmer which I collected in company with my husband, they shall not share them.

To make this decision legal she took it to the *knbt* (court), in year three of Ramses V (1142 BC). The court consisted of the foremen Nekhemmut and Anherkhau, the 'Scribe of the Tomb' Amenakhte and the scribe Harshire, the draftsmen Amenhotep and Pentaweret, the workmen Telmont, To, Userhat, Nebnefer, Amenpahapi and Nebnefer son of Khons, as well as the district officers Ramose and Amennakhte. The reason she gives for disinheriting these children is neglect.

> As for me I am a free woman of the land of Pharaoh. I brought up these eight servants of yours, and gave them an outfit of everything as is usually made for those in their station. But see I am grown old, and see they are not looking after me in my turn. Whoever of

them has aided me, to him I will give of my property but he who has not given to me; to him I will not give any of my property.

As well as disinheriting some of the children she also gave one of her sons, the workman Kenhirkhepshef, special consideration; 'I have given to him a special reward, a washing bowl of bronze over and above his fellows 10 sacks of emmer'.

On one of the documents concerning her will, the bowl is recorded as weighing 13 *debens* of copper, and it is recorded that their father, Khaemnum, ensured the son received it. Another document records that Khaemnum went to the court after the will had been written, with his children to say 'As for the writings that Naunakhte has made, concerning her property, they shall be carried out exactly as prescribed'.

Two of the surviving papyri give a very detailed account of the division of Naunakhte's property, mentioning every piece of furniture and kitchen utensil. There were very few items of value bar the bowl mentioned, and Gardiner comments, that the papyrus she had the arrangements written on was probably the most valuable thing she possessed. Naunakhte clearly wanted to make a point that her children did not deserve her possessions after her death due to the way they neglected her in her old age.

CONCLUSION

Although many details are missing from the life of Naunakhte it is clear that she led a full life after the death of her first husband. Although some people thought he was corrupt she was very fond of him and this affection was passed on to her oldest son by her second husband. It is likely that she had been adopted by Kenhirkhepshef, as she and her family treat him as a revered grandparent rather than a first husband.

FOURTEEN

PANEB

AN ANCIENT ROGUE

INTRODUCTION

Paneb was a rather notorious character from Deir el Medina, who has maintained his reputation for three millennia. We were introduced to him briefly in the previous chapter in connection with bribery of the scribe Kenhirkhepshef.

FAMILY

From Paneb's tomb we learn the names of his parents and some of his children. He was the son of the workman Neferemsenut who died shortly after year 40 of Ramses II (1239 BC). Paneb's mother was called Iuy and his grandfather was a man called Kasa. Paneb is thought to have been about five years old when his father died, so he was probably born in 1244 BC. Shortly after the death of his father, Paneb was adopted by the foreman Neferhotep, in the same sense that Ramose adopted Kenhirkhepshef. Paneb would have worked under the close eye of Neferhotep until he was ready to take over as foreman.

At the end of Ramses II's reign Paneb married a village woman called Wabet and they may have had up to 10 children. In Paneb's tomb one son Apehty and two daughters Iyi and the 'Chantress of Amun' Sheritre are named. A vignette originally named six of his daughters but only Nodjemetsu and Nofret are still legible. Two stelae name more of his children, one currently in the British Museum dedicated to the goddess Meretseger names Apehty, Paneb and Nebmehyt as his sons, and another British Museum stela names another son, Hednakht.

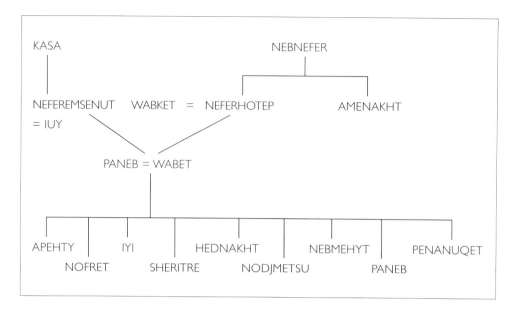

The relationship with his immediate family is unknown, although there is recorded hostility between Paneb and his adopted father Neferhotep, and Neferhotep's family. Despite this hostility Paneb followed tradition and named one of his daughters after a member of Neferhotep's family, showing respect for the man who adopted him.

The brother of Paneb's adopted father Neferhotep, Amenakht was particularly embittered against Paneb and took every possible opportunity to denounce him. In one record Amenakht gleefully tells us that Paneb and his eldest son Apehty did not always get on, which is often the case with any parent and child. Amenakht records that one day Apehty ran away from Paneb's house and went to the doorkeeper and said:

> I cannot bear to be with him; my father made love to the Lady Tuy when she was the workman Kenna's wife, he made love to the Lady Hunro, when she was with Pendua and when she was with Hesysenebef [*later also adopted by Neferhotep*]. And after that he debauched her daughter too.

The seduction of the daughter is slightly unlikely as she was about three years old at the time, so it indicates that this record maybe somewhat exaggerated. It would be interesting to know whether these words really came from Paneb's son or Amenakht himself. It is interesting, however, to know that the Lady Hunro was also said to be debauched by Apehty as well, so if this report was from him it may have been motivated by resentment that his father had seduced someone he had also seduced.

The foreman Neferhotep was married to another village woman called Wabket, and by adopting Paneb, Neferhotep named Paneb as his heir, of his house and the rich furnishings. Neferhotep was a rich man and owned a number of servants which were eventually buried in the same tomb as the servants of Ramose, 'The Honest Scribe'.

CAREER

The earliest definite evidence of the foreman Paneb at Deir el Medina, is from year 66 of Ramses II (1213 BC), although he had not been promoted to foreman at this stage. However, the name Paneb also appears on an undated ostracon recording an inventory of water supplies. The other names on this ostracon can all be traced to year 40 of Ramses II, 26 years earlier (1239 BC) and it is generally thought this could be the same Paneb. By year 50 he definitely was old enough for a junior workman position in the village.

Paneb started life in the village as an ordinary workman and was promoted to 'Foreman' or 'Chief of the Gang' in year five of Sety I (1286 BC) amidst a riot of complaints and accusations of bribery. It would seem that even at this early stage in his career he was not popular amongst the inhabitants of Deir el Medina. Calculations show he was born in approximately 1244 BC, and became foreman when he was approximately 30 years old.

It is thought that Paneb was a follower of Seth, and this is supported by the name of his eldest son, Apehty meaning 'great of strength' and was an epithet of Seth, showing an affiliation with this god. As a reminder of Kenhirkhepshef's description of a follower of Seth we can see how Paneb may have fitted this.

> The god in him is Seth ... he is a man of the people .... He dies by a death of ... the fallings ... sinews.... He is one dissolute of heart on the day of judgment ... discontent in his heart. If he drinks beer he drinks it to engender strife and turmoil. The redness of the white in his eyes is this god. He is one who drinks what he detests. He is beloved of women through the greatness – the greatness of his loving them. Though he is a royal kinsman he has the personality of a man of the people ... he will descend unto the west, but is placed on the desert as a prey to rapacious birds ... he drinks beer so as to engender turmoil and disputes ... he will take up weapons of warfare – he will not distinguish the married woman from ... as to any man who opposes him he pushes ... massacre arises in him and he is placed in the Netherworld.

Paneb did drink quite heavily, leading to violent rages where he threatened to kill people, and as we have heard already he did seduce women whether they were married or not. However, although he was angry and passionate he was one of the best and most effective foremen of the village.

As the adopted son of Neferhotep, Paneb would live in Neferhotep's house which was in the southern part of the town at the end of the main street. Neferhotep was rich and would have provided well for his family. However, in year two of Merenptah's reign it is recorded that Paneb was 'repairing his house' indicating that he had moved out of Neferhotep's home. He petitioned for a brick wall to be built in order to separate the domestic area from the workshop creating extra space. He also bought a number of new household goods, including boxes, baskets, and even a woman's bed. Paneb liked the finer things in life and all of this wooden furniture, sandals, linen and copper cooking vessels were undoubtedly of the finest quality. It is possible that in year two he moved from Neferhotep's house and into his own; perhaps at this time he had started a family with Wabet.

Paneb moving out probably pleased Neferhotep no end, as Paneb was unruly and prone to drunken fights. Neferhotep filled the gap in his life and home by adopting a second son, his young house servant Hesysenebef. He revered Neferhotep and named his eldest son and daughter after him and his wife. Despite this new adoption Paneb was still Neferhotep's successor, and inherited the position and the wealth from him.

When Paneb was promoted to foreman, Kenhirkhepshef must have been over 80 years old and would probably have watched his progress with some amusement. Kenhirkhepshef seems to have been an important village elder, and as an elder he was involved in the continuing dispute between Paneb and Neferhotep's family. Despite his aversion to drinking, Kenhirkhepshef seemed to support Paneb in their dispute. Neferhotep's brother Amenakht even accused him of taking a bribe from Paneb to 'conceal his misdeeds'.

In year one of Sety II there is evidence that Paneb turned against Neferhotep and his family. At about this time Neferhotep became ill but recovered enough to work for four more years, but he died suddenly, being 'killed by the enemy' although who this was, is not specified. Neferhotep was still the foreman in year five of Sety II although it has been speculated that Paneb may have murdered Neferhotep in order to secure his promotion to foreman ahead of Amenakht who had a stronger familial claim. It is, however, more likely that Neferhotep died in a civil conflict in the Theban area during the early years of Sety II. Amenakht also accused Paneb of ensuring the office through bribing higher officials.

When Paneb was first appointed as 'Foreman' he was supervising the carving and decoration of three tombs: those of Siptah, the official Bay and Queen Tausret. When

King Siptah died at age 20 (1187 BC), they started work on Setnakht's tomb. They started it too soon with little forethought and therefore did not choose a good place to build it. Within a year the tomb had collapsed revealing that they had cut through to the tomb of King Amenmesse who had been buried 12 years earlier. They were ordered by the vizier to take mallets and smash the decoration from the wall of the tomb as Amenmesse was a usurper who ruled ahead of Sety II, the rightful heir. Imagine the stress of destroying something you had spent hours labouring over. All the goods found in his tomb would probably have been removed and reused. Once Amenmesse's tomb was destroyed the corridor above, which was intended for Setnakht, was abandoned. They went back to Queen Tausret's tomb and enlarged the doorways and added a second suite of rooms, which would accommodate the burial of King Setnakht. The king was buried two years later behind the queen's suite in this tomb.

Ramses III, Setnakht's son, became king and Paneb saw the start of the cutting of this tomb as well, which was the fifth tomb that he had worked on in his career. Six years into the reign of Ramses III, Paneb and Apehty disappeared from the records, amidst a cloud of intrigue.

As Neferhotep named Paneb as the heir to his position, Paneb did the same with his son. An offering table from the reign of Sety II names the chief workman Paneb (58) and his 'deputy' Apehty, indicating he had made it clear his son was to succeed him after his death. Paneb was already responsible for his son's promotion from workman to 'deputy' during the reign of Sety II. There is evidence that Apehty was still a 'deputy' in year five of Ramses III and then demoted back to 'workman' before the records of him disappear.

There is a record from year one of Siptah (1193 BC) when Apehty was given a beating probably for a minor indiscretion which has not been specified. He was tried in the *knbt* by the vizier Hori who visited the village three days before the punishment. It would seem that Apehty was similar to his father, possessing a fiery temper and womanising tendencies.

CRIMINAL ACCUSATIONS

Throughout Paneb's career at Deir el Medina there were numerous accusations of criminal activities against him. However, the accuracy of some of these could be questioned as well as the frequency of these crimes being committed by other village members which went unrecorded. All of the accusations against Paneb were made by the same man: the brother of Neferhotep, Amenakht. He did not approve of the fact that Paneb, as a family outsider, had inherited his brother's position and wealth. He felt

58 Offering table of Paneb.
*Copyright: The Egypt Centre,
Swansea*

that despite the adoption he should have been the one to inherit this, and rather than accepting this, Amenakht decided to make Paneb's life difficult so he could not enjoy his status and wealth. Initially the accusations were sent to the vizier's office on ostraca, the normal form of communication. Then when Amenakht reached the later years of his life he decided to record every thing that he had ever accused Paneb of during his lifetime, as well as new accusations on *Papyrus Salt*. Papyrus was an expensive commodity and Amenakht obviously felt his task important enough to warrant the expense.

CORRUPTION

One of the first accusations Amenakht made about Paneb was that in order to secure his position as foreman he had bribed the vizier. He may have felt that he was capable of doing the job but that maybe he was unlikely to achieve promotion in his own right, as he was a workman, and not a direct descendant of Neferhotep. It is recorded that Paneb bribed the vizier with five servants which were part of Neferhotep's household. Amenakht is particularly concerned as these servants belonged to the inheritance of his brother, and should therefore have belonged more to the blood relatives than the adopted son although he does admit that Paneb, as an adopted son has as much right to the position as Amenakht.

> I am the son of the chief workman Nebnefer. My father dies and the chief workman Neferhotep, my brother was put in his place. The enemy killed Neferhotep and although I was his brother, Paneb gave five servants of my father to Praemhab, who was then vizier ... and he put him in the place of my father although it was indeed not his place.

The absentee record from Deir el Medina, which recorded who was absent from work and the reason, records that Paneb sent a man from work on the tomb to feed his ox. No other foremen are recorded as doing the same thing although it is a simple enough activity that other foremen were probably doing it too. In year two of Siptah (1194 BC) Nebnefer, the son of Wadjmose, was absent for several days due to 'feeding his [Paneb's] ox'. Paneb in this case, however, was clearly abusing the power that he had, as the ox-feeder was a member of Neferhotep's family.

Paneb was further accused by Amenakht of abusing the workmen by making them and their wives work for him, presumably without pay.

> Charge concerning his ordering the workmen to work on the plaited bed of the Deputy of the temple of Amun, while their wives wove clothes for him. He made Nebnefer, son of Wadjmose feed of his ox for two whole months.

Other entries from the absentee record show further abuse of power. In year one of Siptah (1193 BC) a draftsman, Neferhotep, was absent due to 'painting the coffin of Paneb'.

Although Amenakht appears to have a problem with Paneb's use of labour, it obviously was not unusual as people were often absent from work for similar work with other scribes, or foremen.

Amenakht also accuses Paneb of using government tools for use in his own tomb, in addition to reusing pieces of the Royal tomb. 'He took away the spikes of Pharaoh and the hoe for work in his own tomb'. There was also another:

> Charge concerning his ordering the workmen to cut down stones on the top of the tomb of Sety Merenptah. They took them away to his tomb and he erected four columns in his tomb of these stones.

The actual tomb in which these pillars were supposedly erected has not been discovered so we do not know the accuracy of the accusations.

BODILY HARM

Paneb was also accused of making threats, and even of murdering someone:

> Charge concerning his [Paneb] running after the Chief Workman, Neferhotep, although it was him who reared him. And he (Neferhotep) closed his doors before him, and he [Paneb] took a stone and broke his doors. And they caused men to watch over Neferhotep because he [Paneb] said 'I will kill him in the night'.

It took many guards to drag the enraged Paneb away from his adopted father's door, and they stood watch in case he returned. Unfortunately the exact causes of the argument will remain a mystery, but it would seem that he did not carry out his threat as Neferhotep was possibly killed in the civil war between Sety II and the usurper Amenmesse. It is possible that this violent attack on his adopted father was instigated by alcohol.

This was not the only death threat that Paneb made during his time at Deir el Medina. At the time that Paneb was foreman of the right-hand side of the gang (year five of Sety I to year one of Siptah), Hay was foreman of the left-hand side (year three of Merenptah to year 19 of Ramses III). For some unrecorded reason these two were adversaries and it is recorded that Paneb said to Hay 'I will get you in the mountains and kill you'.

However, yet again he does not appear to have carried out the threat and this may also have been the result of alcohol related bravado.

The death threats to Hay and Neferhotep would make the other accusations of Amenakht believable which may have been what he was hoping. By sending numerous complaints about Paneb he was hoping to sully his general reputation leading to an investigation by the vizier.

A serious petition against Paneb, which does not seem to have been proved, is a case of murder. As the men he was supposed to have killed are not named, it could be a case of hearsay rather than fact. Amenakht informs us:

> Such conduct is indeed unworthy of his office. And he is keeping well although he is like madman. Yet it was he who killed those men that they might not bring a message to pharaoh. Lo, I have caused the vizier to know about his way of life.

The vizier was no doubt inundated with letters from Amenakht and possibly was sick of investigating each of these complaints.

TOMB ROBBERIES

The first three accusations on *Papyrus Salt* concern tomb robberies where Paneb removes objects, whether he sells or keeps them is unclear; Amenakht probably did not know.

When Sety II died Neferhotep's brother Amenakht took the opportunity to denounce Paneb for tomb robbery. A robbery had obviously taken place as a long list including tomb doors, chariot coverings, incense wine and statues would suggest, and apparently it was common knowledge in the village. In case tomb robbery was not enough, when the king was placed in the sarcophagus Paneb sat on top of it drunk. Paneb swore an oath to the vizier in his defence which was 'should the vizier hear my name again I shall be dismissed from my office and become a stone mason once more', which seems to have been enough to acquit him on this occasion.

Amenakht comments 'When the burial of all the kings was made, I reported Paneb's theft of the things of King Sety Merenptah'. This was during the reign of Sety II and may have been in reference to the burial of Merenptah or Amenmesse.

Amenakht also comments that Paneb:

> Went to the tomb of the workman Nakhmin and stole the bed which was under him. He carried off the objects which one gives to a dead man and stole them.

This obviously was a grotesque thing to do but he seems to have had no punishment for this, perhaps suggesting that the accusation was false. The third charge was:

> Concerning his going to the burial of Henutmire [Queen of Ramses II] and taking away a goose [model]. He took an oath by the Lord concerning it saying 'it is not in my possession', but they found it in his house.

213

This accusation was shortly followed by Paneb's disappearance so he may have received punishment for this. Perhaps this was the only crime he had committed or the only crime that could be proved.

None of these accusations appeared to end up in the *knbt* (court). Tomb robbery was seen as a major crime and would generally be punishable by death. Even when they 'found the objects in his house' nothing appears to have been done immediately although shortly after he did disappear from the records.

The charges of tomb robberies may have been a misunderstanding of Paneb and his friend Kenna searching in the over-crowded cemetery of Deir el Medina for a place to build their tombs. Many of the tombs collapsed and there was a lot of rubble, which they may have been rummaging through in order to salvage anything.

ADULTERY

More accusations against Paneb include adultery with Kenna's wife, Hunro, when she was both Tuypendua's wife and Hesysenebef's wife and also possibly with her daughter Webkhet. Paneb's son, Apehty, also 'debauched Webkhet', so it would appear that his son may have inherited some of his father's morals.

One further claim was that Paneb 'stripped the Lady Yemyemwah of her clothes and threw her on top of the wall and seduced her'. She was Amenakht's and Neferhotep's sister and if this actually occurred then Paneb may have done it to annoy Amenakht. This case and that of the seduction of the other three women was probably designed to present Paneb as a 'sower of social discord'.

There is no doubt that these accusations are based on fact, and Paneb was probably a particularly nasty piece of work, although it could also be suggested that so was Amenakht. He seems to be embittered that Paneb has a position of power that he feels should rightfully be his, and this is reflected in his long list of petitions against Paneb. The fact that Paneb was disgraced and found guilty of tomb robbery, shows he was not an honest man, and abuse of his position is also attested by the absentee record. It is, however, possible that Amenakht's accusations may be overzealous, due to jealousy.

Paneb himself complained about the vizier's office and after Amenmesse's death the vizier of the time was dismissed on the strength of this. Paneb probably complained of the vizier allowing 'irregularities' to occur in the Valley of the Kings. Anyone who knew of 'irregularities', which generally were tomb robbery or damage, were as guilty as the robbers in the eyes of the law.

Every time Paneb was approached by the authorities regarding these accusations he would declare an oath which was strong enough for the case to crumble instantly. The oath was 'not to upset a stone in the neighbourhood of the place of Pharaoh'. The penalty for perjury was heavy so the judges believed him as it would be dangerous to lie. However the accusations annoyed Paneb and he became quite hostile to Neferhotep's family after this.

He prevented Amenakht from visiting the tomb chapel of Neferhotep and sent a member of his workforce to enforce it. He also shouted to the villagers 'don't let any member of the family of Neferhotep be seen going to make offerings to Amun, their god'. If he caught anyone carrying out offerings on their behalf Paneb threw stones at them. Fear of the wrath of Paneb probably won out in this matter.

TOMB

Paneb built a vaulted tomb (TT211) in the top end of the Western Cemetery. Above the vault was a pyramid and a causeway similar to that of his adopted father Neferhotep's situated just above it. Unfortunately the tomb is now half destroyed but would originally have been painted with a yellow and white colour scheme. Paneb started building TT211 when he was a workman although it is doubtful he or his family were ever buried in it. The titles in this tomb were never changed from 'Workman' to 'Foreman' indicating it had been abandoned before his promotion. It is likely that with his new position and wealth he would have started another tomb elsewhere although this has not been located.

DEATH

Despite all of the accusations against him throughout his career in the village Paneb appeared to have never been punished, or if he did they were minor penalties and have escaped the records. He was eventually caught and charged with a most serious crime brought to the attention of the authorities by Amenakht:

> Concerning his [Paneb's] going to the burial of Queen Henutmire [wife of Ramses II and daughter of Sety I] and taking away a goose.

This was in reference to a gilded goose which was sacred to Amun. Paneb took an oath by the Lord saying 'It is not in my possession' but they found it in his house as

Amenakht gleefully tells us. It is likely that Paneb was probably removed from the village and possibly executed.

An ostracon states that 'Year five [of Ramses III 1177 BC], the fifth month the killing of the chief' which may record the execution of Paneb. He was approximately 67 years old at this point. His son Apehty also disappeared from the village at this time and it is thought he may have had some connection with his father's activities and therefore shared his fate.

FIFTEEN

RAMSES III
THE LAST GREAT KING

INTRODUCTION

Ramses III from the twentieth dynasty is generally believed to be the last great king of Egypt, as after his reign followed a time of invasions and foreign rule leading to an unstable country both politically and economically. Ramses III, although not a son of Ramses II, greatly admired this king and tried to emulate him. To a certain degree he managed this, although the reign of Ramses III was fraught with more problems than that of Ramses II, and his strength and leadership were regularly tested. Ramses III ruled for 31 years and 41 days from 1182–1151 BC at a time when there was unrest in many of the countries surrounding Egypt, resulting in many displaced people looking for a new place to call home. Nowhere seemed more promising that the ripe fertile land of the Nile Valley.

FAMILY

Ramses III's father King Setnakht was the founder of the twentieth dynasty although how and why he came to the throne is uncertain as there is no firm evidence that he is related to the previous dynasty, although it is thought he could be a grandson of Ramses II. Setnakht's queen was Tiy-Merenese and she could be the mother of Ramses III.

Ramses III had a number of wives although his 'Great Royal Wife' was Isis. However, the cartouches at Medinet Habu that should contain her name have been left blank. Her mother's name was Habadjilat, indicating that she was an Asiatic. This suggests that Ramses's wife herself was Asiatic or half Asiatic. Isis was buried in the Valley of the Queens (QV51). There are numerous tombs in the Valley of the Queens to his wives and sons including Khaemwaset, Parahiremef and Amenhirkhopshef. The tombs for his sons in the Valley of the Queens were carved and painted but had the names left blank in order that the life of the son would not be fated. Other sons are buried in the Valley of the Kings as they became kings after Ramses III (Ramses IV, V, and VI). Many of his children were named after Ramses II or his children, and could suggest a relationship between the two kings. If one of Ramses's sons died then the next child born would be named after them. For example one son Amenhirkhopshef who is buried in QV55 died and another son was given the same name and became the 'Master of the Horse'. Some of the titles bestowed upon the sons were also the same as those bestowed upon Ramses II's son of the same name. Khaemwaset for example was named after a son of Ramses II and was also given the name 'High Priest of Ptah'.

Ramses was also married to his daughter Titi, who outlived him, and is buried in the Valley of the Queens (QV52). She bore many titles including 'Mistress of the Two Lands', 'Chief Royal Wife', 'King's Daughter', 'Beloved Daughter of his Body' as well as 'King's Sister' and 'King's Mother'. It is thought that this marriage may have produced Ramses IV.

A minor wife, Tiye, was a disgruntled spouse and was involved in a conspiracy to assassinate Ramses. She also had a son, Pentewere, although this was not his birth name. Tiye wanted her son to come to the throne, although he was not an heir, and as Ramses had not identified which of his 10 or so sons would be the crown prince, it was open to usurption.

It was traditional throughout the reign of Ramses III to have very public parades of the royal children, which emphasised the importance of the new royal dynasty. The sons of Ramses III appear to have been close to their father and Ramses IV wrote the *Harris Papyrus* which lists all of the good deeds of his father.

BATTLES OF THE 'SEA PEOPLE'

Ramses's father Setnakht only ruled for three years, so Ramses III was able to start the dynasty from scratch and make his mark on it. When Ramses III became king his chosen throne name was Usermaatre–Meryamun (Born of Re, Beloved of Amun) and throughout his life Ramses shows his dedication to the god Amun. Years one to four of his reign were relatively peaceful. However in year five the first of Ramses's Libyan problems began. The new Libyan king Themer, was angered when Ramses tried to impose a young vassal king upon them who was viewed by the Libyans as a child;

he used this as an incentive to invade Egypt. Ramses was faced with a 30,000-strong army comprising a mixture of Libyans and 'Sea People'. After careful consideration he decided that they would wait until the Libyans were 'sitting in Egypt', which would encourage them to lower their guard. Ramses then attacked, and overcame them resulting in 12,535 enemy deaths and 1000 Libyans being taken as slaves, if the Egyptian records are to be believed. The prisoners were branded with the king's name, returned to Egypt, and paraded in front of the king in a victory procession (59).

This victory was not to last long, and after three years of peace the *Harris Papyrus* records that after several bad harvests in the surrounding regions, various nations were on the move towards Egypt in an attempt to escape the Hittites. They were the strongest nation in the Near East, and Sety I and Ramses II had already fought them at Kadesh. These nations were collectively known by the Egyptians as the 'People of the Sea', and were a mixture of Libyans and tribes from the southern coasts of Asia Minor, Philistine and Sicily.

The outer wall of the second pylon at Medinet Habu records the battle of the 'Sea People', as they tried to invade Egypt. Before marching on Egypt this band of people (including wives, children, and possessions piled up on ox-carts) rested in Syria before marching on to the eastern borders of the Delta. Ramses would have heard about this oncoming army before they arrived and had time to plan his attack. He initially sent out despatches to the eastern border of the Delta to weaken the onslaught before the arrival of the rest of the Egyptian army.

As the maritime people of the Aegean had provided the 'Sea People' with ships for the invasion, they were the first army to be strong enough to take on the Hittites and win, as they controlled trade on both the land and the sea. On land the 'Sea People' fought in a similar fashion to the Hittites, with chariots carrying two armed men and a driver. However, their seagoing vessels were smaller than the Egyptian boats and had no separate oarsmen. This meant they could not fight and move at the same time, unless there was a strong wind for the sail. The Egyptians had the advantage as they had 24 oarsmen as well as a contingent of soldiers aboard each ship, with the added benefit of a sail. The rowers on the Egyptian vessels were protected by the high sides of the ships and they benefited from the earliest recorded crows nests, which were used not just for lookout posts but also as a platform from which to fire arrows from.

Ramses III faced the army of the Libyans and 'Sea People' on both land and sea and luckily was successful in both areas. The land battle was relatively quick with the Egyptian charioteers and the archers breaking down the defence of the invading army. Once the land battle was over the 'Sea People' in large battleships aimed for the eastern branch of the Nile. Ramses had predicted this move and the 'Sea People' were greeted in this narrow river by the Egyptian fleet.

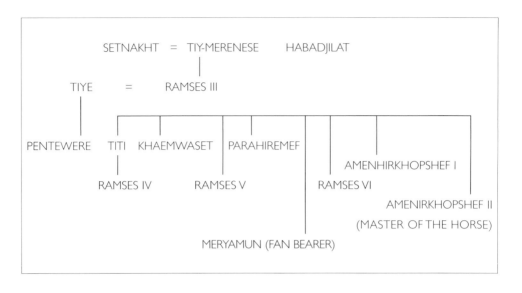

SETNAKHT = TIY-MERENESE   HABADJILAT

TIYE   =   RAMSES III

PENTEWERE   TITI   KHAEMWASET   PARAHIREMEF

AMENHIRKHOPSHEF I

RAMSES IV   RAMSES V   RAMSES VI

AMENIRKHOPSHEF II
(MASTER OF THE HORSE)

MERYAMUN (FAN BEARER)

59 Libyan captives, Medinet Habu. *Photograph Charlotte Booth*

The ensuing naval battle is one of the earliest to be recorded (*60*). The exact location of the battle is unknown and is only referred to as the 'Great Green' generally believed to be the Mediterranean Sea, although it could refer to the fertile land of the Delta region. The Egyptians were not a sea-faring nation and did not pride themselves on being sailors. The Egyptian fleet followed the 'Sea People' into the 'river-mouths' of the Delta, and as the Egyptians had sail and oar power they were able to manoeuvre themselves so as to trap the enemy ships against the shore where the Egyptian archers were waiting to shower them with arrows. The inscriptions suggest that the Egyptians used fire arrows against the enemy, which were greatly feared as the wooden boats caught fire easily. This meant the enemy ships were trapped between the Egyptian navy and the Egyptian archers. There were a number of marine archers lined up on the deck of the Egyptian ships so the enemy were showered from the land and sea simultaneously by arrows. When many of the enemy had been killed the Egyptian ships moved in and rammed the enemy vessels with the decorative prows of their ships. They seized the ships with grappling hooks, and engaged the enemy in hand-to-hand combat. The 'Sea People' were:

> Dragged overturned and laid low on the beach. Slain and made heaps from stern to bow of their galleys, while all their things were cast upon the water.

The battle on the border was harsh with many people killed, although the records never mention Egyptian deaths. Ramses, although primarily the commander of this army, would actually have taken part in the battle leading the chariot troops into the land battle. Although not recorded, Ramses probably chased the 'Sea People' into the Levant to get them far away from the borders of Egypt. Scenes at Medinet Habu, however, show Ramses III attacking fortified Syrian towns which appear to be manned by Hittites and it is believed (although the city is not named) to be Kadesh. However, these skirmishes made no permanent land gains for Egypt although Ramses was able to return to Egypt with booty and tales of victory. Ramses then travelled south to Thebes claiming a victory for Egypt and for Amun, the favoured god of the king. Before the battle commenced Amun had handed the sword of victory to Ramses enabling him to win.

Although the Libyans and the 'Sea People' were defeated, by year 11 the threat from the Libyans reappeared. This battle is also recorded at Medinet Habu on the first pylon. The *Libu* (Libyan tribe) had been attacked by another Libyan tribe called the *Meshwesh* forcing the *Libu* to participate in an invasion of Egypt. They attacked the western border, just west of the canopic arm of the Nile in the Delta. Ramses underwent another Libyan war and killed 2175 *Libu* and *Meshwesh* and took 2000 as prisoner. On the Medinet Habu inscriptions scribes present a pile of enemy hands before the king

60 Sea battle, Medinet Habu. *Photograph Wayne R. Frostick*

to tally the dead, totalling 175. The Egyptians would cut off the right hand, or the penis of the enemies to count how many had been killed. However, as was traditional, the Egyptians did not record their losses in these battles. Ramses then drove the enemy 11 miles into the Western Desert and the possessions of the invading Libyans were taken by the Egyptian army. On the defeat of the enemy Ramses declared a festival day called 'slaying the *Meshwesh*' when there was a victory procession of prisoners, and booty in addition to a public feast with dancing and singing.

There are many other battles recorded at Medinet Habu but it is suggested that other than the Libyans and the 'Sea People', many of the battles did not actually take place. For example one of them is against the Nubians, although evidence suggests that during this reign there were no problems with this region. There are also depictions of invasions of the northern territories, including the country of Amurru, Khatti and Syria, none of whom were considered political enemies at this time. They are recorded in the same manner as those of Ramses II and it is thought that Ramses III may have lifted these scenes directly from the Ramesseum to emulate his ancestor.

This warfare, although victorious appears to have taken its toll on the economy of Egypt. The workmen of Deir el Medina were supposed to get paid on the twenty-eighth day of each month, but on many occasions these rations were late. In year 29 of Ramses III delays in the delivery of rations had been going on for six months resulting in the workmen going on strike, with protests before the funerary temples of Thutmosis III, Ramses II and Sety I. One text describes this event:

> It is because of hunger and because of thirst that we come here. There is no clothing, no ointment, no fish, no vegetables. Send to Pharaoh our good Lord about it and send to the vizier, our superior that sustenance may be made for us.

On this occasion they received their rations, but later that same year Djhutymose, a village scribe, had to go with two bailiffs to collect the grain himself from the local farmers and the temples, as the rations again had not arrived.

It would seem unthinkable that there could be such delays in the payment of rations considering the extreme wealth of the temples in this period. The temple of Amun at Karnak owned 900 square miles of agricultural land, vineyards, quarries and mines. Some of the temples even had their own riverboats and sea-faring vessels. Most of the agricultural land was rented to the peasants and a third of the harvest was paid to the temple as rent. The temple at Medinet Habu had a daily income from its associated land of 2222 loaves of bread, 154 jars of beer, 8000 litres of grain, plus meat and other commodities, which was enough to feed 600 families. Special mud-brick storerooms were built alongside the temples for the storage of this vast quantity of food. Either this income was being deployed to the army or the administration had collapsed.

These economic problems caused great distress to Ramses III as he would require the workmen to continue work on his tomb and the various tombs of his family. No doubt he tried to solve the problem so this work could continue.

THE HAREM CONSPIRACY

The *Harem Conspiracy Papyrus* records the trial of a group of people who plotted to kill Ramses III. Luckily for the king it was not successful and a prosecution of the conspirators was commissioned. However, he did not live long enough to hear the verdicts of the trial and it is thought he may have died due to the assassination attempt, albeit not instantly. It was therefore was Ramses IV who would have presided over the convictions.

There were 14 men who were called to preside as judges, all from different walks of life. There were seven butlers, two treasury overseers, two army standard bearers, two scribes and a herald. They were given the power to call for whatever evidence and witnesses they required to conduct the case. They were also given complete power to carry out the verdict and punishment, which was the death penalty for this type of crime. Ramses III obviously gave this power to them, allowing him to step back or recover whilst knowing that justice will be done.

In total there were over 40 people tried for taking part in the conspiracy; all close to the king, from the harem. Some of main defendants were:

✧ 'Chief of the Chamber' – Pekkamun

✧ Butlers – Mesedsure, Weren, Peluka, Yenini (Libyan)

✧ 'Scribe of the Harem' – Pendua

✧ 'Inspectors of the Harem' – Peynok, Petewnteamun, Keupes, Khamopet, Khammate, Setimperthoth, Setimperamun

✧ 'Overseer of the Palace' – Pere

✧ 'Captain of Archers in Nubia' – Binemwese

✧ Six wives of the people of the harem gate

It is hardly surprising that this plot was discovered as there were a lot of people involved, making it difficult to conceal.

There was also a secondary plot to incite a revolt outside the palace at the same time as the assassination, ensuring the king would not be as well guarded as usual. If this assassination had been successful then there would have been complete chaos and unrest throughout Egypt.

The chief defendant was Ramses minor wife Tiye who wanted her son Pentewere to be king, even though he was not an obvious heir. Her name is real but her son's had been changed in the records as a punishment for this crime. This was a typical punishment and ensured their true names were never repeated which would affect their afterlife. The record of her trial has not survived but it is unlikely that she survived the death penalty.

There were four separate prosecutions outlined on the *Harem Conspiracy Papyrus*. The first prosecution involved 28 people including the major ringleaders. They all were condemned to death possibly by public execution, which acted as a deterrent to others. The second prosecution resulted in six people being forced to commit suicide immediately in the court in front of the judges. The third prosecution involved the trial of four people, including Prince Pentewere, the son of Tiye. They were probably condemned to commit suicide within their cells after the trial, although sadly this sentence is unreadable on the papyrus. The fourth prosecution involved three judges and two officers who were residing over the trial. After their appointment they were accused of 'knowingly entertaining' some of the female conspirators, and a general named Peyes. One of the judges was found to be innocent but all the others were condemned to be mutilated by having their nose and ears cut off. Pebes, one of the judges committed suicide before the sentence was carried out. Clearly mutilation was too much for him to bear.

Whether Ramses would have given the same verdicts is uncertain, but as already mentioned, he died before the verdicts were pronounced.

MONUMENTS

One of the most important monuments that Ramses III built was his mortuary temple, Medinet Habu, which was named 'United with Eternity' (*61*). Prior to Ramses's death a local version of Amun was worshipped at this temple and was the personal god of Ramses III. The temple also had a palace indicating that ritualistic ceremonies may have been carried out here by the king in life as well as in death. The temple follows the standard temple design with an enclosure wall surrounding a pylon-courtyard and hypostyle hall and is a copy of the Ramesseum.

On the two pylons there are propagandistic images of Ramses III in the Libyan battle (of year 11) on the first pylon, the northern war of year eight on the second pylon and the Libyan war of year five in the second court. In addition to the images of battle we see Ramses III participating in the 'Beautiful Festival of the Valley' and the procession of the bark of Ptah-Sokar. In the rear part of the temple there is a suite of darkened rooms that associate Ramses III with various deities. On the northern side there are rooms to associate the king with Re-Harakhty and help symbolise the king's 'Solar rebirth', and on the southern side are rooms to stress the connection with the king and Osiris. In the northern area there is an open-air altar dedicated to Amun. There is also a chapel dedicated to the revered Ramses II, whom Ramses III looked to as a role model for kingship.

61 Medinet Habu from the air. *Photograph Wayne R. Frostick*

The entrance gateway to Medinet Habu is modelled on a *migdol*, a Syrian fortified tower (*62*). As there was no real need for this fortified tower, it was purely decorative. This gateway indicates that Ramses had an interest in foreign architecture which may have developed through his many travels. It has been suggested that this had been built as a tribute to the Syrian campaigns of his ancestors, and in remembrance of the Nubian and Egyptian dead. The images in the third floor of the east side of the gateway show Ramses III in intimate positions with the royal women and suggests this was used as a harem. The complex here consists of two groups of three rooms, in addition to a roof complex with further small structures. However, the inscriptions in the gateway do not tell what it was used for and the excavators of Medinet Habu believe that it is unlikely that the main harem would be placed outside of the enclosure wall where they could be in danger. It is more likely that the gateway was seen as a temporary retreat where the women had views of activities, processions and rituals being carried out in and outside of the temple.

It seems likely that they may have been permanently housed in the second palace at Medinet Habu (so called as it was built over an earlier mud-brick palace), which was built near the end of the reign of Ramses III to celebrate his *heb sed* (*63*).

At the back of the palace there are three apartments which are comparable to the women's quarters at the palace of Amenhotep III at Malkata, and the palace at Amarna. The apartments are reached by a maze of narrow corridors, which separate it from the rest of the palace. The rest of the palace is also likely to be the women's quarters and consists of a shower (64) and bathroom, indicating the sleeping quarters may be at the rear of the palace. There is some archaeological evidence of a pleasure garden, accessible from this palace, including a pool and small garden structures.

62 Migdol, Medinet Habu.
Photograph Wayne R. Frostick

63 Palace, Medinet Habu.
Photograph Geoffrey Webb

64 Shower, Medinet Habu. *Photograph Wayne R. Frostick*

OTHER BUILDING WORKS

The *Harris Papyrus* records the other building work that Ramses III carried out including a shrine to Amun at Karnak, a shrine to Re at Heliopolis, and a shrine to Ptah at Memphis. The bark shrine at Karnak was built outside what would have been the entrance at the time, but is now the second pylon. This shrine was used in the processions of the sacred statues during festivals and acted as a resting place for the bark. Bark shrines were normally only large enough to accommodate the sacred bark of the divine statue for a short period of time, and did not normally contain anything other than an altar upon which the god could be 'refreshed' before continuing on his journey. Ramses bark shrine is in itself a temple and if it had been anywhere but Karnak would have been a large monument. It has a courtyard with 16 Osirid statues for pillars, in a similar way to his temple at Medinet Habu (65).

65 Osirid statues, Medinet Habu. *Photograph Geoffrey Webb*

66 Temple of Khonsu, Karnak. *Photograph Wayne R. Frostick*

Ramses III and his son Ramses IV did substantial work at the temple of Khonsu (*66, 67 and 68*) at Karnak temple, although by the end of the reign of Ramses IV only the inner part of the temple had been completed. Ramses III also started a decorating project at the rear of Luxor temple, in order to maintain and improve the temple built by Ramses II.

He held numerous annual religious festivals and bestowed many gifts on the temple over his 31-year reign. These gifts included vast quantities of barley, oils, herds of cattle, copper, silver, gold, a golden bark of Amun-Re and a vineyard to the temple of Amun at Karnak, which was renowned for making very sweet red wine. These gifts greatly enriched the temple of Amun, and during his reign Karnak received 86 per cent of everything Ramses gave to temples Egypt-wide. It owned a quarter of cultivable land, 9 Syrian towns, 56 Egyptian towns, 433 gardens, 83 ships, half a million cattle and governed 86,000 artisans and therefore all the products they produced. This increase in the wealth and royal favour of the cult of Amun would prove to be the downfall of the later Ramesside Period.

67 Ramses at the temple of Khonsu, Karnak. *Photograph Wayne R. Frostick*

68 Ramses at the Temple of Khonsu, Karnak. *Photograph Wayne R. Frostick*

TOMB

Ramses III was buried in the Valley of the Kings (KVII) in a tomb originally built by his father but abandoned when the tomb corridor cut into the tomb of Amenmesse. Ramses, however, decided to continue with the cutting of this tomb. To avoid the roof of Amenmesse's tomb he altered the angle of the corridor so it sloped upwards before straightening up again. He also added Hathor-headed columns at the entrance to the tomb, which is unique. Ramses clearly liked adding new architectural elements to his monuments.

The tomb has four corridors which were built by Setnakht, and the first two were decorated with the *Litany of Re*, a New Kingdom religious text that praises the 75 forms of the sun god. Ramses added numerous antechambers to these corridors decorated with scenes of the royal armoury including bows, arrows and boats, blind harpers, the luxury items of the king's treasury, including imported Aegean jars which may have contained wine or oils, and even a room full of snake goddesses. All of the decoration is in painted sunk-relief.

These corridors eventually lead to the pillared burial chamber and four side rooms; one on each corner. Unfortunately the burial chamber is very badly water damaged, but some of the reliefs have survived and show that it was decorated with the *Book of Gates*, describing the 12 hours of the nocturnal journey of the underworld. Each hour would be separated by a gate or portal. It was also decorated with the *Book of the Earth* which became very popular during the reign of Ramses VI which also recorded the nocturnal journey of the sun. This journey was separated into four sections with the climax being the sun being raised from the earth by Nun, the deity of the primeval waters, representing the creation of the world. In one of the side rooms there is the text from the *Book of the Divine Cow* which shows the divine cow carrying the sun over the vault of the sky.

The sarcophagus was found in the burial chamber and it is thought that this was originally intended as an outer container for Sety II, although it was never used by him. The sarcophagus lid is currently in the Fitzwilliam Museum in Cambridge. The second innermost coffin was decorated exactly like the cartonnage coffin of Ramses's father and was found in the royal cache at Deir el Bahri housing the body of Amenhotep III. The lid to this coffin was damaged in antiquity by robbers as it was thrown from the case to access the body within.

Of Ramses III's funerary equipment only five cast-bronze shabti figures have been found. It is very likely that, considering the wealth of Egypt, the funeral goods of Ramses III would have been immense. In life he emulated Ramses II so it is likely that he would have wanted to have a burial that would be worthy of his namesake.

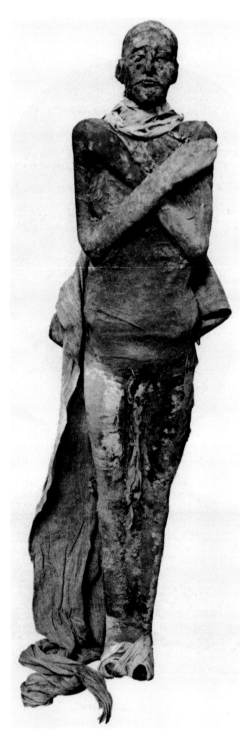

69 Mummy of Ramses III. *Photograph from Elliot Smith 1912*

Two pieces of graffiti in the burial chamber of KVII name Butehamun, a scribe involved in the rewrapping of the royal mummies in the royal caches. This rewrapping was done in year 13 of Smendes I (approximately 1070 BC) and is also recorded on the new bandages of the king's mummy. Graffiti in the tomb from the Third Intermediate Period tells of a tomb inspection and then later in the Third Intermediate Period his tomb was reused, with the burial of a nobleman. This was a common practice in the Third Intermediate Period, as it was a particularly unstable economic era and new tombs were not being built. Ramses's tomb has been open since the Graeco-Roman Period, and was often visited as a tourist attraction.

CONCLUSION

Trying to reach the individual behind the official image of Ramses III is quite difficult but we are able to see that he was a very strong, level-headed king who was ruling in a time of extreme difficulty. He had many problems early in his reign with the invasions of the Libyans and the 'Sea People', but he was able to manoeuvre the Egyptian army into a victory against them. He even encouraged his army to fight by sea, in the first recorded naval battle, even though the Egyptians on the whole feared the sea. He was at the front of the battle in his chariot, which would encourage his army, and assure them he was a true divine king.

Ramses was quite family oriented and there are tombs for his sons in the Valley of the Queens where he is shown accompanying them into the afterlife and personally introducing them to the gods. His children were equally devoted to Ramses as the spectacular *Harris Papyrus* would suggest. Ramses IV chose to dictate this papyrus listing all of his father's deeds in his 31-year rule. Even though Ramses chose not to make it clear who the crown prince was on the monuments it is possible that they were a close family, who made use of their time together when their father was home from his various foreign campaigns.

Ramses also showed devotion for his own father, indicated by the reuse of his abandoned tomb and using the same design for his inner coffins.

Even in an unstable time Ramses devotion to religion remained as strong as ever, with a concentration on building works at the temples of Karnak, Heliopolis, and Luxor. Although the reputation of Ramses III has not survived to the levels of Ramses II he has received a type of eternal notoriety as the inspiration for Boris Karloff's costume in the 1932 horror film *The Mummy* (69).

SIXTEEN

NATSEFAMUN

A PRIEST OF AMUN

INTRODUCTION

The setting for the life of Natsefamun is the temple of Amun, at Karnak. He was a priest here during the reign of Ramses XI in the twentieth dynasty. The temple of Amun had gradually gained in power and wealth throughout the New Kingdom, until, during the reign of Ramses XI, the priests of Amun had actually taken over the throne and ruled the south of Egypt.

In the final years of the New Kingdom between years 12 and 19 of the reign of Ramses XI a civil war started in the south of Egypt. The Viceroy of Nubia, Panehsy, was based at Thebes and came into conflict with the High Priest of Amun, Amenhotep. At this point the High Priests of Amun held almost the same power as the king, although the king had military support. This high priest was denied his position for nine months and eventually turned to Ramses XI for help. Being a man of god, Ramses commanded his army to go on campaign to destroy Panehsy who was exiled to Nubia. At some point between years 12 and 19 of Ramses XI, Herihor takes over the role of 'High Priest' and also the titles of Panehsy. This was the first time that religious and military titles were held by one man, and essentially made Herihor more powerful than the king. This left Ramses XI in a very weak position and he became king in name only ruling alongside Herihor. Herihor places his names and title of 'High Priest' in cartouches in the manner of a king. Herihor died before Ramses XI and his successor, Piankhy, may have been his son-in-law. After Ramses XI died Egypt divided in two, with Lower Egypt being ruled by King Smendes from Tanis who legitimised his claim to the throne by marrying a daughter of Ramses XI, and Upper Egypt being ruled by Piankhy, albeit briefly. This started a dynasty of Theban

High Priests, all successors of Piankhy and all holding military and religious titles. It is generally believed that Piankhy was himself of Libyan origin and may have been from a line of settled mercenaries in the Egyptian army.

Despite the divided Egypt the Tanite and Theban families were related by marriage and were amicable, making a peaceful but economically weak society. This weakened economy had many downfalls for the Egyptians, and for the king meant that royal building works were not as grand and tombs for officials were not built. Therefore officials reused older tombs or were buried in undecorated rock-cut tombs.

It was during the reign of Pinedjem I, the son of Piankhy, that the reburial of New Kingdom royalty was carried out, which produced the royal caches. However, their reburial was not solely for religious purposes, as this re-wrapping was a perfect opportunity for the priests to 'recycle' the gold that the tomb robbers may have missed.

Gold was rare during this period as Nubia was now lost to Egypt. Egypt had controlled Nubia from the Old Kingdom, exploiting the gold mines for millennia. Trading expeditions to the Levant were also rare during this period, cutting off another major trade route. Egypt during this time was not the powerful, respected country that it once was.

Natsefamun was a priest, with the title 'Scribe of the accounts of the Sacred White Bulls of Amun' and would not have held a position of great responsibility, but was located at one of the richest temples in the whole of Egypt. His duties involved caring for the bulls at Karnak, which were dedicated and sacrificed in honour of the divine Theban triad of Amun, Mut and Khonsu. No doubt he was responsible for feeding them, and recording the quantity and quality of grain that they were fed. He was also an incense bearer for the ritual ceremonies which were carried out on a daily basis. As he was not a senior priest, he may only have been expected to perform his priestly duties for three months every year before returning back to his village and his family. This was common in Egypt; most young men were conscripted into the temple for a few months on an annual rotary system. Only the high priest and other senior priests made a vocation out of the priesthood and worked at the temple permanently.

When Natsefamun died he was middle aged, 45–55 years old, and showed signs of numerous diseases that would make his life difficult. One of the most interesting is traces of the parasitic worm that causes elephantiasis. This type of disease is very difficult to detect in mummies due to primarily affecting soft tissues. An examination of the scrotum of his mummy presented evidence of the adult parasitic filaria worm. It is impossible to see at which stage of the disease Natsefamun had reached, although if he had been in the later stages of the disease he may have had a grossly enlarged scrotum and swollen legs. Examination of the femoral arteries of the legs show marked plaques of atheroma, caused by high levels of cholesterol and saturated fat in his diet. This probably great caused discomfort in his life and could have eventually led to gangrene and amputation of his legs and feet. Currently there have been no other reports since this autopsy carried out in 1992, of filaria parasites being discovered in other mummies.

Two species of mosquito carry lymphatic filariasis, one that bites primarily at night and the second that breeds in unclean water, drains and cesspools. The filaria worms lay larvae instead of eggs, which gestate in the stomach of the mosquito for about 10 days. When the mosquito bites a human these microfilariae (larvae) infect the host. They then take 8-24 months to mature into adult worms. The adult worms then have a lifespan of two to five years. The adult worms block up the lymphatic channels causing swelling in the legs, scrotum and vulva. It could take up to 20 years for the infection to develop into fully-fledged elephantiasis. The areas affected by elephantiasis caused by filaria worms in decreasing order are the legs, scrotum, arms, penis, breasts, vulva and the head. Elephantiasis is characterised by nodular, warty changes to the thickening skin.

Natsefamun would suffer from dizzy spells and chronic pains in his legs and feet where plaques of atheroma would have started to clog his arteries. This would make walking difficult, and if he had not died when he had he may have had to suffer the added problem of having one or both of his legs amputated. His groin might have been swollen and ungainly, or at best painful or uncomfortable.

In addition to this he also had osteoarthritis in his hip, and changes in his cervical spine indicate that he had pains all the way up to his neck. These problems would make standing and walking painful.

He also may have suffered from an eye condition called peripheral neuritis, which is caused by the degeneration of the nerve fibres. This would mean that Natsefamun would suffer from headaches due to eye strain and it may have led ultimately to blindness.

A study of his teeth show that he did not have too many dental problems other than extensive wear which may have led to tooth ache. This wear may have been caused by a diet consisting of excessive amounts of acidic fruits. Strangely enough the wear was not just on the biting surface of the teeth as was normal, but also between the teeth indicating that he over-cleaned his teeth, causing damage. Teeth would have been cleaned using a twig and natron.

LIFE IN THE TEMPLE

Food was plentiful for the priests of Karnak temple. Most temples were supported by their own estates, which were given by the king or wealthy members of the community. In the reign of Ramses III, for example, the temple of Amun at Karnak owned 900 square miles of agricultural land, vineyards, quarries and mines. This would mean that Natsefamun, even as a part-time priest was well-fed.

The daily rituals of the temple revolved around the care of the sacred statue of the deity. There were elaborate rituals, involving dressing, washing and feeding the divine statue twice a day. The contents of the type of meal offered to the god are inscribed on the inner sanctuary walls and probably would include:

◇   Bread (various kinds)

◇   Ox, cow and goat meat

◇   Antelope and gazelle meat

◇   Vegetables (onions and leeks)

◇   Fruit (dates, figs and pomegranates)

◇   Water, milk, wine and beer

After the god had 'eaten', the 'left-over' food was then offered to the statues of former kings and officials before being distributed among the priesthood. As Natsefamun participated with religious rituals he would have eaten and drunk the best produce that Egypt had to offer; food suitable for a god. This resulted in his health problems, of high cholesterol, obesity and very worn teeth.

The mummy of Natsefamun was clean shaven with no evidence of hair on his head or face. This was customary for priests, as they shaved all their body hair on a daily basis to eliminate the problems of lice, ensuring they were clean before entering the temple. All of these cleansing rituals took place in the sacred lake at Karnak where the priests jumped into the water that filled up naturally from the Nile. They then donned gowns or kilts of pure white linen.

As well as having to shave all of his hair, whilst he was performing his priestly duties Natsefamun would adhere to numerous other rules and regulations. This included not eating fish, due to the preparation being similar to that of mummification. They also were not supposed to wear wool, or have sex within the temple complex. Ideally the priests were celibate but as Natsefamun was a part-time priest it was unreasonable to insist he did not marry, so it is more likely that during the three months as a priest he did not participate in sexual intercourse.

DEATH

Natsefamun, probably died due to an insect bite to the tongue, as his mummy shows that it was so swollen that it could not be pushed back into his mouth, possibly causing suffocation. The insect may have got into his mouth via his food. Although this is the favoured cause of death it has also been suggested that he may have died due to a tongue disease or strangulation.

It would seem that Natsefamun was plagued by insect bites, as the bite from a mosquito carrying the filariasis worm and the fatal sting on his tongue would suggest. Working closely with the bulls for three months a year involved being surrounded by insects all of the time and the villages were breeding grounds for insects with cess pools, irrigation channels and stagnant water in the canals off the main river.

BURIAL

His body was found at Gournah in 1823 and was first scientifically studied at Leeds Museum shortly afterwards, the examination taking several months to complete (*colour plate 19*).

Natsefamun was buried in a highly decorated coffin which was an 'off the peg' example, made and decorated with the names and titles left blank for the new owner to add his own. His body was mummified to a high standard ensuring that he had a beautifully preserved body for the afterlife. Natsefamun was obviously not poor.

CONCLUSION

With the priest Natsefamun there is little evidence of his life, both in the temple and out of it. It is likely that as he worked as the 'Scribe of the White Bulls of Amun' in the temple he may have owned cattle in his village. He was probably chosen for this priestly role due to his abilities with his own cattle. He was also literate indicating he may have hailed from a middle-class literate family who were land owners rather than farmers.

However, it would appear that it may have been his occupation that killed him, being bitten by an insect on his tongue that made it swell to such proportions that it suffocated him. He may have been plagued by insect bites throughout his life, leading to parasitic worm infections which in their extremity could have led to elephantiasis, which although not an immediate killer can make life difficult if not impossible.

SEVENTEEN

HOREMKENISI

A THIRD INTERMEDIATE PERIOD PRIEST

INTRODUCTION

Horemkenisi was a scribe and priest who lived in approximately 1070 BC in the twentieth dynasty, in the Third Intermediate Period, and may have been a contemporary of Natsefamun.

LIFE OF HOREMKENISI

During the civil war in the final years of Ramses XI, Horemkenisi was a young man working in Thebes and watching the events with nervous anticipation.

His name Horemkenisi was a rare one and means 'Horus in the embrace of Isis', but this makes it easy to identify him from various items of graffiti in the Theban area. From this graffiti we are aware of the titles that he held as well as his movements.

His main title, and the position that took up most of his time, was that of 'Chief of the Gang in the Place of Truth' which was a late variation of the New Kingdom title 'Chief Workman' or 'Foreman', the position held by Paneb in the nineteenth dynasty.

Other titles included 'Scribe of the task in the Horizon of Eternity' (the royal tomb), which refers to his work at Deir el Medina as a scribe. He also held priestly titles of '*Wab* Priest in front of Amun in the temple United with Eternity' which identifies him as low-ranking purification priest at Medinet Habu. He also held the similar title '*Wab* Priest of Amun-Re, King of the Gods' at Karnak temple on the east bank of the Nile and in this role may have met Natsefamun.

From the graffiti we are able to identify his father as Huysheri, who was also a 'Wab Priest' at Medinet Habu, indicating it was a hereditary title passed on from father to son. As Horemkenisi was only a low-ranking priest, his priestly titles would not have prevented him from marrying and having children but there is no evidence that he had a family.

Horemkenisi started his scribal and priestly career during the reign of Ramses XI, and was still active in year 20 of Pinedjem I. In his life Horemkenisi did not receive much promotion, as he remained a *wab* priest, the lowest ranking religious position, and his last promotion in the village was to 'Chief Workman'; it is thought he may have died a few years later.

Horemkenisi was probably taught to read and write at a young age either at classes held in Deir el Medina or at Medinet Habu. He showed a particular talent for reading and writing, and became a temple scribe.

Through his three positions as 'Chief Workman', 'Scribe' and 'Wab' Priest' Horemkenisi had a diverse working life. As he was promoted no higher than a *wab* priest it is thought that his main job was the 'Chief Workman' and 'Scribe' and the priestly title was a secondary role.

As 'Chief Workmen' he was responsible for the workforce at Deir el Medina, although during the twenty-first dynasty the population here had dwindled to a few workmen, the 'Scribe of the Tomb' and the two 'Chief Workmen'. As the building of elaborate royal monuments had ceased, their role was very different from the New Kingdom population of the village. They were more concerned with inspection tours of the necropolis and the supervision of new burials, restoration and reburial of older mummies. Graffiti tells of these inspections:

> Year 20, second month of summer the coming by the *wab* priest of Amun-Re King of the Gods, the great one of the Gang in the Place of Truth, Horemkenisi, to make initial inspection of the Great Valley, with the agents of the gang who were under his direction Heramunpehaef, Kenamun and Sapaankh.

They probably carved the graffiti during these inspections, either as a record of attendance or as a way of ensuring their names were recorded for eternity. From the graffiti we can see that Horemkenisi was responsible for a large area, as his name has been found from the Valley of the Kings to 1.7km south of Medinet Habu indicating he may have spent time searching for old tombs in these areas. This inspection and search for tombs was not purely for the protection of the deceased from robbery. Once tombs had been found the bodies could be searched for valuables, before being rewrapped and reburied. Once old mummies had been discovered they would be taken to Medinet

Habu or an unused tomb to be rewrapped, labelled, placed in a coffin and put into a tomb which formed the royal caches found at the end of the nineteenth century. The removal of jewellery from mummies and gilding from coffins aided the weak economy and formed an ulterior motive for the reburial of these ancient kings.

As a scribe, Horemkenisi was literate in hieratic and perhaps in hieroglyphs as well, and as mentioned learnt this at a young age. He was responsible for keeping records of the work of his subordinates and he may have carried with him a scribal palette and pens made from hollowed-out reeds. This would make note taking and graffiti writing convenient and easy.

Wab priests were the lowest of the priestly ranks, and were known as 'Purification Priests' suggesting that cleaning was a major part of their role, but they also were bearers of the god's image in procession. At the time of Horemkenisi the oracle of the god parading through the streets was at its most popular due to a mistrust of the legal court, or *knbt*. Horemkenisi helped with the manipulation of the god during these oracle processions. The questions were addressed directly to the god or handed over in written form, and the way the god moved through the swaying of the priests below would dictate an answer.

On his coffin Horemkenisi has the title '*Wab* in front' indicating he was either the *wab* priest who walked in front of the bark carrying a chest and who was allowed to wear silver sandals, or he was placed at the front when carrying the sacred bark on his shoulders. Either way he was singled out for a specific role.

It is possible that he was never promoted from *wab* priest as his father and ancestors had never progressed further than this position. It is, however, probable that Horemkenisi's administration roles took up most of his time and he was unable to commit fully to the role of a priest.

As a *wab* priest (albeit part-time) he had a shaved head and face, which is supported by his mummy which also shows short stubble re-growth revealing that his hair and eyebrows were black, and his beard was black with streaks of white.

During this period the workers of Deir el Medina actually lived within the compound of Medinet Habu as there were general fears of attacks by Libyan tribes, from the western desert. His house at Medinet Habu has not yet been identified, but that of his companion Butehamun has, and it was a rather grand house. Horemkenisi was not as wealthy as Butehamun, so his house would have been smaller and plainer. The walls were of mud brick and he would have had a door frame made of reused stone. The flat roof of the house may have been used as a recreational garden or as a storage area.

As Horemkenisi came from such an economically poor and unstable period we know very little about his life, although the examination of his body tells us that he was relatively healthy. He was short and plump, probably about 5ft 5in tall although the osteoarthritis in his spine made him stoop a little in later life. Numerous folds of skin on the mummy hint towards obesity, which may be due to a liking of honey cakes. He may have also had his ears pierced, although no jewellery was found on his person.

The most noticeable injury that he suffered was a heavy blow to the face, which fractured and displaced his nasal bone. It was not properly fixed and set slightly to the right, causing a constriction of the left nostril which may have caused him some breathing difficulties. This blow to the face may have been accidental or it may have been caused by an irate subordinate punching him in the face.

Like many ancient Egyptians Horemkenisi suffered from bilhazia, a parasitic infection caught from water snails that breed in stagnant water. He also suffered from untreated malaria, which is contracted from the mosquito, indicating that like Natsefamun he may have been partial to insect bites.

Horemkenisi also had a rare condition in his thoracic vertebrae known as diffuse idiopathic skeletal hyperostosis (DISH), a deformity of the bone that has an appearance of dripped wax; he may not have had any symptoms other than stiffness in the back, shoulders and neck.

Despite all of these minor ailments chronic toothache may have made Horemkenisi incredibly grouchy. His teeth were all heavily worn due to his advanced age. He had lost three teeth in life due to abscesses, although whether they fell out or were pulled is uncertain. The pus from abscesses eats through the root of the tooth and the gums before the tooth falls out, amidst great pain. Two other teeth were so worn the pulp was exposed, allowing bacteria to get in causing more abscesses to develop. The pus was starting to penetrate into his maxillary sinuses, as indicated by a patch of wrinkled skin on his cheek. This would have caused great pain in most of his face and jaw. There were very few cures for toothache other than a mouth wash although it was possible to drain the abscess by sticking a hollow reed into it; albeit without an anaesthetic. Horemkenisi also had two caries (decay), which was unusual for Egyptians as there was very little sugar in their diet. Coupled with the caries his obesity suggests he could have a liking for honey, which was often made into cakes.

His mummy gives no clue as to what killed him, although we know that he was in his 60s when he died. The good condition of his hands, feet and eyes indicate that he may have died of a heart attack or stroke causing him to fall face down in the sand. The rest of his body had been attacked by insects and was in an advanced state of decomposition indicating he may have been lying where he fell for two or more days until he was found. Maybe he died in the course of duty whilst inspecting the tombs. He seemed to have died with his mouth open and due to the level of decomposition the embalmers decided to leave it and continue quickly with the embalming.

TOMB

Horemkenisi was embalmed somewhere close to the Nile as the study of floral remains found in his bandages suggest. Most leading members of the family of priests of Amun were buried in various tombs at Deir el Bahri, and it was in these tombs that the royal caches were found. Horemkenisi was no different. He was buried in a royal tomb in the temple of Mentuhotep II at Deir el Bahri. His coffin was placed at the bottom of the 16ft burial shaft of Mentuhotep's wife, Sadeh. Her remains were in the tomb with a cartonnage mask, leather sandals and canopic equipment. They clearly just swept the original occupant to one side to make room for Horemkenisi.

The temple of Mentuhotep II was a pilgrimage site until a rock fall damaged it at the end of the twentieth dynasty, whilst Horemkenisi was a young man. It is possible that he visited this site when he was alive and chose this tomb himself as it was discreet and may be missed by the robbers.

As finance was an issue with Horemkenisi his funeral was probably a very simple affair with his coffin being carried by his friends rather than being pulled on an ox-drawn sled or cart. There were no burial goods at all with him so he would not have had an entourage of offering bearers that we see regularly in tomb art. He probably was accompanied just by a priest with a papyrus to read the last rites, which may have been performed in the nearby temple of Hatshepsut. These rites would primarily have consisted of the 'Opening of the Mouth' ceremony ensuring the deceased was able to breath, speak and eat in the afterlife. Then the coffin was taken to the tomb and lowered into the burial shaft. Horemkenisi did not have any papyrus or shabtis as was common for this period suggesting that he was not wealthy enough to purchase them. His coffin was laid undisturbed in the centre of the burial chamber and the breast of the coffin was still draped with garlands of plaited rush leaves. The only other funerary goods were papyrus stalks and sticks with leaves on the top. The weakened economy explains the decline in elaborate funerary goods, which were replaced with religious texts written on the coffin of Horemkenisi.

He only had one coffin and a mummy board, when two coffins and a mummy board were more common; this is another indication of his economic problems. It was an 'off the peg' coffin with standard images and texts with spaces left for the deceased's name to be written. Both the coffin and mummy board were made of *ficus sycamors* (sycamore wood), a native Egyptian wood. Once the shape of the arms, wig and raised abdomen were carved from the planks of wood, the whole lid was plastered which provided a good painting surface for the artists. The hands and the false beard were made of separate pieces of wood.

The mummy board was made by hollowing out a tree trunk and cutting it in half, which fitted over the mummified body. The mummy of Horemkenisi was well wrapped in alternate layers of bandages and large sheets, with folds of linen used to pad out any hollows creating a life-like appearance. The limbs were wrapped individually with the ankles, knees and elbows tied with twisted linen to keep them in place. A large sheet was placed over the head and twisted to make a false beard. Inscriptions in black ink on one of the bandages have Horemkenisi's name clearly identifying him as the mummified individual.

Many beetles have been found within the wrappings indicating that the body was decomposing before it was wrapped. The brain had not been removed by the embalmers, and it appears to have disappeared through a combination of natural decomposition and the activity of beetles. The embalmers possibly thought that the late arrival of the body made it pointless to remove the brain, as it was time consuming and would not have prevented the decomposition that had already started.

His internal organs were removed through a typical incision in the abdomen, although this opening was not stitched up, but sealed with resin. The empty abdomen was filled with linen, mud, seeds and straw. His heart had also been removed which was very unusual. The internal organs were not mummified and they do not appear to have been buried with the mummy. If these were found they could tell us more about the diseases that Horemkenisi may have suffered from.

CONCLUSION

Horemkenisi is a particularly interesting character as he helped to create the royal caches, which have been so important for modern egyptological research. If he had not carried out the inspections of the royal tombs many of the royal mummies may have been destroyed over the centuries. Horemkenisi is therefore an example of how an unimportant individual can make a very important contribution to history, albeit without realising it at the time.

EIGHTEEN

ASRU

CHANTRESS OF AMUN

INTRODUCTION

Asru was a 'Chantress of Amun' in the temple of Amun at Karnak around 900 BC in the Third Intermediate Period. This was a period of political unrest, between the New Kingdom and the Late Period and saw Egypt divided with the High Priests of Amun ruling Southern Egypt and the Tanis kings ruling the North. Despite the division of Egypt in this manner the two rulers were amicable with no animosity in Egypt at this time.

She was of noble birth, being perhaps the daughter of a priest, elite workman or government official. On her coffin, only her matrilineal connections are mentioned indicating that she had inherited the position from her mother, Tadu-Amen, who had inherited it from her mother. The exact role of the chantress is obscure, but numerous images on the walls of Karnak temple show they took part in religious processions, singing, dancing and playing instruments. They may have participated in the daily rituals of the temple, possibly accompanying the priests in their chants and prayers, prior to dressing, and washing the statue of the god and making offerings to him.

The role of chantress as a full-time position sometimes proved an effective, yet acceptable, way of employing older unmarried women, and although Asru inherited the position from her mother there seems to be no evidence that she had married. There is no evidence on her mummified remains to indicate that she had children, and there is no mention on her coffin of a husband. Perhaps she dedicated her life to Amun voluntarily or it was used as an escape for an elderly spinster (*70*).

70 Nefertari 'Chantress of Amun'. *Copyright: Petrie Museum of Egyptian Archaeology, University College London, UC 38042*

Asru's body was discovered in two highly decorated coffins indicating that she had personal wealth, although we do not know how well paid her role as chantress was (*colour plate 20*). It is likely that she had residency at the temple or on temple land, which was plentiful during this period; she also was given rations in the form of grain. On a daily basis she was given a share of the offerings of Amun. Despite her wealth and the access to good food, the mummy of Asru was very thin. There was no sign of external disease that could have caused this weight loss so the Manchester Mummy Project examined the mummy closer to find further evidence.

AILMENTS

Asru suffered from a large number of diseases. Remains of her lung and bladder were found inside her abdomen and these were examined closely. She also arrived at Manchester with a package of preserved viscera on her legs. The x-ray showed striped scars on the lung, evidence of the parasitic worm ecchinoccus, commonly known as the dog tapeworm. The cyst causing the scarring was 20cm in diameter and contained immature forms of the tapeworm. The dog tapeworm starts developing in the intestines and burrows through the intestinal wall to the liver, kidney, lungs and brain, developing into a cyst, where the eggs are laid. A cyst in the brain can kill quite rapidly, but with Asru it would only have caused breathlessness and pleurisy. It is also possible that Asru may have noticed some live worms in her stools, although there was no available cure. The dog tapeworm normally lives in sheep, but has been found in numerous mummies who have had contact with contaminated dog faeces. This could suggest that Asru had some contact with a domestic dog, which may have been a pet or part of the temple menagerie.

Asru's lungs also provide evidence of sand pneumoconiosis, a very common disease in ancient Egypt, associated with the inhalation of the wind-blown sand of the desert environment. This can potentially be fatal, and would also have lead to breathlessness and frequent bouts of coughing. Eventually it can affect circulation, causing heart failure. It is likely that Asru may have taken cough remedies made of honey to aid her coughing fits. However, the breathlessness was a major problem in her active life within the walls of Karnak temple.

She also hosted the parasite strongyloides, which is often caught through walking barefoot in water. The worm gets into the blood stream through the hands or feet and travels via the blood cells first to the heart, then the lungs, then the throat and windpipe where they are swallowed into the intestines. Here they grow into adult worms and lay their eggs. These eggs cause bowel problems displayed by blood in stools, chronic diarrhoea and anaemia, which may have ultimately led to her death. The larvae leave the body via the stools and the cycle starts again. Through all these visible signs, Asru may have had some indication that there was something wrong. However, as the annual flood of the Nile meant there were often many stagnant pools and streams of water, avoiding these parasites was virtually impossible.

Asru's bladder tissue produced evidence of bilhazia, another common disease in ancient and modern Egypt. These worms are carried by a water snail present in stagnant water, which gets into the body through blisters or cuts. Via the blood stream they reach the intestines, where the adults lay the eggs, which are spiked and attach themselves to the intestinal wall, causing intestinal tears which can eventually lead to cancer. The eggs laid in the intestines, end up in the bladder via the bloodstream, and are then expelled through urine and the cycle starts again. This disease was particularly common amongst farmers and fishermen due to their constant contact with stagnant water. The species of bilhazia that Asru was carrying, can lead to blood in the urine; eventually the bladder calcifies causing water retention resulting in swelling, pain, exhaustion and sickness. Despite this pain and sickness there was no cure for this common disease.

The fourth parasitic worm was inside her skull where larval skins from the parasite, chrysomyia were found. These caused a cyst on her brain and may have been what killed her.

When Asru died she was elderly by Egyptian standards and she had evidence in her fingers of osteoarthritis, with numerous changes to her joints. She also had calcification in the aorta, the bronchi and the lower legs and feet, as well as chronic arthritis throughout the body. All of this would suggest that she was over 50 years old, although there were no signs of the changes that would occur if she were over 70, placing her age at death at over 60. A few years before her death she fractured her lumbar vertebrae, as indicated by the bone growth over the lumbar area. Increased calcification of the spine in the lower region joined with this old injury, would send sciatica-like pain down her left leg due to pressure on the nerve endings of the spine. This fracture was caused by a severe fall. X-rays of her spine also show a 'slipped disc' and the presence of abnormal cells in her right mastoid bone indicative of infection and may have caused her earache.

As a chantress of Amun, Asru may have been expected to play an instrument, sing or dance. If she regularly played the harp this may have contributed to the damage evident in her finger joints. In her later years she would not have been able to play the harp at all, as septic arthritis in her left hand had completely destroyed her third digit.

Further investigation was carried out to find out what her occupation really was through finger and toe prints taken by Chief Inspector Fletcher of the Greater Manchester Police. As her fingers could not be easily manoeuvred, putty was applied to her hands and feet. The casts were then painted with acrylic, which was then pealed off. This was then inked and printed. This suggested to the police that she was a lady in her late 40s, which is an underestimate as the rest of her body indicates her late 50s or 60s (*colour plate 21*). Her hands show she was unaccustomed to hard work and her fingers did not show signs of prolonged harp playing. Her feet also did not show the flattening and wear of a barefoot dancer. This indicates that Asru may have been a singer rather than dancer or musician. This obviously was problematic if she was breathless or in pain.

Her surviving front teeth show that she had a substantial overbite; her upper incisors completely cover the lower ones. Many of her back teeth were missing and she suffered painful toothache for most of her later life. There was a serious infection in her jaw, with damage caused to the bone around the roots of her teeth, due to abscesses, resulting in tooth loss. This immense pain would affect her singing substantially. The remaining teeth, of which there were not many, did not have any caries as the diet in ancient Egypt did not consist of many sweet foods, but they were very worn and showed signs of marked periodontal disease. The airborne sand, plus sand and sometimes granite dust added to the grain when making bread to help it grind easier contributed to this wear. There was minimal pain relief and the *Ebers Medical Papyrus* lists a few remedies although the effectiveness is uncertain:

> The beginning of remedies to fasten a tooth: powdered *ammi*, yellow ochre and honey are mixed together and the tooth is filled therewith.
>
> To expel growth of purulence in the gums: sycamore fruit, beans, honey, malachite and yellow ochre are ground and applied to the tooth.
>
> To treat a tooth which is eaten away where the gums begin: cumin, frankincense and carob pulp are powdered and applied to the tooth.

It would be interesting to know what remedies Asru used.

CONCLUSION

Although Asru was probably born to the Egyptian upper classes and would have led a privileged life, she still was clearly affected by the hazards of the harsh Egyptian climate.

From all of these ailments she experienced increasing pain as she got older, and would relish any painkillers that were available, and it has been suggested that she may have partaken in a painkiller made of Lotus flowers mixed with wine. This mixture may have had opiate properties which would have eased the pain a little. However, the ancient Egyptians had a much stronger constitution than a modern westerner, and her pain threshold would have been higher.

Her mummy had a shaved head, with hair that had just started to re-grow, which was not unusual in the Egyptian society. The hair was shaved on men and women of all statuses, to prevent fleas and lice. Most people wore headdresses, caps or elaborate wigs to disguise the bald head. The hair was removed using tweezers, razors and hair removal wax made of bird bones and fly dirt, which was applied and ripped off, removing the hair. Although her parasitic infections were caused by unhygienic living conditions, she would have been very clean, using perfumes, soap and make-up which was normal for all Egyptians but which also formed part of her ritualistic duties as an employee of Karnak. Her head had been anointed with aromatic oils before she was wrapped. However, for much of the time she probably walked around bare foot and therefore could be stepping into all sorts of things; any blisters or open wounds would be ideal for these worms to enter into the body.

Despite hosting a number of these parasitic worms Asru led a long and probably full life in the very powerful temple of Amun at Karnak. Even when she was wracked with pain, she no doubt took part in the daily rituals for as long as she was capable.

We do not know what she died of, but considering her advanced years it may simply have been old age although anaemia or a cyst on the brain could have been the cause. She was mummified to a high standard and was placed in a nest of two decorated coffins. Her body is currently residing in the Manchester Museum.

NINETEEN

CLEOPATRA
THE LAST QUEEN OF EGYPT

INTRODUCTION

The last queen of Egypt, Cleopatra VII is one of the most famous. There are many details available about her life and therefore it is possible to paint an elaborate image of the woman behind the legend.

FAMILY AND CHILDHOOD

Life in the Ptolemaic royal family was one of deceit and danger, and Cleopatra's childhood was built primarily on mistrust. Cleopatra's father was Ptolemy XII Dionysus, nicknamed Auletes or 'Flute-Player,' who came to the throne in 80 BC after his two predecessors had been murdered. His father was Ptolemy XI and his mother was a Syrian concubine. In order to reinforce his royal lineage and therefore lessen the damage of his non-royal mother he stressed the link with his father by adopting the name *Philopater* (Father-lover) and adding this to his titles.

He married his sister Cleopatra V Tryphaena to further reinforce his claim, and even in the Ptolemaic Period incestuous marriages were reserved purely for the royal family. Auletes Ptolemy XII had other wives, as was traditional, and fathered six children. The children of his first wife Cleopatra V were: Cleopatra VI, Berenice IV and Cleopatra VII (born 70 BC). The children of his second wife were: Arsinoe IV, Ptolemy XIII (born in 61 BC) and Ptolemy XIV.

Despite these numerous children Auletes had a reputation for homosexuality. On a stela at Philae there is graffiti where a number of men claim to have been his lover. He was thought to be a decadent king, and it is recorded that he danced around dressed as Dionysus and became enraged if others did not accompany him. He was not very popular in Egypt due to what was considered his fawning attitude to Rome, as well as being a weak and cruel ruler. In 57 BC Rome took Cyprus which was ruled by Auletes' brother who then committed suicide. The indifference of Auletes to this death gained the wrath of the Alexandrian mob, who were already angered at the bribes given to Rome by their king, leading to Auletes fleeing Egypt in 60 BC. He fled to Rome while his eldest daughter, Berenice, took the throne. When Auletes started his journey back to Egypt with the support of Rome, she married a cousin in order to strengthen her claim to the throne. He was not a suitable husband and was nicknamed 'The Salt Fishmonger' so she had him strangled so that she could marry another man, Archelaus, the illegitimate son of King Mithridates of Pontus, an enemy of Rome. At some point during Berenice's three-year reign Cleopatra VI died of unknown causes.

Whilst in Rome Auletes borrowed heavily (10,000 talents) from a Roman financier Rabinus Postumus in order to gain his throne back. When he returned from Rome, with their power behind him, Berenice was executed for treason, and Archelaus died in battle against the Romans and had an honourable burial, against Auletes's wishes. Cleopatra VII was now the pharaoh's oldest child, and the legitimate female heir to the throne.

Ptolemy XII died aged 50 in 52 BC and left his children in Pompey's care. Pompey had helped Auletes to return to Egypt as king and the Romans were demanding repayment for his debts, meaning that Julius Caesar now had a foothold in Egypt. Cleopatra at 19 married her half-brother Ptolemy XIII who was 10 years old and they ascended to the throne in 51 BC. As her husband was still a child she was hailed as king at the Festival of the Apis Bull at Memphis, in the same manner as a co-regent, with the understanding that when Ptolemy XIII was old enough she would give the throne back to him. However, she issued a coin which bore only her image as if her brother and co-ruler did not exist.

Cleopatra held the title 'Lady of the Two Lands' adopted from the kingly title 'Lord of the Two Lands,' also used by Hatshepsut and Nefertari. When she came to the throne, Egypt was in great debt to Rome and in an attempt to lower this debt, she changed the metal content of Egyptian silver and bronze coins by having other metals added to them; then the numerical value of the coins were stamped onto them to prevent them from being devalued due to the changed metal content.

Although of Macedonian decent Cleopatra adopted the Egyptian religion and customs and won the hearts of the Egyptian people in a way her father never had. She, however, remained loyal to her father and continued with her father's work in restoring the temple of Hathor at Dendera which further endeared her to the people of Egypt.

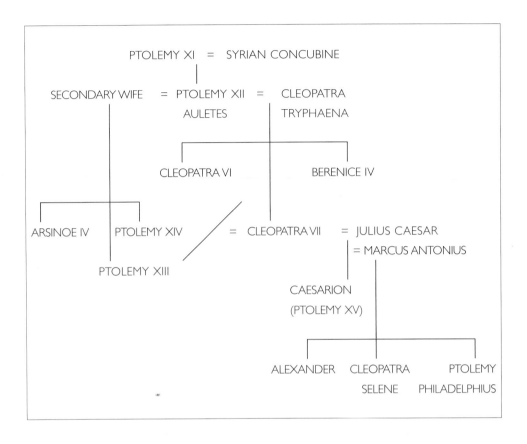

BUILDING PROJECTS

The Greeks associated Hathor with the Greek goddess Aphrodite and throughout the Ptolemaic Period Hathor was very popular. Dendera was originally built by Ptolemy VIII and was added to throughout the reigns of Ptolemy X, XI, XII and Cleopatra VII. The latest work to this temple is from the reign of the Emperor Tiberius; a building period from 116 BC–34 AD. At the rear of the temple beneath the lion-shaped water spouts, directing water away from the decorated walls, is a large image of Cleopatra VII with her son Caesarion Ptolemy XV (*colour plate 22*).

Cleopatra also built at the temple of Koptos in Middle Egypt, whose main deity was Min, the fertility god, worshipped here since the Pre-dynastic Period. The small temple at the back of the complex was dedicated to Geb, the earth god, and was originally started by Nectanebo II. Cleopatra and Caesarion built a new inner shrine to the temple which housed the sacred statue and would only have been accessible to the king and the high priests. This temple was the site of an oracle where people came to seek the advice of the gods, and the remains of a small chamber behind the shrine are still visible where a priest sat and answered the questions on behalf of the god.

Further work was built in the name of Cleopatra and her son at Armant, and in Middle Egypt at the ancient site of Hermopolis. The site was sacred to the war god Montu whose fame spread throughout Egypt. Cleopatra added a birth-house to the site and a sacred lake to celebrate the divine birth of the god Montu. Very little remains on the site now as in the nineteenth century it was all but destroyed for sugar-refining factories.

Cleopatra is commonly shown wearing the vulture headdress associated with the goddess Mut, the consort of Amun. She also associated herself with the goddess Isis and in her marriage ceremony with Antony she dressed as Isis and he as Osiris to reinforce the legitimacy of their marriage, as well as to re-enact one of the most valued love stories of ancient Egypt. The Ptolemies in general adopted the brother–sister marriages to re-enact the Isis–Osiris relationship.

PROBLEMS

The loyalty the people of Upper Egypt had for Cleopatra was used against her by the spin-doctors of Ptolemy XIII who wanted him to receive the power he deserved as pharaoh. Ptolemy's advisors led by a eunuch named Pothinus resented Cleopatra's independence and conspired against her. In 50 BC there was a bad harvest and the supporters of Ptolemy XIII decreed in both Ptolemy's and Cleopatra's name that all the available grain should be sent to Alexandria and none to Middle and Upper Egypt, where Cleopatra's supporters were mostly situated. This angered the Egyptian populace, and they turned against her. They stripped her of her power and forced her into exile in Syria. She fled to Ashkelon on the coast, north of Gaza, along with her sister Arsinoe.

In 48 BC Julius Caesar headed towards Egypt, as he was loyal to Cleopatra's deceased father and had promised him that Cleopatra would remain on the throne. Cleopatra herself had not been idle whilst in Syria and, determined to regain her throne, had amassed an army on Egypt's border. At this time Pompey was fighting with Julius Caesar for control of the Roman Empire. After losing the battle of Pharsalos, Pompey sailed to Alexandria, pursued by Caesar, to seek Ptolemy's protection. Ptolemy's advisors thought it would be safer to side with Caesar, and when Pompey arrived he was stabbed to death while Ptolemy XIII watched. Three days later Caesar reached Alexandria, but before he entered the city, Ptolemy's courtiers brought him a gift, Pompey's head. Pompey had once been Caesar's friend and Caesar was appalled by his brutal murder. He marched into the city, seized control of the palace, and began issuing orders. Both

Ptolemy and Cleopatra were to dismiss their armies and meet with Caesar, who would settle their dispute. However, Cleopatra knew that if she entered Alexandria openly, Ptolemy's henchmen would kill her so she is reputed to have smuggled herself into the palace to Caesar inside an oriental rug. When the rug was unrolled, Cleopatra tumbled out. It is said that Caesar was bewitched by her charm, and became her lover that very night. Her bravery and spirit would no doubt have been what first endeared Caesar to her. When Ptolemy XIII saw Caesar and Cleopatra together the next day, he was furious. He stormed out of the palace, shouting that he had been betrayed. Caesar had him arrested, but Ptolemy's army, led by the eunuch Pothinus and Cleopatra's sister Arsinoe laid siege to the palace. In hopes of appeasing the attackers Caesar released Ptolemy XIII, but the Alexandrian war continued for almost six months and only ended when Pothinus was killed in battle and Ptolemy XIII drowned in the Nile whilst trying to flee. Alexandria then surrendered to Caesar, who captured Arsinoe and restored Cleopatra VII to her throne. Cleopatra then married her brother Ptolemy XIV, who was 11 or 12 years old. Julius Caesar gave them Cyprus as a wedding gift, even though his own interest in Cleopatra had been awakened. Julius Caesar, however, had a reputation for being a womaniser; a contemporary, Suetonius, records:

> Home we bring our bald whoremonger. Romans lock your wives away. All the bags of gold you lent him, when his Gallic tarts to pay.

Although she was obliged to marry her brother, Cleopatra soon dropped his name from any official documents despite the fact that the male presence should be first among co-rulers. She also had her own portrait and name on coins of that time, and very much ruled independently of her brother.

ADULTHOOD

Cleopatra is not reputed as being a great beauty but she was considered witty, charming and intelligent with a huge amount of sex appeal and this was what attracted Julius to her (*colour plate 23*). In Plutarch's *Life of Marcus Antonius* he describes Cleopatra:

> For (as they say) it was not because her [Cleopatra's] beauty in itself was so striking that it stunned the onlooker, but the inescapable impression produced by daily contact with her: the attractiveness in the persuasiveness of her talk, and the character that surrounded her conversation was stimulating. It was a pleasure to hear the sound of her voice, and she tuned her tongue like a many-stringed instrument expertly to whatever language she chose.

She is depicted on ancient coins with a long hooked nose and masculine features, yet she was clearly a very seductive woman. She had an enchantingly musical voice and exuded charisma. Because of this appeal to powerful men, she was reputed as being a whore who could have any lover that she wanted. However, she is only recorded as ever having two lovers, Julius Caesar and Mark Antony, both of which she appeared to love very much. However, the power she held over them was enough to cause envy throughout the world, and bitterness as both of these powerful men abandoned their loyal Roman wives to be with her, leading what was believed by all to be a debauched life of eroticism and pleasure.

Plutarch records that Cleopatra spoke a total of eight languages; several African languages, Hebrew, Aramaic plus her native Greek. She was also the only Ptolemaic ruler to speak Egyptian, which would endear her to the Egyptian population. It has been suggested that her father taught her these languages as he was looking further ashore than the boundaries of Egypt for eventual rule.

For pleasure Cleopatra also studied the science of fragrant and protective unguents and even wrote a beauty book on how to mix substances to moisturise and protect the skin from the harsh climate. Unfortunately this book has not survived into modern archaeology. The Greeks and Romans saw her obsession with beauty as evidence of her exotic nature. However, in Egypt this was seen as normal, as everyone, men and women took care of their skin, and would wear make-up, for beauty enhancement and for medical reasons. They were aware of the connection between dirt and disease and in the climate of Egypt bathing daily was common.

The relationship between Cleopatra and Julius blossomed and in 47 BC they went on a boat trip down the Nile. The boat would probably have been made from Lebanese cedar with a combination of Egyptian and Greek decoration. Cleopatra was 23 years old and pregnant with Caesar's child. This trip also had political motivations as travelling with Caesar to Upper Egypt showed the people that they had the support of both the newly re-appointed queen and Rome, and may have re-established favour lost after the decree of Ptolemy XIII.

When they returned to Alexandria Julius Caesar left Egypt for Rome, and not long after, their son Caesarion was born. His name means 'Little Caesar' and although Caesar had a wife, Calpurnia, in Rome and a daughter from this marriage, he acknowledged Caesarion as his own in the Roman senate. Plutarch records that Caesar claimed Cleopatra was his 'sister' which in ancient Egypt was a term of endearment that often used to address wives. Soon after the birth of Caesarion a coin was minted in Cyprus, showing Cleopatra suckling her new-born child.

In the temple of Hathor at Dendera Cleopatra presents her son Caesarion to the gods, naming him as 'Ptolemy Caesar son of Julius Caesar and Cleopatra'. North of

Thebes at Hermonthis a birth-temple was built celebrating the combined birth of Horus and Caesarion, not only showing him to be the living Horus but also the heir apparent to the throne of Egypt.

When Caesar returned to Rome, he left three legions in Egypt to protect Cleopatra. A year later he invited Cleopatra to visit him in Rome. She arrived in the autumn of 46 BC, accompanied by Caesarion and her young brother/husband, Ptolemy XIV. In September, Caesar celebrated his war triumphs by parading through the streets of Rome with his prisoners, including Cleopatra's sister Arsinoe.

Cleopatra lived in Caesar's villa near Rome for almost two years. During this time he showered her with gifts and titles and even had a statue of her erected in the temple of Venus Genetrix. The Romans were scandalised by his extra-marital affair and it was even rumoured that Caesar intended to pass a law allowing him to marry Cleopatra and make their son his heir. It was also rumoured that Caesar, who had accepted a lifetime dictatorship and sat on a golden throne in the Senate, intended to become the king of Rome in the manner of Egyptian royalty.

In 44 BC, whilst Cleopatra was still in Rome, Julius Caesar was murdered in the Roman senate at which time his great-nephew Octavian, declared himself Caesar. Cleopatra saw this as a threat to the life of her son Caesarion, who was only three years old, and she quickly returned to Egypt. Before or on their return to, Egypt, her husband Ptolemy XIV died aged 15, possibly poisoned at Cleopatra's command. Cleopatra then made Caesarion her co-regent, who was crowned Ptolemy XV.

Caesar's assassination caused anarchy and civil war in Rome. Eventually the empire was divided among three men; Caesar's great-nephew Octavian, who later became the emperor Augustus; Marcus Lepidus; and Marcus Antonius, better known today as Mark Antony.

It would appear that one episode in the life of Cleopatra was closed, and a new one was opening with the arrival of Mark Antony. Cleopatra met him for the first time when her father was alive in 55 BC. She was about 15 years old and he was approaching 30. He was a successful cavalry officer in the army and travelled to Egypt in support of Cleopatra's father. When she next met him, in 42 BC she was 28 years old. As a member of the triumvirate he had chosen the Eastern sector in support of Julius Caesar and Cleopatra's father, and he was posted to Egypt.

From Tarsus (in modern-day Turkey) Mark Antony had summoned Cleopatra to question her about whether she had assisted his enemies. Plutarch describes the boat in which she arrived; a barge with a gilded stern, purple sails and silver oars. The boat was sailed by her maids, who were dressed as sea nymphs. Cleopatra herself was dressed as Venus, the goddess of love. She reclined under a gold canopy, fanned by boys in Cupid costumes. Antony, an unsophisticated, pleasure-loving soldier, was impressed by this blatant display of luxury, just as Cleopatra had intended. Cleopatra entertained him on her barge that night to maintain the upper hand by ensuring he met her on Egyptian territory. The next night Antony invited her to supper, hoping to outdo her in magnificence. He failed, but joked about it in his good-natured way. Like Caesar before him, Antony was enthralled with Cleopatra, becoming the second great love in her life, and this love eventually caused the downfall of both these great leaders.

Forgetting his responsibilities, he accompanied Cleopatra to Alexandria and spent the winter of 41-40 BC with her. Their revelry was recorded by Plutarch. Apparently eight boars were roasted for a dinner of 12 people, one after another, so a perfect meal would be ready whenever Antony and Cleopatra decided to dine, displaying extravagance and waste, which was not received well in Rome. Plutarch also records other forms of relaxation enjoyed by the couple.

> She played at dice with him, drank with him, hunted with him; and when he exercised in arms, she was there to see. At night she would go rambling with him to disturb and torment people at their doors and windows, dressed like a servant-woman, for Antony also went in servant's disguise .... However, the Alexandrians in general liked it all well enough, and joined good-humouredly and kindly in his frolic and play.

The relationship between Antony and Cleopatra was clearly one of frivolity; she shared all of his activities, causing criticism from both the Roman and the Egyptian people. She had a lot of influence over him and convinced Antony to continue his campaign to annex Parthia, which was attacking the eastern provinces at this time, as she believed this would strengthen his position in the Roman triumvirate, and would benefit both Rome and Egypt. Whilst he was away Cleopatra bore him twins, a boy Alexander Helios (the sun) and a girl Cleopatra Selene (the moon). It was four years until she saw him again. Both children were acknowledged by Antony and he actually offered Alexander in marriage to the king of Armenia's daughter, in an attempt to appease a quarrel. The king of Armenia refused and Antony attacked him in 34 BC.

Octavian Caesar wanted to stop Antony from returning to Egypt from Parthia and rejoining Cleopatra, and so married Antony to his sister Octavia during the four years of absence. Antony, widowed from his first wife Fulvia, had never claimed to be married to Cleopatra although he admitted a relationship. Although his official mourning period was not over, Roman law was overruled and he married Octavia.

In 37 BC, on his way to invade Parthia, Antony enjoyed another rendezvous with Cleopatra. He rushed through his military campaign in order to hurry to her. From then on Alexandria was his home and Cleopatra was his life. He married her in 36 BC, in Antioch in North Syria, despite his marriage to Octavia. He dressed as Osiris and she dressed as Isis, and they referred to themselves as the New Isis and New Dionysus which horrified those in Rome. Antony gave her Phoenicia, Syria, Cyprus, Judea and the Coastal strip of Arabia down to the Red Sea as a wedding gift. Shortly after this wedding she gave birth to another son, Ptolemy Philadelphus.

Meanwhile, back in Rome, Octavia remained loyal to her bigamous husband. She decided to visit Antony in Alexandria but by the time she reached Athens she received a letter from him saying that he would meet her there. However, Cleopatra was determined to keep Antony away from her. She cried, fainted and starved herself and got her way. Antony cancelled his trip, and Octavia returned home without seeing her husband. The Roman people were disgusted by the way Antony had treated Octavia. To make matters worse, in 34 BC Antony made Alexander Helios the king of Armenia, Cleopatra Selene the queen of Cyrenaica and Crete, and Ptolemy Philadelphus the king of Syria. Caesarion was proclaimed the 'King of Kings,' and Cleopatra was the 'Queen of Kings.'

After three years of political tension in Rome, Octavian decided to rule alone and turned on Cleopatra and Antony. In 31 BC Antony's forces fought the Romans in a sea battle off the coast of Actium, aided by Cleopatra and 60 Egyptian ships. When she saw that Antony's cumbersome, badly-manned galleys were losing to the Romans' lighter, swifter boats, she fled the scene. Antony abandoned his men to follow her. Although they may have pre-arranged their retreat, the Romans saw it as proof that Antony was enslaved by his love of Cleopatra, unable to think or act on his own.

For three days Antony sat alone in the prow of Cleopatra's ship, refusing to see or speak to her. They returned to Egypt, where he lived alone, brooding, while Cleopatra prepared for an invasion by Rome. Cleopatra began experimenting with poisons to learn which would cause the most painless death. She also built a mausoleum to which she moved all of her gold, silver, emeralds, pearls, ebony, ivory, and other treasure to prevent the Roman troops from appropriating them.

Antony then received word that his forces had surrendered at Actium and his allies had gone over to Octavian; he left his solitary home and returned to Cleopatra to party away their final days before the arrival of the Roman army.

In 30 BC Octavian reached Alexandria. Mark Antony marched what remained of his army out of the city to meet the enemy. He stopped on high ground to watch what he expected would be a naval battle between his fleet and the Roman fleet. Instead he saw his fleet salute the Romans with their oars and join them. At this Antony's cavalry also deserted him. His infantry was soon defeated and Antony returned to the city, shouting that Cleopatra had betrayed him. She was terrified and locked herself in her mausoleum. In order to calm Antony down and encourage him to return to her Cleopatra sent word to him that she had died. This did not have the desired affect and Antony tried to kill himself by falling on his sword as was noble for Roman officers. However, he did not kill himself and asked his friend Eros to finish the job. Eros, however, fell on his own sword. When Cleopatra heard the news that he had attempted to commit suicide, she immediately sent a message to him saying that she was not dead. Antony demanded that his bleeding body be taken to her. Cleopatra was afraid to open the door because of the approach of Octavian's army, but she and her two serving women let down ropes from a window and pulled him up. Distraught, Cleopatra laid Antony on her bed and he died in her arms.

Octavian meanwhile had taken Cleopatra's palace. He intended to take Cleopatra back to Rome and drag her through the streets in chains, and needed to capture her alive. When Octavian and his men reached her monument Cleopatra refused to let them in. She negotiated with them through the barred door, demanding that her kingdom be given to her children. Octavian ordered one man to keep her talking while others set up ladders and climbed through the window. When Cleopatra saw the men she pulled out a dagger and tried to stab herself, but she was disarmed and taken prisoner. Octavian allowed Cleopatra to arrange Antony's funeral, and she buried him with royal splendour. After the funeral she took to her bed, sick with grief. She wanted to kill herself, but Octavian kept her under close guard. One day he visited her and she flung herself at his feet, and told him she wanted to live. Octavian was lulled into a false sense of security.

Cleopatra was determined to die, due to grief, and because she knew Octavian intended to humiliate her, as her sister Arsinoe had been humiliated. With Octavian's permission she visited Antony's tomb. Then she returned to her mausoleum, took a bath, and ordered a feast. While the meal was being prepared a man arrived at her monument with a basket of figs. The guards checked the basket and found nothing suspicious, so they allowed the man to deliver it. However a follower of hers had placed a poisonous asp within this basket so that when she reached into the basket it bit her and killed her.

After she had eaten and was in her final moments, Cleopatra wrote a letter, sealed it, and sent it to Octavian. He opened it and found Cleopatra's plea that he would allow her to be buried in Antony's tomb. Alarmed, Octavian sent messengers to alert her guards that Cleopatra planned to commit suicide. However, they reached her too late and she was already dead. It is thought that she was buried alongside her Antony although her tomb has not yet been found.

Octavian then killed her son Caesarion, and other Egyptian, and Greeks in power, so there were no more links to the Egyptian throne. Cleopatra Selene married King Juba II of Mauretania and had two children, Ptolemy and Drusilla. No one knows what happened to Alexander Helios and Ptolemy Philadelphus.

Cleopatra was 40 years old when she committed suicide in this manner on 12 August 30 BC.

CONCLUSION

Considering the violent upbringing and moral values of the Ptolemaic household, it is quite surprising that Cleopatra grew up to be a sophisticated, intelligent woman capable of feeling great passion for her lovers, as well as great loyalty to these men and her country.

Cleopatra's defeat by the Romans saw an end to Egypt as an independent country, as it became yet another province of Rome. However, despite this she has been prominent in history since then, and has inspired writers, artists and film makers to recreate her life in various media. She has left no written documentation of her life. The earliest record of her is that of Plutarch who wrote 200 years after her demise, and although he had access to eye-witness accounts of Cleopatra these are now lost. Everyone else has used accounts from Octavian's propaganda and also their own imagination. Many portray her as an unnatural woman who went against the current culture by choosing her own lovers and then exerting political and erotic power over them. Over the ages, the imagery and reputation of Cleopatra has changed to reflect the morals of the time.

Writers before Shakespeare believed that there was a certain nobility, as dying for love fell into the character of courtly love that was fashionable at the time. In these pre-Shakespeare days it is recorded that before she died Cleopatra admits all her wrong doings and renders Antony innocent.

Elizabethan writers saw Antony and Cleopatra's suicides as a morality tale about fidelity and passion, and by the time Shakespeare wrote *Antony and Cleopatra* it was a tale of the dangers of excessive love.

The seventeenth and eighteenth centuries portray her as a weak and passionate woman who got caught up in politics beyond her understanding. She is often portrayed as an icon of feminine manipulation and commercial seduction.

Regardless of the reputation it is spectacular that even 2000 years after her death she still inspires people, and research is still being done to discover exactly what happened to her in her final years.

TWENTY

THE LADY TAIMHOTEP

INTRIGUE OF A PTOLEMAIC FAMILY

INTRODUCTION

The family of Taimhotep lived during the reign of Cleopatra VII, the final queen of Egypt before Roman domination. The story of the life of Taimhotep and her family is recorded on three funerary stelae, currently in the British Museum.

The stelae dedicated to Taimhotep have an inscription in hieroglyphs (71) and also in the more commonly used demotic. Although written in a formulaic fashion it is fundamentally the story of one woman's life; her joy in her children and her natural fears about death.

The hieroglyphic stela starts by introducing the characters involved in her life: herself, her husband Psherenptah: and her son Imhotep, including an account of his remarkable conception and birth. The final section is her lamentation of death and her burial.

The colophon (or scribal signature) at the end of the text claims the scribe who carved the stela was Imhotep son of Khahapi, which may be Taimhotep's brother although the text was probably written by her husband, indicated in this verse, spoken by Taimhotep to her widower:

> Weary not of drink and food
> Of drinking deep and loving!
> Celebrate the holiday,
> Honour your heart day and night,
> Value the years spent on earth.

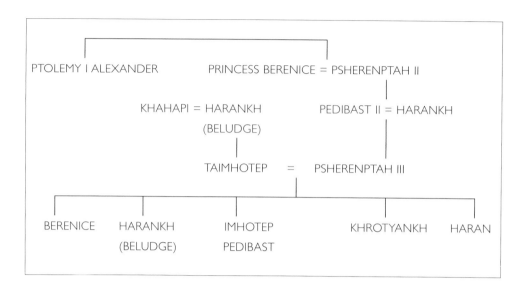

What more could a husband want, than permission from his deceased wife to continue enjoying life without her, and to make the most of the time on earth without a prolonged period of grief?

Other signs of her husband's penmanship are reflected in the introductory passage, which lists his titles and achievements with greater flourish than those of Taimhotep. However, if the stela was written by her brother, as the colophon would suggest, he may have been praising his sister's husband as a compliment to her.

The verse which introduces Psherenptah as Taimhotep's new husband gives us an insight into some of the social structures of the period. Taimhotep claims 'My father gave me as wife to the Prophet of Ptah'.

In ancient Egypt, the marriage ceremony, per se, did not exist, as all that was required for a couple to be married was for the woman to move into her husband's home. In Taimhotep's case her father arranged the 'marriage' and chose a suitable husband for her. As this stela gives all of the dates of the events in her life we know that Taimhotep was 14 years old when she left her father's house to live with her husband.

Throughout the text very few terms of endearment are used by Taimhotep about her husband, as after the long, elaborate list of titles, she simply refers to him as 'High Priest' or 'my husband'. Even when she is referring to him performing her funerary rites, she uses all of his official titles when it may have been appropriate to suggest this was the last act of kindness of a dedicated husband, rather than the duty of a high priest. Her husband was probably trying to maintain protocol of the inscription, and felt terms of endearment were unsuitable. However, when she tells him to continue

71 Stela of Taimhotep, British Museum. *Photograph Clare V. Banks. Copyright: The Trustees of the British Museum, London*

with his life after her death, she uses terms of affection; 'O my brother, my husband, friend, High Priest' which may have been added to support the sentiment being voiced by a loving, doting wife.

To identify the woman (72) behind the formulaic inscription we should outline some of the known facts about her. She was born on 17 December 73 BC, during the reign of Ptolemy XII Neos Dionysos. When she was 14 years old, in 59 BC, she married Psherenptah III, the High Priest of Ptah; her father's choice of husband. She was married to him for 16 years and gave birth to four children, of which the only birth date recorded is that of her son Imhotep, born on 15 July 46 BC. Her three daughters were named Berenice, Harankh, nicknamed Beludge (after Taimhotep's mother) and Khrotyankh. Taimhotep died when she was 30 years old, on 15 February 42 BC, when her son was only four years old.

Her father Khahapi was a prophet and Memphite priest, and her mother Harankh (nicknamed Beludge), was a priestess of Ptah. Taimhotep herself was a sistrum (or sacred rattle) player and a priestess of Ptah, so it was expected that she would marry a High Priest and continue with the religious tradition of her family.

CONCEPTION OF IMHOTEP

A large proportion of the stela concerns the conception of Taimhotep's only son, Imhotep Pedibast. In addition to the traditional roles of a son (i.e. looking after his parents in old age and preparing their burials) Imhotep Pedibast's main role would be to inherit the title of 'High Priest of Ptah' at the death of his father.

The god that was called upon during the conception of Taimhotep's son was Imhotep, 'Son of Ptah', who was primarily a deity of medicine but was also reputed to give children to barren women (see chapter 1). After his death it is probable that pilgrimages to his tomb were organised in order to cure the sick. The pilgrims spent the night in the temple next to the tomb, where they were given a hallucinogenic drug to enable the god to make revelations to them in their sleep. The priests would then interpret the dreams and relay the information to the pilgrim. In the story of Taimhotep and her husband there is no mention of them spending the night in the temple sanatorium but the god did reveal himself to Psherenptah in a dream. The god demanded a sanctuary to be built in his tomb at Ankhtawi, for which in return he would give them a male child. Naturally Psherenptah commissioned the sanctuary and Taimhotep conceived her son Imhotep Pedibast. So strong was her belief in the powers of Imhotep that she thought she even saw the 'god's likeness' in her new-born son, although I am sure this can be put down purely to the strength of a mother's love.

72 Stela of Taimhotep (detail), British Museum. *Photograph Clare V. Banks. Copyright: The Trustees of the British Museum, London*

Although Ptah was the principle god in the lives of Taimhotep and Psherenptah a large part of this funerary stela is dedicated to Imhotep due to their gratitude at receiving a son.

As members of the Priesthood of Ptah, the assumption can be made that Taimhotep and her family believed in the creation story recorded on the Shabaka Stone, that Ptah created the world through speech and thought alone; and therefore she would believe that Ptah was an all-powerful god. On the other hand Taimhotep's beliefs surrounding death are quite un-Egyptian and do not correspond well with the traditional funerary beliefs.

DEATH

Taimhotep personifies death and gives it a name, 'Come', in a way the Egyptians never did. To the Egyptians, death was an abstract concept viewed more as a journey to rebirth. The Egyptian god of the dead, Osiris, guided the deceased through the underworld to their place of rebirth, but he was not the reason for their death. Taimhotep's ideas may have had Greek influence and although she calls him 'Come' he could be a counterpart of the Greek deity Thanatos, the god of Death. In the Greek myth Sisyphos, the king of Korinth, escaped Hades a number of times. On one occasion when Thanatos came to take him to Hades, Sisyphos tied him in chains; until Thanatos was released no one died. Sisyphos' punishment was to eternally push a rock up a hill with no hope of ever reaching the top. In Egyptian mythology if Osiris was harmed, people would still die and would still travel in the underworld but without his guidance.

Taimhotep describes Death as being merciless, and unreasonable, rendering mortals fearful and powerless in his presence. She indicates that death is even more powerful than the gods as 'Of gods and men no one beholds him', in direct contrast to her belief that Ptah is the all-powerful creator god. Her opinion on this has probably derived from her fear of his invisibility, and as we all know, if you cannot see something you cannot fight it. However, fighting death did not appear to be in the forefront of her mind: 'He is not seen that one might give him any gift' suggesting her desire to bribe this phantom in an attempt to escape death. However, there has to be something physical to lay gifts to. In her everyday life in the temple of Ptah she would leave offerings to the statue of the god and this was seen as a way of requesting help. Without this she does not know how to appease Death. She sees no logic in his choice of victims, as:

> He snatches the son from his mother
> Before the old man that walks by his side.

It is clear she believes those who are old, or those that 'pray for him ... who praises him' should be the ones to die not those who have to be snatched away, or plead with him to leave them or their kin. This is a sentiment that many people hold, as no one likes to see the untimely death of children, or the particularly kind-hearted. Therefore no one was safe from death as he chose the victims, rendering mortals powerless against him.

An earlier passage is devoted to Taimhotep's lamentation of the physical state of being dead. She is unhappy, that she is part of the land of the dead and the realisation that:

> They wake not to see their brothers,
> They see not their fathers, their mothers.
> Their hearts forgot their wives, their children.

This does not reflect the standard Egyptian belief that she will be reunited with her ancestors in the afterlife. She worries that she will be left in the desert, thirsting for the life-giving water, just out of her reach, destined to sleep eternally. She does not have the image of death as a journey to a better life, just the end of life altogether.

It would be interesting to know if these ideas were developed during an illness that led to death, or whether they are the thoughts of her husband (or brother) who developed their own doubts about death and the afterlife.

MOTHERHOOD

Taimhotep seems to be a typical proud mother, like all mothers through history. She was immensely proud of her only son, to the point of recording the hour of his birth on her stelae. She claims to be able to see in the child's appearance that of the god Imhotep. This reflects the thoughts of a doting mother who sees things in her child that other people cannot see:

> There was jubilation over him by the people of Memphis ...
> Everyone rejoiced over him.

Every new mother assumes everyone has her enthusiasm for her new-born. Among the Priesthood of Ptah there may have been a mild interest as this child would potentially be the new high priest upon the death of Psherenptah, but it is doubtful there was jubilation all over Memphis.

If the stelae are to be believed Taimhotep was popular, with many friends. She was described as:

> Greatly valued, greatly praised,
> Full of charm, well-disposed,
> Much beloved by everyone,
> Highly praised by her friends,
> The worthy young woman, skilled in speech
> Whose words please and her council helps.

This conjures up an image of a quiet and serene women, who was a good listener, and was able to offer good advice. You can almost imagine her friends dropping into her house for a chat, bringing their children, and discussing various issues going on in their lives.

Her training as a priestess may have contributed greatly to the tranquillity of her character, although maybe her tranquillity of character contributed to her choice of training as a priestess. However, like priestly titles, the office of priestess was hereditary, and she inherited the role from her mother. She showed great obedience and loyalty as she obeyed her father without question with his choice of husband for her.

PSHERENPTAH III

Her husband Psherenptah III and her son Pedibast III also have funerary stelae.
There were two funerary inscriptions each, one in hieroglyphs and one in demotic
(73). As well as giving further insight into an elite Ptolemaic family, these stelae are
very important for information regarding the takeover of Egypt by the Romans, as
Imhotep Pedibast died three days before the sacking of Alexandria.

The majority of the stelae of Psherenptah III are filled with 38 of his titles, many
of which are probably epithets describing the responsibilities of his real title 'Chief
of Artificers', a title common to all of the High Priests of Ptah. Many of his titles
begin with 'scribe' representing different aspects of one job. The word 'scribe' is
often followed by a deity's name which could be united under a general title 'Sacred
Scribe' responsible for the writing of the sacred books of these deities. His title
'Prophet in the Library' shows he was responsible for the maintenance and upkeep
of the religious libraries in Memphis.

Psherenptah also holds five titles starting with 'superintendent of the confidential
affairs' which could refer to 'religious mysteries', or the control of state secrets and
other matters not made public knowledge. He also is called 'scribe of the god's seal',
which shows he was a 'state secretary' in charge of the administration of the temple
accounts, at Memphis in particular, but also other temple complexes in Alexandria
and possibly Thebes. Being in control of so many confidential matters meant the
king kept the role of high priest in one family, hence the other common title to this
position is 'Hereditary Prince'. The information would be passed down from father
to son and Psherenptah records spending 13 years under the supervision of his father;
also a High Priest of Ptah.

The High Priests of Ptah at Memphis held a very high position in the royal house
of Ptolemy and Psherenptah is described as the:

> Eyes of the Upper Egyptian King,
> Ears of the Lower Egyptian King.

However, Psherenptah appears to have been very pompous with ideas above his
station, as he claims he was born 'Egypt's sovereign'; a presumptuous claim. However,
Psherenptah's grandfather, Psherenptah II, married a princess of royal blood,
Berenice daughter of Eugertes II and sister to Ptolemy Alexander I, which could
be a legitimate claim to the throne should the house of Ptolemy collapse. This royal
connection massaged Psherenptah's ego, and he makes frequent claims of being the
king's favourite or 'great of love in every man's heart'.

Pompous boasting aside there is a lot of real information that can be learnt about Psherenptah from his stelae. He was born on the twenty-first of the month of Paopi (20 September) in 90 BC, year 25 of Ptolemy X. He died at aged 49 on the fifteenth day of Epep (11 June) in 41 BC during year 11 of the reign of Cleopatra VII. His mother was Harankh, a sistrum player of Ptah (74), and his father was the High Priest, Pedibast II.

From birth Psherenptah spent 13 years under the supervision of his father being trained as High Priest. The king then passed the position of 'Chief of Artificers' to Psherenptah when he was just 14 years old. Not only did this young boy have to cope with the loss of his father, but also the acquisition of a great deal of responsibility. Psherenptah was allowed no time in which to get used to his position as his first task would be a daunting one, especially to a 14 year old boy. This was the coronation of the king at the temple at Memphis. Not only did he have to perform all of the secret rites in connection to this coronation but also the public ones, including placing the diadem upon the new king's head. The tradition of having the High Priest of Ptah perform this rite was started by Alexander the Great when he was crowned at Memphis according to Egyptian law. Although Psherenptah also lived through the coronation of Cleopatra VII his part in the ceremony is not mentioned in either of his stelae, but it can be assumed that he was involved in her coronation ceremony. The title which would normally be given to the priest who crowned the Pharaohs was 'Prophet of the Window of Appearances' but this seems to be omitted from the titles of Psherenptah, although it is in the list of his son's titles, even though there is no record of Imhotep Pedibast actually attending a coronation, as he was born and died during the reign of Cleopatra VII.

Psherenptah married Taimhotep in 59 BC, in year 23 of Ptolemy XII, when he was 31 years old and she was just 14. From her stelae we learn that the marriage was arranged by her family. It would be interesting to know what they thought of each other, whether she regarded him an old man and he regarded her as a child. It is likely that Taimhotep's father knew Psherenptah's father, as his titles ranked him high up in the priesthood. It would also be interesting to know at what age Taimhotep was when she was offered to Psherenptah as wife. Their marital roles in life may have been mapped out from birth.

Psherenptah also mentions the birth of his son Imhotep Pedibast and credits the god Imhotep with the conception. Psherenptah was 43 when his son was born in 46 BC. In the hieroglyphic stela he fails to mention his daughters but in his demotic stela he names all four of his daughters, whereas Taimhotep only mentions three. This fourth daughter Haran, could be a daughter of a concubine or mistress. Later in the stela Psherenptah boasts of his 'harem of fair maidens' and this may have produced the mother of this daughter. As the high priests were supposed to be monogamous, Psherenptah boasts of this privilege:

Above left: 73 Stela of High Priest of Ptah, reign of Cleopatra and Caesarion (either Pshereptah or Pedibast). *Copyright: Petrie Museum of Egyptian Archaeology, University College London,* UC *14357*

Above right: 74 Bronze figure of Ptah, thirtieth dynasty. *Copyright: Petrie Museum of Egyptian Archaeology, University College London,* UC *30491*

> Because I am a noble, splendid of possession of every kind.
>
> To me belongs even a harem of fair maidens.

Psherenptah uses this gift of a harem to reinforce his statement that he is 'loved by the king, more than his favourite'.

Psherenptah also held the title 'Prophet of the King' indicating a high position in the Egyptian cult of the king. This title was bestowed upon him on a visit by Ptolemy XII and Psherenptah to the temple of Isis. After the king had made offerings to the goddesses he left the temple in his war chariot for a procession. Psherenptah suggests it was a somewhat spontaneous event as the king halts his chariot in front of him and adorns his head with a golden diadem encrusted with jewels and the ureaus on the top, and in Psherenptah's own words 'I was made his Prophet' which held more significance to him than any number of jewels. The king also assured Psherenptah would always be cared for:

> I have granted to him income from the Temples of Upper and Lower Egypt for numerous years.

At this time all the temples of Upper and Lower Egypt were taxed in support of this favoured priesthood, so the king was assuring Psherenptah that his position would not change, because although hereditary, the king had the power to dispose of anyone who fell out of favour.

A royal visit to Memphis on a festival day is also recorded where the king was accompanied by his household (wives and concubines, royal children and courtiers). Although the date of this trip is not recorded it is believed to have occurred between 76 BC, when Psherenptah became high priest, and 46 BC when his son Imhotep was born. Psherenptah's death occurred six years after the birth of his son Imhotep, although very little is mentioned about the death and burial other than the day, month and year.

IMHOTEP PEDIBAST

The stela of Taimhotep and Psherenptah's son Imhotep Pedibast does not have a demotic twin, although it consists of six lines of hieroglyphs followed by nine lines of demotic, giving personal details of his life. Pedibast led a short life, ending at a time of great political upheaval, when the Romans took over Egypt.

Pedibast was born on the 15 July 46 BC, year 6 of Cleopatra VII's reign, and according to the demotic text this was on the festival day of Bastet. From Taimhotep's stela we discover it was the day after the god Imhotep's birthday. His mother died when he was four years old and his father died when he was six years old, so from a very young age he was alone, with his sisters and the priesthood responsible for his upbringing. When his father died he became high priest in his place, at the age of seven years and 10 days. He was not old enough to fully understand the power he held, and therefore created a weak link in the resistance against Rome. He died in year 22 of Cleopatra in 30 BC when he was just 16 years and 21 days old.

The text does not record any major events in this young priest's life, although it does mention how his father needed to be reburied and re-mummified in year 22 of Cleopatra after being buried for 11 years. It has been suggested that Psherenptah was originally buried in Alexandria, and when the Romans sacked the city the tomb was defiled requiring another burial, this time in Memphis. However, although this seems probable there is no evidence of the High Priest of Ptah being buried at anywhere other than Memphis. It is also possible that other priests of Ptah moved the body when they realised the impending crisis waiting to befall Egypt, and wanted to protect the body *from* being defiled by the Romans.

Although the death of Pedibast is reported in a rather unremarkable way it was part of a long line of events leading to the collapse of the Ptolemaic dynasty.

First the son of Mark Antony and Fulvia was killed in Rome due to his recognition in Egypt as co-ruler with Cleopatra. Then Caesarion, the child of Julius Caesar and Cleopatra, was killed. Therefore the only threat left to Roman rule in Egypt was Pedibast who, due to his great-grandfather's marriage to a Ptolemaic princess, had a legitimate claim to the throne of Egypt, as well as having the power of the priesthood as support. By murdering the last legitimate claim to the throne, Egypt was open for Roman rule. Until the body of this high priest is discovered we will be unsure of the exact cause of death, but it is likely that he was murdered, only three days before Alexandria was captured by the Romans. With the death of Pedibast, the Ptolemaic dynasty and the reign of his own family as high priests, after 200 years, ended.

CONCLUSION

The burial of Pedibast, according to the demotic text, was carried out according to the correct rituals, on the sixth day of Mesore (2 July), year 22 of Cleopatra. In the hieroglyphic inscription it claims he was buried by his cousin, a priest of Ptah, Psenamunis. Pedibast III was recorded as having a traditional burial with all the pomp and splendour that was expected, including a funerary statue with 'gold and silver ornaments' and a number of semi-precious amulets to protect him in the afterlife. A statue of Pedibast III was discovered outside Egypt at Cherchel, in the capital of Juba II. Whether this statue was the funerary statue mentioned, is not known. It is possible that the statue was removed from Memphis when the political situation in Egypt became delicate along with the fleeing of the rest of the family in an attempt to preserve their own safety.

Although the stela claims that everything was carried out for his burial, Pedibast's mummy, remained in the embalmers' workshop for six years, eight months and 10 days before he was buried. The high priests were probably waiting for a time to bury him when the political situation had calmed somewhat. Even if burial did not go according to Egyptian tradition, the stela suggests that the embalming was carried out in the appropriate manner; his body was anointed with unguents, myrrh and incense with a number of amulets of precious stones secreted in the bandages. There were also ceremonies involved with the receiving of linen for the wrappings. Even if they were not donated physically, the written record of receiving bandages would change into reality in the afterlife. The unusual content of this stela, concentrating on the burial rather than the life of this last high priest could be an indication that the process was not followed and in order to ensure Pedibast would be reborn in the afterlife they recorded his ceremonial wrapping and burial.

Despite what must have been a frightening time of his life, in which he had to endure much of it as an orphan, in his final prayer of the demotic text, he is assured that his parents will be waiting for him in his burial chamber where they can all be once again united in death.

REFERENCES

INTRODUCTION

David R. (2003) *Religion and Magic in Ancient Egypt*. (London. Penguin)
Lichtheim M. (1980) *Ancient Egyptian Literature. Volume III*. (Berkeley. University of California Press)
Partridge R. (2002) *Fighting Pharaohs; weapons and warfare in ancient Egypt*. (Manchester, Peartree Publishing)
Robins G. (1993) *Women in Ancient Egypt*. (London. British Museum Press)
Sauneron S. (2000) *The Priests of Ancient Egypt*. (Ithaca & London. Cornell University Press)
Shaw I. (1991) *Egyptian Warfare and Weapons*. (Princes Risborough. Shire Egyptology)
Watterson B. (1998) *Women in Ancient Egypt*. (Stroud. Sutton Publishing)

ONE – IMHOTEP: FROM ROYAL BUILDER TO GOD

Hurry J.B. (1928) *Imhotep: the Vizier and physician of King Zoser and afterwards the Egyptian god of medicine*. (Oxford. Oxford University Press)
Ray J. (2001) *Reflections of Osiris: Lives from Ancient Egypt*. (London. Profile Books)

TWO – TETY: THE ASSASSINATION OF AN OLD KINGDOM KING

Arnold D. (2003) *The Encyclopaedia of Ancient Egyptian Architecture*. (London. I.B. Tauris Publishers)
Clayton P. (1994) *The Chronicle of the Pharaohs*. (London. Thames and Hudson)
Kanawati N. (1977) *The Egyptian Administration in the Old Kingdom*. (Warminster. Aris and Phillips)
Kanawati N. (2003) *Conspiracies of the Egyptian Palace*. (London. Routledge)
Lehner M. (1997) *The Complete Pyramids*. (London. Thames and Hudson)
Lichtheim M. (1975) *Ancient Egyptian Literature. Volume II*. (Berkeley. University of California Press)
Macy-Roth A. (1954) *Egyptian Phyles in the Old Kingdom: the evolution of a system of social organization*. (Chicago. Oriental Institute of the University of Chicago)
Oakes L. & Gahlin L. (2002) *Ancient Egypt*. (London. Anness Publishing)
Shaw I. & Nicholson P. (1997) *British Museum Dictionary of Ancient Egypt*. (London. British Museum Press)
Wilkinson R. (2000) *The Complete Temples of Ancient Egypt*. (London. Thames and Hudson)

THREE – KHNUMNAKHT AND NAKHTANKH: TWO BROTHERS

Adams B. (1998) *Egyptian Mummies.* (Princes Risborough. Shire Egyptology)
David R. (1979) *Manchester Museum Mummy Project.* (Manchester. Manchester University Press)
David R. & Archbold R. (2000) *Conversations with Mummies: new light on the lives of ancient Egyptians.* (London. Harper Collins)
David R. & Tapp E. (1984) *Evidence Embalmed: modern medicine and the mummies of ancient Egypt.* (Manchester. Manchester University Press)
Murray M. (1910) *Tomb of the Two Brothers.* (Manchester. Sherrat and Hughes)
Petrie W.M.F. (1907) *Gizeh and Rifeh.* (London. British School of Archaeology in Egypt)
Prag J. and Neave R. (1997) *Making Faces: using forensic and archaeological evidence.* (London: British Museum Press)
Reeder G. (2005) 'The Eunuch and the Wab Priest' in *KMT Volume 16 number 1.* p.54-63

FOUR – AHMOSE: THE END OF AN ERA

Booth C. (2005) *The Hyksos Period in Egypt.* (Princes Risborough. Shire Egyptology)
Clayton P. (1994) *The Chronicle of the Pharaohs.* (London. Thames and Hudson)
Forbes D. (2003) 'Women of the House of Tao' in *KMT Volume 14 number 3.* p.54-65
Goedicke H. (1995) *Studies about Kamose and Ahmose.* (Baltimore. Halgo Inc.)
Lehner M. (1997) *The Complete Pyramids.* (London. Thames and Hudson)
Thomas S. (2003) *Ahmose, Liberator of Egypt.* (New York. Rosen Publishing Groups)
Wilkinson R. (2000) *The Complete Temples of Ancient Egypt.* (London. Thames and Hudson)

FIVE – HATSHEPSUT: THE FEMALE PHARAOH

Bickerstaffe D. (2002) 'The Discovery of Hatshepsut's Throne' in *KMT Volume 13 Number 1.* p.71-7
Bierbrier M. L. (1995) 'How Old Was Hatshepsut?' in *Gottinger Miszellen 144* p.15-9
Bunson M. (1991) *The Encyclopaedia of Ancient Egypt.* (New York. Gramercy Books)
Clayton P. (1994) *Chronicles of the Pharaohs.* (London. Thames and Hudson)
Dodson A. (2000) *Monarchs of the Nile.* (Cairo. American University in Cairo Press)
Habachi L. (1957) 'Two graffiti at Sehel from the reign of Hatshepsut' in *Journal of Near Eastern Studies 16.* p.88-104
Ray J. (2001) *Reflections of Osiris: lives from ancient Egypt.* (London. Profile Books)
Robins G. (1993) *Women in Ancient Egypt.* (London. British Museum Press)
Ryholt R.S.B. (1997) *The Political Situation in Egypt during the Second Intermediate Period.* (Copenhagen. Museum Tusculanum Press)
Tyldesly J. (1996) *Hatshepsut.* (London. Penguin)
Watterson B. (1991) *Women in Ancient Egypt.* (Stroud. Sutton Publishing)

SIX – SENENMUT: LOVER OF AN EGYPTIAN QUEEN

Bunson M. (1991) *The Encyclopaedia of Ancient Egypt.* (New York. Gramercy Books)
Dorman P. (1948) *The Tombs of Senenmut: the architecture and decoration of tombs 71 and 353.* (New York: Metropolitan Museum of Art)
Tyldesly J. (1996) *Hatshepsut.* (London. Penguin)

SEVEN – REKHMIRE: THE VIZIER OF THUTMOSIS III AND AMENHOTEP II

De Garis Davies N. (1973) *The Tomb of Rekh-mi-Rē at Thebes*. (New York. Arno Press)

Johnson G. (2003) 'Monument for a Vizier' in *KMT Volume 14 number 2*. p.28-44

Manniche L. (1987) *The Tombs of the Nobles at Luxor*. (Cairo. American University in Cairo Press)

Van den Boorn, G.P.F. (1988) *The Duties of the Vizier: civil administration in the early New Kingdom*. (London. Kegan Paul)

EIGHT – AKHENATEN: THE HERETIC KING

Aldred C. (1988) *Akhenaten King of Egypt*. (London. Thames and Hudson)

D'Auria S. (2000) 'Pharaohs of the Sun' in *Egyptian Archaeology 16* p.20-4

Ertman E. (2001) 'An Electrum Ring of Nefertiti; More Evidence of her Co-Kingship?' in *KMT Volume 12 number 4*. p.27-8

Filer J. (2000) 'The kv55 Body: the facts' in *Egyptian Archaeology 17* p.13-4

Fletcher J. (2004) *The search for Nefertiti*. (London. Hodder and Stoughton)

Harrell J. (2001) 'Ancient Quarries near Amarna' in *Egyptian Archaeology 19* p.36-8

Hornung E. (1995) *Akhenaten and the Religion of Light*. (London. Cornell University Press)

James S. (2001) 'Who is the Mummy Elder Lady' in *KMT Volume 12 number 2*. p.42-50

Kemp B. (2002) 'Resuming the Amarna Survey' in *Egyptian Archaeology 20*. p.10-2

Lichtheim M. (1975) *Ancient Egyptian Literature. Volume II*. (Berkeley. University of California Press)

Owen G. (2000) 'The Amarna Courtiers Tombs' in *Egyptian Archaeology 17* p.21-4

Spence K. (1999) 'The North Palace at Amarna' in *Egyptian Archaeology 15* p.14-6

Watterson B. (1984) *Gods of Ancient Egypt*. London. Sutton Publishing Ltd

Watterson B. (1999) *Amarna; Ancient Egypt's Age of Revolution*. (Gloucestershire. Tempus Publishing)

NINE – TUTANKHAMUM: THE BOY KING

Aldred C. (1968) *Akhenaten; Pharaoh of Egypt*. (London. Abacus)

Davies B. G. (1995) *Egyptian Historical Records of the Later Eighteenth dynasty. Fascicle VI*. (Warminster. Aris & Phillips)

Forbes D.C. (1998) *Tombs, Treasures, Mummies: seven great discoveries of Egyptian archaeology*. (Sebastopol. KMT Communications)

Filer J. (1995) *Disease*. (London. British Museum Press)

Hawass Z. (2005) Press Release – *Tutankhamun CT scan*

Janssen J. (1975) *Commodity Prices from the Ramesside Period: an economic study of the village of necropolis workmen at Thebes*. (Leiden. Brill)

Johnson. W.R. (1992) *An Asiatic Battle Scene of Tutankhamun from Thebes: a late Amarna antecedent of the Ramesside battle narrative*. (Unpublished PhD Thesis. University of Chicago)

Nims C.F. (1965) *Thebes of the Pharaohs*. (London. Elek Books Ltd)

Tyldesley J. (2000) *The Private Lives of the Pharaohs* (London. Pan Macmillan)

United Press International (2005) *King Tut liked Red Wine Best*. (www.sciendaily.com)

Vogelsang-Eastwood G.M. (1999) *Tutankhamun's Wardrobe*. (Rotterdam. Barjesteh van Waalwijk van Doorn & Co.)

Welsh F. (1993) *Tutankhamun's Egypt*. (Princes Risborough. Shire Egyptology)

Wilkinson R.H. (2000) *The Complete Temples of Ancient Egypt*. (London. Thames and Hudson)

TEN – HOREMHEB: THE RESTORER OF EGYPT

Aldred C. (1988) *Akhenaten*. (London. Thames and Hudson)

Breasted H. (1906) *Ancient Records of Egypt. Volume III*. (Chicago. University of Chicago Press)

Breasted H. (1951) *A History of Egypt*. (London. Hodder & Stoughton)

Clayton P.A. (1994) *Chronicles of the Pharaohs*. (London. Thames and Hudson)

Davis T.M. (1912) *The Tombs of Harmhabi and Touatankhamanou*. (London. Duckworth Egyptology)

De Garis Davies N. (1905). *The Rock Tombs of El-Amarna: smaller tombs and boundary stelae Pt. 5*. (London. Egypt Exploration Fund)

Dodson A. & Hilton D. (2004) *The Complete Royal Families*. (London. Thames and Hudson).

Forbes D. (2004) 'Where Tourists Seldom Venture' in *KMT Volume 15* p.64-76

Johnson. W.R. (1992) *An Asiatic Battle Scene of Tutankhamun from Thebes: a late Amarna antecedent of the Ramesside battle narrative*. (Unpublished PhD Thesis. University of Chicago)

Gardiner A. (1953) 'The Coronation of King Haremhab' in *Journal of Egyptian Archaeology 39* p.13-31

Hölscher U. (1932) *Excavations at Ancient Thebes 1930/31*. (Chicago. University of Chicago Press)

Martin G.T. (1989) *The Memphite Tomb of Horemheb: Commander in Chief of Tutankhamun. Volume II* (London/Leiden. The Rijksmuseum Van Oudheden and The Egypt Exploration Society)

Martin G.T. (1991) *The Hidden Tombs of Memphis*. London. Thames and Hudson

Pfluger K. (1946) 'The Edict of King Haremhab' in *Journal of Near Eastern Studies (JNES) 51* p.260-76

Ray J. (2001) *Reflections of Osiris: lives from ancient Egypt*. (London. Profile Books)

Reeves N., Wilkinson R. (1996) *The Complete Valley of the Kings*. (London. Thames and Hudson)

Romer J. (1981) *Valley of the Kings*. (London. Michael O'Mara Books)

ELEVEN – RAMSES II: THE GREATEST KING OF THE NEW KINGDOM

Gardiner A.H. (1960) *The Kadesh Inscriptions of Ramses II*. (Oxford. Griffith Institute)

Gardiner A.H. (1920) 'The Ancient Military Road Between Egypt and Palestine' in *Journal of Egyptian Archaeology 6* p. 99-116

Kitchen K. (1982) *Pharaoh Triumphant*. (Cairo. University of Cairo Press)

Lichtheim M. (1975) *Ancient Egyptian Literature Vol II*. (Berkeley. University of California Press)

Morschauser S. (1985) 'Observations on the Speeches of Ramses II in the Literary Record of the Battle of Kadesh' in Goedicke. H. (ed) *Perspectives on the Battle of Kadesh*. (Baltimore. Halgo Inc.)

Tyldesley J. (2000) *Ramses; Egypt's Greatest Pharaoh*. (London. Penguin)

TWELVE – RAMOSE: AN HONEST SCRIBE

Bierbrier M. (1982) *The Tomb Builders of the Pharaohs*. (New York. Charles Scribners Sons)

Corteggiani J-P. (1986) *The Egypt of the Pharaohs at the Cairo Museum*. (London. Scala Books)

Cerny J. (1973) *A Community of Workmen at Thebes in the Rammeside Period*. (Cairo. Bibliothèque D'Etude)

Davies B. (1999) *Who's Who at Deir el Medina*. (Leiden. Nederlands Instituut Voor Het Nabije Oosten)

Lesko L. (1994) 'Literature, Literacy and Literati' in Lesko, L. (ed) *Pharaoh's Workers*. (London. Cornell University Press)

McDowell A. (1991) 'Contact with the Outside World' in Lesko. L. (ed) *Pharaoh's Workers*. (London. Cornell University Press)

Montserrat D. & Meskell L. (1997) 'Mortuary Archaeology and the Religious landscape at Graeco-Roman Deir el Medina' in *Journal Egyptian Archaeology 83* p.179-98

Romer J. (1984) *Ancient Lives*. (London. Phoenix Press)

THIRTEEN – KENHIRKHEPSHEF & NAUNAKHTE: AN EARLY HISTORIAN & HIS WIFE

Bierbrier M. (1982) *The Tomb Builders of the Pharaohs*. (New York. Charles Scribners Sons)
Corteggiani J-P. (1986) *The Egypt of the Pharaohs at the Cairo Museum*. (London. Scala Books)
Cerny J. (1945) 'The Will of Naunakhte and the Related Documents' in *Journal of Egyptian Archaeology 31* p.29-53
Cerny J. (1973) *A Community of Workmen at Thebes in the Rammeside Period*. (Cairo. Bibliothèque D'Etude)
Davies B. (1999) *Who's Who at Deir el Medina*. (Leiden. Nederlands Instituut Voor Het Nabije Oosten)
Edwards I.E.S. (1968) 'Kenhirkhepshef's Prophylactic Charm' in *Journal of Egyptian Archaeology 54* p.155-60
Janssen J. (1980) 'Absence From Work by the Necropolis Workmen of Thebes' in *Studien zur Altagyptischen Kultur. Band 8*. p127-52
Lesko L. (1994) 'Literature, Literacy and Literati' in Lesko, L. (ed) *Pharaoh's Workers*. (London. Cornell University Press)
Montserrat D. & Meskell L. (1997) 'Mortuary Archaeology and the Religious landscape at Graeco-Roman Deir el Medina' in *Journal Egyptian Archaeology 83* p.179-98
Romer J. (1984) *Ancient Lives*. (London. Phoenix Press)

FOURTEEN – PANEB: AN ANCIENT ROGUE

Bierbrier M. (1982) *The Tomb Builders of the Pharaohs*. (New York. Charles Scribners Sons)
Corteggiani J-P. (1986) *The Egypt of the Pharaohs at the Cairo Museum*. (London. Scala Books)
Cerny J. (1973) *A Community of Workmen at Thebes in the Rammeside Period*. (Cairo. Bibliothèque D'Etude)
Davies B. (1999) *Who's Who at Deir el Medina*. (Leiden. Nederlands Instituut Voor Het Nabije Oosten)
Janssen J. (1980) 'Absence From Work by the Necropolis Workmen of Thebes' in *Studien zur Altagyptischen Kultur. Band 8*. p127-52
Montserrat D. & Meskell L. (1997) 'Mortuary Archaeology and the Religious landscape at Graeco-Roman Deir el Medina' in *Journal Egyptian Archaeology 83* p.179-98
Romer J. (1984) *Ancient Lives*.(London. Phoenix Press)

FIFTEEN – RAMSES III: THE LAST GREAT KING

Clayton P. (1994) *The Chronicle of the Pharaohs*. (London. Thames and Hudson)
Dodson A. (1997) 'The Sons of Ramses III' in *KMT Volume 8 number 1*. p 29-43
Newby P.H. (1980) *The Warrior Pharaohs*. (London. Faber and Faber)
Partridge R.B. (2002) *Fighting Pharaohs; weapons and warfare in ancient Egypt*. (London. Peartree Publishing)
Reeves N. & Wilkinson R. (1996) *The Complete Valley of the Kings*. (London. Thames and Hudson)
Redford S. (2002) *The Harem Conspiracy; the murder of Ramses III*. (Dekalb. Northern Illinois University Press)
Wilkinson R. (2000) *The Complete Temples of Ancient Egypt*. (London. Thames and Hudson)

SIXTEEN – NATSEFAMUN: A PRIEST OF AMUN

David R. (1979) *Manchester Museum Mummy Project*. (Manchester. Manchester University Press)
David R. & Archbold R. (2000) *Conversations with Mummies: new light on the lives of ancient Egyptians*. (London. Harper Collins)
David R. & Tapp E. (1984) *Evidence Embalmed: modern medicine and the mummies of ancient Egypt*. (Manchester. Manchester University Press)

Nims C.F. (1965) *Thebes of the Pharaohs: pattern for every city.* (London. Elek Books)
Snape S. (1996) *Egyptian Temples.* (Princes Risborough. Shire Egyptology)
Wilkinson R. (2000) *The Complete Temples of Ancient Egypt.* (London. Thames and Hudson)

SEVENTEEN – HOREMKENISI: A THIRD INTERMEDIATE PERIOD PRIEST

Adams B. (1998) *Egyptian Mummies.* (Princes Risborough. Shire Egyptology).
Taylor J.H. (1995) *Unwrapping a Mummy.* (London. British Museum Press).

EIGHTEEN – ASRU: CHANTRESS OF AMUN

David R. (1979) *Manchester Museum Mummy Project.* (Manchester. Manchester University Press)
David R. & Archbold R. (2000) *Conversations with Mummies: new light on the lives of ancient Egyptians.* (London. Harper Collins)
David R. & Tapp E. (1984) *Evidence Embalmed: modern medicine and the mummies of ancient Egypt.* (Manchester: Manchester University Press)
Tyldesley J. (2000) *The Private Lives of the Pharao hs.* (London. Channel 4 Books)

NINETEEN – CLEOPATRA: THE LAST QUEEN OF EGYPT

Foss M. (1998) *In Search for Cleopatra.* (New York. Arcade Publishing)
Samson J. (1985) *Nefertiti and Cleopatra: Queen-Monarchs of ancient Egypt.* (London. Rubicon Press)

TWENTY – THE LADY TAIMHOTEP: INTRIGUE OF A PTOLEMAIC FAMILY

Birch S. (1863) 'On two Egyptian Tablets of the Ptolemaic Period' in *Archaeologica 39*
Griffith F.L. (1900) *Stories of the High Priests of Memphis.* (Oxford. Clarendon Press)
Gunn B. (1941) 'Notes on Ammenemes I' in *Journal of Egyptian Archaeology 27* p.2-6
Hall H.R. (1930) *A General Introductory Guide to the Egyptian Collections in the British Museum.* (London. British Museum Press) p.216
Hart G. (1990) *Egyptian Myths.* (London. British Museum Publications)
Hurry J.B. (1928) *Imhotep.* (Oxford. Oxford University Press)
Lichtheim M. (1980) *Ancient Egyptian Literature Vol III.* (Berkeley. University of California Press) p.59-65
Petrie F.W. (1909) *Memphis I.* (London. Bernard Quaritch). p.7 pl.XIII
Quaegebeur J. (1977) 'Inventaires des Steles Funeraires Memphites d'Epoque Ptolemaique' in Bevan E. (1977) *A history of Egypt under the Ptolemaic Dynasty.* (London. Methuen) p.347
Reymond E.A.E & Barns J.W.B (1977) 'Alexandria and Memphis' in *Orientalia 46* p.24
Reymond E.A.E. (1981) 'From the Records of a Priestly Family of Memphis' Volume I in *Agyptologische Abhandlungen Band 38.* (Otto Harrassowitz. Weisbaden)
Sandman-Holberg M. (1946) *The God Ptah.* (Gleerup. Lund C.E.K)
Schefold K. (1964) *Gods and Heroes in Late Archaic Greek Art.* (Cambridge. Cambridge University Press)
Thompson D. (1988) *Memphis under the Ptolemies.* (Guildford. Princeton University Press)
Wildung D. (1977) 'Imhotep and Amenhotep' in *Muncher Agyptologische Studien 36* p.68-70

INDEX

If you are interested in purchasing other books published by Tempus,
or in case you have difficulty finding any Tempus books in your local bookshop,
you can also place orders directly through our website

www.tempus-publishing.com